*G*AINA SÛTRAS

SACRED BOOKS OF THE EAST

*G*AINA SÛTRAS

TRANSLATED FROM PRÂKRIT
BY
HERMANN JACOBI

Part I

THE ÂKÂRÂṄGA SÛTRA

THE KALPA SÛTRA

ATLANTIC PUBLISHERS & DISTRIBUTORS
4215/1, Ansari Road, Darya Ganj
New Delhi-110002

Published by :
Atlantic Publishers & Distributors,
4215/1, Ansari Road, Darya Ganj,
New Delhi-110002

Head Office :
B-2, Vishal Enclave, Najafgarh Road,
New Delhi-110027
Phone : 5413460

Printed at :
MEHRA OFFSET PRESS
1979, Chandni Mahal
DELHI-110006

CLASSICAL REPRINTS PUBLISHED BY US

SACRED BOOKS OF THE EAST

EDITOR: F. Max Müller

These volumes of the Sacred Books of the East Series include translations of all the most important works of the seven non-Christian religions. These have exercised a profound influence on the civilizations of the continent of Asia. The Vedic Brahmanic System claims 21 volumes, Buddhism 10, and Jainism 2; 8 volumes comprise Sacred Books of the Parsees; 2 volumes represent Islam; and 6 the two main indigenous systems of China, thus placing the historical and comparative study of religions on a solid foundation.

VOLUMES

1, 15. THE UPANISADS: in 2 Vols. *F. Max Müller*

2, 14. THE SACRED LAWS OF THE ARYAS: in 2 Vols. *Georg Bühler*

3, 16, 27, 28, 39, 40. THE SACRED BOOKS OF CHINA: in 6 Vols. *James Legge*

4, 23, 31. THE ZEND-AVESTA: in 3 Vols. *James Darmesteter & L. H. Mills*

5, 18, 24, 37, 47. PAHALVI TEXTS: in 5 Vols. *E. W. West*

6, 9. THE QUR'AN: in 2 Vols. *E. H. Palmer*

7. THE INSTITUTES OF VIṢṆU: *J. Jolly*

8. THE BHAGAVADGĪTĀ with the Sanatsujātiya and the Anugītā: *K. T. Telang*

10. THE DHAMMAPADA: *F. Max Müller*
SUTTA-NIPĀTA: *V. Fausböll*

11. BUDDHIST SUTTAS: *T. W. Rhys Davids*

12, 26, 41, 43, 44. THE ŚATAPATHA-BRĀHMAṆA: in 5 Vols. *J. Eggeling*

13, 17, 20. VINAYA TEXTS: in 3 Vols. *T. W. Rhys Davids & H. Oldenberg*

19. THE FO-SHO-HING-TSAN-KING: *Samuel Beal*

21. THE SADDHARMA-PUṆḌARĪKA or THE LOTUS OF THE TRUE LAWS: *H. Kern*

22, 45. JAINA SUTRAS: in 2 Vols. *Hermann Jacobi*

25. MANU: *Georg Bühler*

29, 30. THE GṚIHYA-SŪTRAS: in 2 Vols. *H. Oldenberg & F. Max Müller*

32, 46. VEDIC HYMNS: in 2 Vols. *F. Max Müller & H. Oldenberg*

33. THE MINOR LAW-BOOKS: *J. Jolly*

34, 38. THE VEDĀNTA SŪTRAS: in 2 Vols. with Śaṅkarācārya's Comm.: *G. Thibaut*

35, 36. THE QUESTIONS OF KING MILINDA: in 2 Vols.: *T. W. Rhys Davids*

42. HYMNS OF THE ATHARVA-VEDA: *M. Bloomfield*

48. THE VEDĀNTA-SŪTRAS with Rāmānuja's Śrībhāṣya: *G. Thibaut*

49. BUDDHIST MAHĀYĀNA TEXTS: *E. B. Cowell, F. Max Müller & J. Takakusu*

50. INDEX : *M. Winternitz*

CONTENTS

THIRD PART

FOURTH PART

KALPA SÛTRA.

INTRODUCTION.

THE origin and development of the *G*aina sect is a subject on which some scholars still think it safe to speak with a sceptical caution, though this seems little warranted by the present state of the whole question; for a large and ancient literature has been made accessible, and furnishes ample materials for the early history of the sect to all who are willing to collect them. Nor is the nature of these materials such as to make us distrust them. We know that the sacred books of the *G*ainas are old, avowedly older than the Sanskrit literature which we are accustomed to call classical. Regarding their antiquity, many of those books can vie with the oldest books of the northern Buddhists. As the latter works have successfully been used as materials for the history of Buddha and Buddhism, we can find no reason why we should distrust the sacred books of the *G*ainas as an authentic source of their history. If they were full of contradictory statements, or the dates contained in them would lead to contradictory conclusions, we should be justified in viewing all theories based on such materials with suspicion. But the character of the *G*aina literature differs little in this respect also from the Buddhistical, at least from that of the northern Buddhists. How is it then that so many writers are inclined to accord a different age and origin to the *G*aina sect from what can be deduced from their own literature? The obvious reason is the similarity, real or apparent, which European scholars have discovered between *G*ainism and Buddhism. Two sects which have so much in common could not, it was thought, have been independent from each other, but one sect must needs have grown out of, or branched off from the other. This à priori opinion has prejudiced the discernment of many critics, and still does so. In the following pages I shall try to destroy this prejudice, and to vindicate that authority and credit of the sacred books of the *G*ainas to which they are entitled. We begin our discussion with an inquiry about Mahâvîra, the founder or, at least, the last prophet of the *G*aina church. It will be seen that enough is known of him to invalidate the suspicion that he is a sort of mystical person, invented or set up by a younger sect some centuries after the pretended age of their assumed founder.

The *G*ainas, both *S*vetâmbaras and Digambaras, state that Mahâvîra was the son of king Siddhârtha of Ku*nd*apura or Ku*nd*agrâma. They would have us believe that Ku*nd*agrâma was a large town, and Siddhârtha a powerful monarch. But they have misrepresented the matter in overrating the real state of things, just as the Buddhists did with regard to Kapilavastu and *S*uddhodana. For Ku*nd*agrâma is called in the Â*k*ârâṅga Sûtra a sa*m*nivesa, a term which the commentator interprets as denoting a halting-place of caravans or processions. It must therefore have been an insignificant place, of which tradition has only recorded that it lay in Videha (Â*k*ârâṅga Sûtra II, 15, § 17). Yet by combining occasional hints in the Baud-dha and *G*aina scriptures we can, with sufficient accuracy, point out where the birthplace of Mahâvîra was situated; for in the Mahâvagga of the Buddhists[1] we read that Buddha, while sojourning at Ko*t*iggâma, was visited by the courtezan Ambapâli and the Li*kkh*avis of the neighbouring capital Vesâli. From Ko*t*iggâma he went to where the *Ñ*âtikas[2] (lived). There he lodged in the *Ñ*âtika Brick-hall[2], in the neighbourhood of which place the courtezan

[1] See Oldenberg's edition, pp. 231, 232; the translation, p. 104 seq., of the second part, Sacred Books of the East, vol. xvii.

[2] The passages in which the *Ñ*âtikas occur seem to have been misunderstood by the commentator and the modern translators. Rhys Davids in his translation of the Mahâparinibbâna-Sutta (Sacred Books of the East, vol. xi) says in a note, p. 24: 'At first Nâdika is (twice) spoken of in the plural number; but then,

Ambapâli possessed a park, Ambapâlivana, which she bequeathed on Buddha and the community. From there he went to Vesâli, where he converted the general-in-chief (of the Likkhavis), a lay-disciple of the Nirgranthas (or Gaina monks). Now it is highly probable that the Kotiggâma of the Buddhists is identical with the Kundaggâma of the Gainas. Apart from the similarity of the names, the mentioning of the Ñâtikas, apparently identical with the Gñâtrika Kshatriyas to whose clan Mahâvîra belonged, and of Sîha, the Gaina, point to the same direction. Kundagrâma, therefore, was probably one of the suburbs of Vaisâlî, the capital of Videha. This conjecture is borne out by the name Vesâlie, i. e. Vaisâlika given to Mahâvîra in the Sûtrakritânga I, 3[1]. The commentator explains the passage in question in two different ways, and at another place a third explanation is given. This inconsistency of opinion proves that there was no distinct tradition as to the real meaning of Vaisâlika, and so we are justified in entirely ignoring the artificial explanations of the later Gainas. Vaisâlika apparently means a native of Vaisâlî: and Mahâvîra could rightly be called that when Kundagrâma was a suburb of Vaisâlî, just as a native of Turnham Green may be called a Londoner. If then Kundagrâma was scarcely more than an outlying village of Vaisâlî, it is evident that the sovereign of that village could at best have been only a petty chief. Indeed, though the Gainas fondly imagine Siddhârtha to have been a powerful monarch and depict his royal state in glowing, but typical colours, yet their statements, if stripped of all rhetorical ornaments, bring out the fact

thirdly, in the last clause, in the singular. Buddhaghosa explains this by saying that there were two villages of the same name on the shore of the same piece of water.' The plural Ñâtikâ denotes, in my opinion, the Kshatriyas, the singular is the adjective specifying Giñgakâvasatha, which occurs in the first mention of the place in the Mahâparinibbâna-Sutta and in the Mahâvagga VI, 30, 5, and must be supplied in the former book wherever Nâdika is used in the singular. I think the form Nâdika is wrong, and Ñâtika, the spelling of the Mahâvagga, is correct. Mr. Rhys Davids is also mistaken in saying in the index to his translation: 'Nâdika, near Patna.' It is apparent from the narrative in the Mahâvagga that the place in question, as well as Kotiggâma, was near Vesâli.

[1] See Weber, Indische Studien, XVI, p. 262.

that Siddhârtha was but a baron; for he is frequently called merely Kshatriya — his wife Trisalâ is, so far as I remember, never styled Devî, queen, but always Kshatriyânî. Whenever the Gñâtrika Kshatriyas are mentioned, they are never spoken of as Siddhârtha's Sâmantas or dependents, but are treated as his equals. From all this it appears that Siddhârtha was no king, nor even the head of his clan, but in all probability only exercised the degree of authority which in the East usually falls to the share of landowners, especially of those belonging to the recognised aristocracy of the country. Still he may have enjoyed a greater influence than many of his fellow-chiefs; for he is recorded to have been highly connected by marriage. His wife Trisalâ was sister to Ketaka, king of Vaisâlî[1]. She is called Vaidehî or Videhadattâ[2], because she belonged to the reigning line of Videha.

Buddhist works do not mention, for aught I know, Ketaka, king of Vaisâlî; but they tell us that the government of Vesâli was vested in a senate composed of the nobility and presided over by a king, who shared the power with a viceroy and a general-in-chief[3]. In Gaina books we still have traces of this curious government of the Likkhavis; for in the Nirayâvalî Sûtrâ[4] it is related that king Ketaka, whom Kûnika, al. Agâtasatru, king of Kampâ, prepared to attack with a strong army, called together the eighteen confederate kings of Kâsî and Kosala, the Likkhavis and Mallakis, and asked them whether they would satisfy Kûnika's demands or go to war with him. Again, on the death of Mahâvîra the eighteen confederate kings, mentioned above, instituted a festival to be held in memory of that event[5], but no separate mention is made of Ketaka, their pretended sovereign. It is therefore probable that Ketaka was simply one of these confederate kings and of equal power with them. In addition to this, his power was checked by the

[1] See Kalpa Sûtra, my edition, p. 113. Ketaka is called the maternal uncle of Mahâvîra.

[2] See Kalpa Sûtra, Lives of the Ginas, § 110; Âkârâṅga Sûtra II, 15, § 15.

[3] Turnour in the Journal of the Royal As. Soc. of Bengal, VII, p. 992.

[4] Ed. Warren, p. 27.

[5] See Kalpa Sûtra, Lives of the Ginas.

constitution of Vesâli. So we are enabled to understand why the Buddhists took no notice of him, as his influence was not very great, and, besides, was used in the interest of their rivals. But the *G*ainas cherished the memory of the maternal uncle and patron of their prophet, to whose influence we must attribute the fact, that Vai*s*âlî used to be a stronghold of *G*ainism, while being looked upon by the Buddhists as a seminary of heresies and dissent.

We have traced the connection of Mahâvîra's family not out of mere curiosity, which indiscriminately collects all historical facts however insignificant in themselves, but for the reason that the knowledge of this connection enables us to understand how Mahâvîra came to obtain his success. By birth he as well as Buddha was a member of a feudal aristocracy similar to that of the Yâdavas in the legends about K*ri*sh*n*a, or that of the Râjpoots of the present day. In feudal societies family ties are very strong and long remembered[1]. Now we know for certain that Buddha at least addressed himself chiefly to the members of the aristocracy, that the *G*ainas originally preferred the Kshatriyas to the Brâhmans[2]. It is evident that both Mahâvîra and Buddha have made use of the interest and support of their families to propagate their order. Their prevalence over other rivals was certainly due in some degree to their connection with the chief families of the country.

Through his mother Mahâvîra was related to the ruling dynasty in Magadha; for *K*e*t*aka's daughter *K*ellanâ[3] was married to Se*n*iya Bimbhisâra[4] or Bimbisâra, king of Magadha, and residing in Râ*g*ag*ri*ha. He is praised by the *G*ainas and Buddhists, as the friend and patron of both

---

[1] The *G*ainas are very particular in stating the names and gotras of Mahâvîra's relations, of whom they have recorded little else. Kalpa Sûtra, Lives of the *G*inas, § 109.

[2] See Kalpa Sûtra, Lives of the *G*inas, §§ 17 and 18.

[3] See Nirayâvalî Sûtra, ed. Warren, p. 22. She is commonly called by the Buddhists Vaidehî; in a Thibetan life of Buddha her name is *S*rîbhadrâ, which reminds us of the name of *K*e*t*aka's wife Subhadrâ. See Schiefner in Mémoires de l'Académie Impériale de St. Pétersbourg, tome iv, p. 253.

[4] He is usually called only Se*n*iya or *S*re*n*ika; the full name is given in the Da*s*â*s*rutaskandha, Weber, Ind. Stud. XVI, p. 469.

Mahâvîra and Buddha. But Kûnika or, as the Buddhists call him, Agâtasatru[1], his son by Kellanâ, the Videhan lady, showed no favour to the Buddhists in the earlier part of his reign; only eight years before Buddha's death he became his patron. We should go wrong in believing him to have sincerely been converted. For a man who avowedly murdered his father[2], and waged war against his grandfather[3], is not likely to have cared much about theology. His real motive in changing his religious policy we may easily guess. He planned to add Videha to his dominions, just as his father had added Aṅga to his kingdom of Magadha; he therefore built the fort at Pâtaligrâma[4], in order not to repel but subdue the Vaggians or Vrigis, a tribe of Videha, and at last fixed a quarrel on the king of Vaisâlî, his grandfather. As the latter was the maternal uncle of Mahâvîra, Agâtasatru, by attacking this patron of the Gainas, lost in some degree their sympathy. Now he resolved on siding with their rivals, the Buddhists, whom he formerly had persecuted as friends of his father's, whom, as has been said above, he finally put to death. We know that Agâtasatru succeeded in conquering Vaisâlî, and that he laid the foundation of the empire of the Nandas and Mauryas. With the extension of the limits of the empire of Magadha a new field was opened to both religions, over which they spread with great rapidity. It was probably this auspicious political conjuncture to which Gainism and Buddhism chiefly owed their success, while many similar sects attained only a local and temporal importance.

The following table gives the names of the relations of Mahâvîra, or, as we should call him when not speaking of

---

[1] That the same person is intended by both names is evident from the fact that according to Buddhist and Gaina writers he is the father of Udâyin or Udayibhaddaka, the founder of Pâtaliputra in the records of the Gainas and Brâhmans.

[2] The story is told with the same details by the Buddhists; see Kern, Der Buddhismus und seine Geschichte in Indien, I, p. 249 (p. 195 of the original), and the Gainas in the Nirayâvalî Sûtra.

[3] See above.

[4] Mahâparinibbâna-Sutta I, 26, and Mahâvagga VI, 28, 7 seq.

him as a prophet of the *G*ainas, Vardhamâna or *Gñâ*-*tri*putra[1]:—

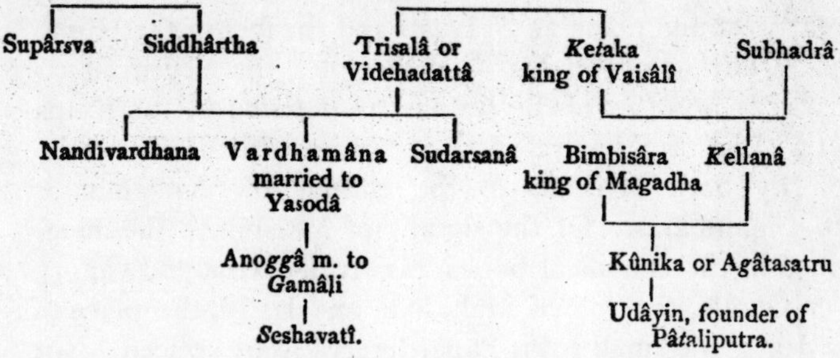

I do not intend to write a full life of Mahâvîra, but to collect only such details which show him at once a distinct historical person, and as different from Buddha in the most important particulars. Vardhamâna was, like his father, a Kâsyapa. He seems to have lived in the house of his parents till they died, and his elder brother, Nandivardhana, succeeded to what principality they had. Then, at the age of twenty-eight, he, with the consent of those in power, entered the spiritual career, which in India, just as the church in Roman Catholic countries, seems to have offered a field for the ambition of younger sons. For twelve years he led a life of austerities, visiting even the wild tribes of the country called Râ*dh*â. After the first year he went about naked[2]. From the end of these twelve years of preparatory self-mortification dates Vardhamâna's Kevaliship. Since that time he was recognised as omniscient, as a prophet of the *G*ainas, or a Tîrthakara, and had the titles *G*ina, Mahâvîra, &c., which were also given to *S*âkyamuni. The last thirty years of his life he passed in teaching his religious system and organising his order of ascetics, which, as we have seen above, was patronised or at least countenanced chiefly by those princes with whom he was related through his mother, viz. *K*e*t*aka, *S*re*n*ika, and Kûnika, the

[1] Nâtaputta in Pâli and Prâkrit. The Buddhists call him Niga*nth*a Nâtaputta, i.e. *Gñ*âtriputra the Nirgrantha or *G*aina monk.

[2] This period of his life is the subject of a sort of ballad incorporated in the Â*k*ârâṅga Sûtra (I, 8).

kings of Videha, Magadha, and Aṅga. In the towns which lay in these parts he spent almost all the rainy seasons during his spiritual career[1], though he extended his travels as far west and north as *S*râvastî and the foot of the Himâlaya. The names of his chief disciples, the eleven Ga*n*adharas or apostles of the *G*ainas, as detailed in the Kalpa Sûtra (List of Sthaviras, § 1), are given without any variation by both divisions of the church, the *S*vetâmbaras and Digambaras. Of the details of Mahâvîra's life, mentioned in the canonical books, his rivalry with, and victory over Go*s*âla, the son of Makkhali, and lastly, the place of his death, the small town Pâpâ, deserve to be noticed. Nor are we by any means forced to rely on the tradition of the *G*ainas only, since for some particulars we have the testimony of the Buddhists also, in whose writings Mahâvîra is mentioned under his well-known name Nâtaputta, as the head of the Niga*nth*as or *G*aina monks and a rival of Buddha. They only misstated his Gotra as that of Agnivai*s*yâyana; in this particular they confounded him with his chief apostle Sudharman, the only one of all the apostles who survived him and took the lead in the church after his teacher's death. Mahâvîra being a contemporary of Buddha, they both had the same contemporaries, viz. Bimbisâra and his sons, Abhayakumâra and A*g*âta*s*atru, the Li*kkh*avis and Mallas, Go*s*âla Makkhaliputra, whom we accordingly meet with in the sacred books of either sect. From the Buddhist Pi*t*akas it appears, as we have seen above, that Mahâvîra's followers were very numerous in Vai*s*âlî, a fact that is in perfect accordance with what the *G*ainas relate about his birth in the vicinity of that town, and which at the same time well agrees with his connection with the chief magistrate of the place. In addition to this, some tenets of the Niga*nth*as, e.g. the Kiriyavâda and the belief that water is inhabited by souls, are mentioned in the sacred books of the Buddhists, in perfect accordance with

[1] See Kalpa Sûtra, Lives of the *G*inas, § 122; *K*ampâ, 3; Vai*s*âlî, 12; Mithilâ, 6; Râ*g*ag*ri*ha, 14; Bhadrikâ, 2; Âlabhikâ, 1; Pa*n*itabhûmi, 1; *S*râvastî, 1; Pâpâ, 1. All these towns, with the exception of Pa*n*itabhûmi, *S*râvastî, and perhaps Âlabhikâ, lay within the limits of the three kingdoms mentioned in the text.

the *G*aina creed. Lastly, the Buddhists are correct in assuming the town Pâpâ as the scene of Nâtaputta's death.

Comparing this outline of Mahâvîra's life with that of Buddha's, we can detect little or nothing in the former which can be suspected as having been formed after the latter by tradition. The general resemblance between the lives of both is due to their being lives of ascetics, which from the nature of the things must present some uniformity, which certainly will appear greater to the mind of a European historian of our times than to that of an ancient Hindu. Some names of Mahâvîra's relations are similar to those of Buddha's: the former's wife was Ya*s*odâ, the latter's Ya*s*odharâ; the former's elder brother was Nandivardhana, the latter's step-brother Nanda; Buddha's name as a prince was Siddhârtha, which was the name of Mahâvîra's father. But if the similarity of these names proves anything, it proves no more than that names of this description were much used then among the Kshatriyas, as surely they were at all times[1]. Nor is it to be wondered at that two Kshatriyas should have founded sects in opposition, or at least in disregard to the authority of the Brâhmans. For, as I shall try to prove in the sequel, the Kshatriyas were the most likely of all to become what the Brâhmans would call 'untrue ascetics.'

We shall now put side by side the principal events of Buddha's and Mahâvîra's lives, in order to demonstrate their difference. Buddha was born in Kapilavastu, Mahâvîra in a village near Vai*s*âlî; Buddha's mother died after his birth, Mahâvîra's parents lived to see him a grown-up man; Buddha turned ascetic during the lifetime and against the will of his father, Mahâvîra did so after the death of his parents and with the consent of those in power; Buddha led a life of austerities for six years, Mahâvîra for twelve; Buddha thought these years wasted time, and that all his penances were useless for attaining his end, Mahâvîra was convinced of the necessity of his

[1] See Petersburg Dictionary, ss.vv.

penances[1], and persevered in some of them even after becoming a Tîrthakara. Amongst Buddha's opponents Gosâla Makkhaliputra is by no means so prominent as amongst Mahâvîra's, nor among the former do we meet Gamâli, who caused the first schism in the Gaina church. All the disciples of Buddha bear other names than those of Mahâvîra. To finish this enumeration of differences, Buddha died in Kusinagara, whereas Mahâvîra died in Pâpâ, avowedly before the former.

I have dwelt so long on the subject of Mahâvîra's life in order to make the reader acquainted with facts which must decide the question whether the origin of Gainism was independent of Buddhism or not. Though most scholars do not go the length of denying that Mahâvîra and Buddha were different persons, yet some will not admit that this decides the question at issue. Professor Weber, in his learned treatise on the literature of the Gainas[2], says that he still regards 'the Gainas merely as one of the oldest sects of Buddhism. According to my opinion,' he writes, 'this is not precluded by the tradition about the origin of its founder having partly made use of another person than Buddha Sâkyamuni; nay, even of one whose name is frequently mentioned in Buddhist legends as one of Buddha's contemporary opponents. This rather suggests to me that the Gainas intentionally disowned Buddha, being driven to this extremity by the animosity of sect. The number and importance of coincidences in the tradition of either sect regarding their founders is, on the whole, overwhelming.'

Professor Weber's last argument, the very one on which he seems to base his theory, has, according to my opinion, been fully refuted by our preceding inquiry. This theory, in itself, would require the strongest proof before we could admit it as even probable. Generally, heterodox sects claim to be the most authentic and correct interpreters of the words and

[1] These twelve years of penance were indeed always thought essential for obtaining perfection, and every ascetic who endeavours to quit this life with the best claims to enter one of the highest heavens, or even Nirvâna, has to undergo a similar course of preparatory penance, which lasts twelve years.

[2] Indische Studien, XVI, 210.

tenets of their founders. If a sect begins to recognise another authority than that of the original founder of the main church, it either adopts another faith already in existence, or starts a new one. In the first case the previous existence of the *G*aina faith in some form or other has to be admitted; in the second we must suppose that the malcontent Buddhists searched in their scriptures for an opponent of Buddha, on whom they might foist their heretical theories, a course in which they were not followed by any other of the many sects of Buddhism. Now, granted for argument's sake, that they really did what they are charged with, they must have proceeded with the utmost dexterity, making use of, and slightly altering all occasional hints about the Nigan*th*as and Nâtaputta which they were able to hunt up in their ancient scriptures, inventing new facts, and fabricating documents of their own, which to all, not in the secret, would seem just as trustworthy as those of their opponents. Indeed the Buddhistical and *G*aina traditions about Mahâvîra, the circumstances in, and the people with whom he lived, so very well tally with, complete and correct each other that the most natural and plausible way to account for this fact, which our preceding inquiry has established, seems to be that both traditions are, in the main, independent of each other, and record what, at the time of their attaining a fixed form, was regarded as historical truth.

We shall now consider the resemblance between Buddhism and *G*ainism which has struck so many writers on this topic and greatly influenced their opinion regarding their mutual relation. Professor Lassen[1] adduces four points of coincidence which, according to his opinion, prove that the *G*ainas have branched off from the Bauddhas. We shall discuss them one after the other.

Both sects give the same titles or epithets to their prophets: *G*ina, Arhat, Mahâvîra, Sarva*gñ*a, Sugata, Tathâgata, Siddha, Buddha, Sambuddha, Parinivr*i*ta, Mukta, &c. All these words occur more or less frequently in the writings of both sects; but there is this difference, that with the exception

[1] Indische Alterthumskunde, IV, p. 763 seq.

of *G*ina, and perhaps *S*rama*n*a, the preference is given to some set of titles by one sect, and to another set by the rival sect; e.g. Buddha, Tathâgata, Sugata, and Sambuddha are common titles of *S*âkyamuni, and are only occasionally used as epithets of Mahâvîra. The case is exactly reverse with regard to Vîra and Mahâvîra, the usual titles of Vardhamâna. More marked still is the difference with regard to Tîrthakara, meaning prophet with the *G*ainas, but founder of an heretical sect with the Bauddhas. What then may be safely inferred from the peculiar choice which either sect made from these epithets and titles? That the *G*ainas borrowed them from the older Buddhists? I think not. For if these words had once been fixed as titles, or gained some special meaning beyond the one warranted by etymology, they could only have been adopted or rejected. But it was not possible that a word which had acquired some special meaning should have been adopted, but used in the original sense by those who borrowed it from the Buddhists. The most natural construction we can put on the facts is, that there was and is at all times a number of honorific adjectives and substantives applicable to persons of exalted virtue. These words were used as epithets in their original meaning by all sects; but some were selected as titles for their prophets, a choice in which they were directed either by the fitness of the word itself, or by the fact that such or such a word was already appropriated by heterodox sects as a title for their highest authority. Thus the etymological meaning of Tîrthakara is founder of a religion, prophet, and accordingly this title was adopted by the *G*ainas and other sects, whereas the Buddhists did not adopt it in this sense, but in that of an heterodox or heretical teacher, showing thereby their enmity towards those who used Tîrthakara as an honorific title. Again, Buddha is commonly used in about the same sense as mukta, that is a liberated soul, and in this meaning it is still employed in *G*aina writings, whilst with the Buddhists the word has become a title of their prophet. The only conclusion which might be forced from these facts is, that the Buddhists at the time when they formed their terminology were opponents of the *G*ainas, but not vice versâ.

Lassen, as a second argument in favour of the priority of Buddhism, adduces the fact that both sects worship mortal men, their prophets, like gods, and erect statues of them in their temples. As Buddhism and *G*ainism excepted none of the many sects, the founders of which pretended, like Buddha or Mahâvîra, to omniscience and absolute perfection, have continued long enough to come within the reach of our knowledge—and all or many of them may, for aught we know, have given the same divine honours to their saints, as the Buddhists and *G*ainas did to their own prophets—it cannot be alleged that the practice of the Buddhists rather than of any other sect was imitated by the *G*ainas, or vice versâ. On the contrary, there is nothing in the notion of Buddha that could have favoured the erecting of statues and temples for his followers to worship them, but rather much that is inconsistent with this kind of adoration, while the *G*ainas commit no inconsistency in worshipping Mahâvîra in his apotheosis. But I believe that this worship had nothing to do with original Buddhism or *G*ainism, that it did not originate with the monks, but with the lay community, when the people in general felt the want of a higher cult than that of their rude deities and demons, and when the religious development of India found in the Bhakti the supreme means of salvation. Therefore instead of seeing in the Buddhists the originals, and in the *G*ainas the imitators, with regard to the erection of temples and worship of statues, we assume that both sects were, independently from each other, brought to adopt this practice by the perpetual and irresistible influence of the religious development of the people in India.

The third point of resemblance between both sects, the stress which is laid on the ahi*m*sâ or not killing of living beings, will be treated more fully in the sequel. For this reason I quickly pass over to Professor Lassen's fourth argument, viz. that the Buddhists and *G*ainas measure the history of the world by those enormous periods of time which bewilder and awe even the most imaginative fancy.

It is true that regarding this the Gainas outdo the Buddhists, but they have the idea of such periods in common not only with the latter but also with the Brâhmans. The main features of the chronological system of the Gainas equally differ from those of the Buddhists as from those of the Brâhmans. For it is impossible to derive the Utsarpi*n*î and Avasarpi*n*î eras, with their six Aras, from the Buddhistical four great and eighty smaller Kalpas, which are as it were the acts and scenes in the drama of the successive creations and dissolutions of the universe, nor from the Yugas and Kalpas of the Brâhmans. I am of opinion that the Buddhists have improved on the Brahmanic system of the Yugas, while the Gainas invented their Utsarpi*n*î and Avasarpi*n*î eras after the model of the day and night of Brahmâ.

We have postponed the discussion of Professor Lassen's third argument, the ahi*m*sâ, because it will be better treated together with the other moral precepts of both sects. Professor Weber[1] has pointed out the near relation existing between the five great vows of the Gainas and the five cardinal sins and virtues of the Buddhists; and Professor Windisch[2] has compared the Gaina vows (mahâvrata) with the ten obligations of the Buddhists (dasasil).

The Ten Precepts for the Buddhist ascetics are the following[3]:

1. I take the vow not to destroy life.
2. I take the vow not to steal.
3. I take the vow to abstain from impurity.
4. I take the vow not to lie.
5. I take the vow to abstain from intoxicating drinks which hinder progress and virtue.
6. I take the vow not to eat at forbidden times.
7. I take the vow to abstain from dancing, singing, music, and stage plays.
8. I take the vow not to use garlands, scents, unguents, or ornaments.

[1] Fragment der Bhagavatî, II, pp. 175, 187.

[2] Zeitschrift der Deutschen Morgenländischen Gesellschaft, XXVIII, p. 222, note.

[3] Rhys Davids, Buddhism, p. 160.

9. I take the vow not to use a high or broad bed.

10. I take the vow not to receive gold or silver.

The Buddhists have also Eight Precepts (a*tth*angasîla), of which the first five (pa*ñk*asîla) are binding on every Buddhist, while the rest are only recommended to pious laymen[1]:

1. One should not destroy life.
2. One should not take that which is not given.
3. One should not tell lies.
4. One should not become a drinker of intoxicating drinks.
5. One should refrain from unlawful sexual intercourse—an ignoble thing.
6. One should not eat unseasonable food at nights.
7. One should not wear garlands or use perfumes.
8. One should sleep on a mat spread on the ground.

The five Buddhist vows nearly agree with those of the *G*aina ascetics, viz.:

1. Not to destroy life (ahi*m*sâ).
2. Not to lie (sûn*ri*ta).
3. Not to take that which is not given (asteya).
4. To abstain from sexual intercourse (brahma*k*arya).
5. To renounce all interest in worldly things, especially to call nothing one's own (aparigraha).

The fifth precept of the *G*ainas is much more comprehensive than the corresponding one of the Buddhists, but the other precepts are the same, in a different order, as Nos. 1–4 of the Buddhists. The agreement is indeed so striking that it would seem hard to avoid the conclusion that one sect borrowed their precepts from the other. Yet the question whether the Buddhists or the *G*ainas were the borrowers, would still remain an open one. It can be shown, however, that neither the Buddhists nor the *G*ainas have in this regard any claim to originality, but that both have only adopted the five vows of the Brahmanic ascetics (sa*m*nyâsin). The latter must keep the following five vows[2]:

[1] Rhys Davids, Buddhism, p. 139.

[2] Baudhâyana II, 10, 18; see Bühler's translation, Sacred Books of the East vol. xiv, p. 275.

1. Abstention from injuring living beings.
2. Truthfulness.
3. Abstention from appropriating the property of others.
4. Continence.
5. Liberality.

And five minor vows:

6. Abstention from anger.
7. Obedience towards the Guru.
8. Avoidance of rashness.
9. Cleanliness.
10. Purity in eating.

The first four great vows of the Samnyâsin agree with those of the Gaina Bhikshu, and are enumerated in the same order. It is therefore probable that the Gainas have borrowed their own vows from the Brâhmans, not from the Buddhists, because the latter have changed the order of the vows, making truthfulness either the third or fourth cardinal virtue instead of giving it the second place. Besides it is highly improbable that they should have imitated the Buddhists, when they had in the Brahmanic ascetics much older and more respected models.

It is worth remarking that the fifth great vow or precept is peculiar to each of the three religious systems, probably because the Brahmanic fifth vow, viz. liberality, could not be enjoined on mendicants such as the monks of the Buddhists and Gainas were. The Gainas previous to Mahâvîra's time had only four great vows, since the fourth was included in the fifth. But Mahâvîra brought the number of the vows again up to five, a number which seems to have been regarded as solemn, since the Buddhists have adopted it likewise in their moral code.

Our foregoing inquiry suggests where we have to look for the originals of the monastic orders of the Gainas and Buddhists. The Brahmanic ascetic was their model, from which they borrowed many important practices and institutions of ascetic life. This observation is not an entirely new one. Professor Max Müller has already, in his Hibbert Lectures (p. 351), started a similar opinion; likewise Professor Bühler, in his translation of the Baudhâyana Sûtra (passim); and Professor Kern, in his History of Buddhism in India. In order to show to what extent the life of *G*aina monks is but an imitation of the life of the Brahmanic ascetics, I shall now compare the rules given to the latter in Gautama's and Baudhâyana's law-books[1] with the rules for *G*aina monks. In most cases the Buddhists conform to the same rules; this will also be briefly noticed.

11. 'An ascetic shall not possess (any) store[2].' The *G*aina and Buddhist monks are also forbidden to have anything which they could call their own. See the fifth vow of the *G*ainas (aparigraha). Even those things which the *G*aina monk always carries about himself, as clothes, alms-bowl, broom, &c., are not regarded as his property, but as things necessary for the exercise of religious duties (dharmopakara*n*a).

12. '(He must be) chaste.' This is the fourth great vow of the *G*ainas and in Baudhâyana, the fifth of the Buddhists.

13. 'He must not change his residence during the rainy season[3].' Bühler remarks in a note: 'This rule shows that the Vasso of the Bauddhas and *G*ainas is also derived from a Brahmanic source.'

14. 'He shall enter a village only in order to beg.' The *G*ainas are not so strict in this respect, as they allow a monk to sleep in a village or town. However he must not stay too long[4]. Mahâvîra did not stay longer than one night in a village or five nights in a town[5].

15. 'He shall beg late (after people have finished their meals), without returning twice[6].' The *G*aina monks collect food in the morning or at noon, probably to avoid meeting with their rivals. They generally but once in a day go out begging; but one who has fasted for more than one day may go a begging twice a day[7].

---

[1] See Bühler's translation, Sacred Books of the East, vol. ii. pp. 191, 192. The numbers in the text refer to the paragraphs in Gautama's third book. The similar passages of Baudhâyana are referred to in the notes.

[2] Compare Baudhâyana II, 6, 11, 16.

[3] Baudhâyana II, 6, 11, 20.

[4] Âkârâṅga Sûtra II, 2, 2, § 6.

[5] Kalpa Sûtra, Lives of the *G*inas, § 119.

[6] Baudhâyana II, 6, 12, 22.

[7] Kalpa Sûtra, Rules for Yatis, § 20.

16. 'Abandoning all desires (for sweet food).' The same is prescribed in the fourth clause of the fifth great vow of the *G*ainas[1], and is, besides, the apparent motive in many rules for the acceptance or rejection of alms.

17. 'He shall restrain his speech, his eyes, (and) his actions.' This nearly agrees with the three Guptis of the *G*ainas, or the restraining of the mind, speech, and body[2].

18. 'He shall wear a cloth to cover his nakedness[3].' The *G*aina rules about dress are not so simple; for they allow a *G*aina to go naked or to wear one, two, or three garments, but a young, strong monk should as a rule wear but one robe[4]. Mahâvîra went about naked[5], and so did the *G*inakalpikas, or those who tried to imitate him as much as possible. But they also were allowed to cover their nakedness[6].

19. 'Some (declare that he shall wear) an old rag after having washed it.' Baudhâyana[7] says: 'He shall wear a dress dyed yellowish-red.' This rule agrees more with the practice of the Buddhists than that of the *G*ainas. The latter are forbidden to wash or dye their clothes, but they must wear them in the same condition in which they are given[8]. However, the *G*ainas have only carried into the extreme the original intention of the Brahmanic rule, viz. that the dress of ascetics should be as simple and mean as possible. For they seem to take a sort of pride in outdoing their Brahmanic rivals as regards rigorous conduct, mistaking nastiness and filthiness for the highest pitch of ascetic virtue[9], while on the other hand the Buddhists studied to bring their conduct in accordance with the dictates of humanity.

20. 'He shall not take parts of plants and trees except such as have become detached (spontaneously).' The *G*ainas have the same precept, but they go still farther

---

1 Â*k*ârâṅga Sûtra II, 15, v, § 15.
2 Kalpa Sûtra, Lives of the *G*inas, § 118.
3 Baudhâyana, l. c. § 16.
4 Â*k*ârâṅga Sûtra II, 5, 1, § 1.
5 Kalpa Sûtra, Lives of the *G*inas, § 117.
6 Â*k*ârâṅga Sûtra I, 7, 7, 1
7 L. c. § 21.
8 Â*k*ârâṅga Sûtra II, 5, 2, 1, and I, 7, 5, 2.
9 Compare Â*k*ârâṅga Sûtra II, 2, 2, 1.

in allowing a *G*aina to eat only such vegetables, fruits, &c. as have no trace of life left[1].

21. 'Out of season he shall not dwell a second night in (the same) village.' We have seen above that Mahâvîra carried out this precept whatever may have been the practice of the monks in general.

22. 'He may either shave or wear a lock on the crown of the head.' The *G*ainas have improved on this rule as they make baldness binding for all monks. According to Baudhâyana[2] a Brâhman on becoming an ascetic had to cause 'the hair of his head, his beard, the hair on his body, and his nails to be cut.' The same practice, at least as regards the cutting of the hair, was observed by the *G*ainas on the same occasion. Hence the phrase: 'becoming bald (or tearing out one's hair) to leave the house and enter the state of houselessness[3].'

23. 'He shall avoid the destruction of seeds.' The reader will observe, in many passages of the second book of the Â*k*ârâṅga Sûtra, how careful *G*aina monks should be of avoiding to injure eggs, living beings, seeds, sprouts, &c. It seems therefore that the *G*ainas have only generalised the above rule in applying it to all small beings of the animal and vegetable world.

24. '(He shall be) indifferent towards (all) creatures, whether they do him an injury or a kindness.'

25. 'He shall not undertake (anything for his temporal or spiritual welfare).'

The last two rules could just as well be taken from a sacred book of the *G*ainas, for they are in full accordance with the drift of their religion. Mahâvîra strictly carried them out. 'More than four months many sorts of living beings gathered on his body, crawled about it, and caused there pain[4].' 'Always well guarded, he bore the pains (caused by) grass, cold, fire, flies, and gnats; manifold pains[5].' 'He with equanimity bore, underwent, and suffered all pleasant

---

1 Â*k*ârâṅga Sûtra II, 1, 7, 6, and 8th Lesson.

2 Baudhâyana II, 10, 17, 10.

3 Mu*m*de bhavittâ agârâo a*n*agâriya*m* pavvaie.

4 Â*k*ârâṅga Sûtra I, 8, 1, 2.

5 Â*k*ârâṅga Sûtra I, 8, 3, 1.

or unpleasant occurrences, arising from divine powers, men, or animals[1].' It is frequently said of the ascetic in the last stage of his spiritual career that 'he does desire neither life nor death[2].'

There are some more precepts in Baudhâyana which bear a close resemblance to such of the Gainas. 'With the three means of punishment, (viz.) words, thoughts, and acts, he shall not injure created beings[3].' This is only an amplification of the first great vow (see above). 'Means of punishment' is what the Gainas call weapon (sastra[4]).

'He shall carry a cloth for straining water for the sake of purification.' 'He shall perform the necessary purifications with water which has been taken out (of a well or a tank) and has been strained[5].' These rules are strictly observed by the Gaina monks. They also carry a cloth for straining water. The commentator Govinda explains pavitra, 'a cloth for straining water,' by 'a bunch of Kusa grass for removing insects from the road[6].' If Govinda be right, and had the authority of a really old tradition, which I do not doubt, we have here the Brahmanic counterpart of the broom (ragoharana or pâdaproñkhana) with which the Gaina monks sweep the road and the place where they walk or sit down, for removing insects.

The outfit of a Brahmanic ascetic consists in 'sticks, a rope, a cloth for straining water, a water vessel, and an alms-bowl[7].' The Gaina monks also carry sticks, at least now-a-days, though I remember no passage in the Pitakas expressly allowing the use of a stick. They have also a rope belonging to the alms-bowl[8], an alms-bowl, and a water vessel[9]. Of the cloth for straining water, and the broom, we have already spoken. The filter for the mouth (mukhavastrika) remains as the only article exclusively used

---

[1] Kalpa Sûtra, Lives of the Ginas, § 117, towards the end.

[2] E. g. Kalpa Sûtra, Rules for Yatis, § 51.

[3] Baudhâyana II, 6, 11, 23.

[4] Âkârâṅga Sûtra, p. 1, note 2.

[5] Baudhâyana II, 6, 11, 24, 25.

[6] See Professor Bühler's translation, p. 260, note.

[7] Baudhâyana II, 10, 17, 11.

[8] Âkârâṅga Sûtra, p. 67, note 3.

[9] Though a monk is allowed to carry a water vessel besides his alms-bowl, still it is thought more meritorious to have but one bowl.

by the *G*ainas. On the whole, therefore, the *G*ainas were outfitted very much like their Brahmanic models, the Sa*m*nyâsins or Bhikshus.

'Let him eat food, given without asking, regarding which nothing has been settled beforehand, and which has reached him accidentally, so much only as is sufficient to sustain life[1].' The reader will find on perusing the *G*aina 'rules for begging[2]' that only that food is considered 'pure and acceptable' which has been obtained under exactly the same circumstances as have been laid down in the above rule of Baudhâyana for Brahmanic ascetics. The Buddhists are not so strict in this regard, as they accept invitations for dinner, of course, prepared especially for them.

From the comparison which we have just instituted between the rules for the Brahmanic ascetic and those for the *G*aina monk, it will be apparent that the latter is but a copy of the former. But now the question may be raised whether the Nirgrantha is a direct copy of the Sa*m*nyâsin, or an indirect one. For it might be assumed that the Nirgrantha copied the Buddhist Bhikkhu, who himself was but a copy of the Sa*m*nyâsin. As I have hinted above, this suggestion is not a probable one, for there being a model of higher antiquity and authority, the *G*ainas would probably have conformed rather to it than to the less respected and second-hand model of their rivals, the Buddhists. But besides this primâ facie argument against the assumption in question, the adoption of certain Brahmanic rules, noticed above, by the *G*inas, which were not followed by the Buddhists, proves that the latter were not the model of the former.

There remains another possibility, but a still more improbable one, viz. that the Brahmanic ascetic copied the Buddhist Bhikkhu or *G*aina monk. I say still more improbable, because, firstly, the Sa*m*nyâsin makes part of the system of the four stages, or Â*s*ramas, which if not so old as Brahmanism itself, is at least much older than both Buddhism and *G*ainism; secondly, the Brahmanic ascetics were scattered all over India, while the Buddhists were

[1] Baudhâyana II, 10, 18, 13.

[2] Â*k*ârâṅga Sûtra II, 1.

confined, at least in the first two centuries of their church, to a small part of the country, and therefore could not have been imitated by all the Samnyâsins; thirdly, Gautama, the lawgiver, was certainly older than the rise of Buddhism. For Professor Bühler thinks that the lower limit for the composition of the Âpastamba Sûtra must be placed in the fourth or fifth century B.C.[1] Baudhâyana is older than Âpastamba; according to Bühler[2], the distance in years between them must be measured rather by centuries than by decades. Again, Gautama is older than Baudhâyana[3]. Gautama, therefore, and perhaps Baudhâyana, must have lived before the rise of Buddhism, and as the former teaches already the complete system of Brahmanic ascetism, he cannot have borrowed it from the Buddhists. But if Bühler should be wrong in his estimation of the time when those codes of sacred laws were composed, and if they should turn out to be younger than the rise of Buddhism, they certainly cannot be so by many centuries. Even in that case, which is not a probable one, those lawgivers are not likely to have largely borrowed from the Buddhists whom the Brâhmans at that time must have despised as false pretenders of a recent origin. They would certainly not have regarded laws as sacred which were evidently appropriated from heretics. On the other hand the Buddhists had no reason not to borrow from the Brâhmans, because they greatly respected the latter for the sake of their intellectual and moral superiority. Hence the Gainas and Buddhists use the word Brâhmana as an honorific title, applying it even to persons who did not belong to the caste of Brâhmans.

It may be remarked that the monastical order of the Gainas and Buddhists though copied from the Brâhmans were chiefly and originally intended for Kshatriyas. Buddha addressed himself in the first line to noble and rich men, as has been pointed out by Professor Oldenberg[4]. For

---

[1] Sacred Laws of the Âryas, part i, introduction, p. xliii.

[2] L. c. p. xxii.

[3] L. c. p. xlix.

[4] Buddha, sein Leben, &c., p. 157 seq.

Buddha, in his first sermon at Benares, speaks of his religion as that yass' atthâya kulaputtâ sammad eva agârasmâ anagâriyam pabbaganti: for the sake of which sons of noble families leave the house and enter the state of houselessness[1]. That the Gainas too gave the Kshatriyas the preference over the Brâhmans is proved by that curious legend about the transfer of the embryo of Mahâvîra from the womb of the Brâhmanî Devânandâ to that of the Kshatriyânî Trisalâ, it being alleged that a Brâhmanî or another woman of low family was not worthy to give birth to a Tîrthakara[2].

On the other hand it is probable that Brahmanic ascetics did not regard fellow-ascetics of other castes as quite their equals, though they were just as orthodox as themselves. For in later times the opinion prevailed that only Brâhmans were entitled to enter the fourth Âsrama, and as a

[1] Mahâvagga I, 6, 12.

[2] This legend is rejected as absurd by the Digambaras, but the Svetâmbaras staunchly uphold its truth. As it is found in the Âkârânga, the Kalpa Sûtra, and many other books, it cannot be doubted that it is very old. However, it is not at all clear for what reason so absurd a legend could have been invented and have gained currency. Yet I may be allowed to offer my opinion on this dark point. I assume that Siddhârtha had two wives, the Brâhmanî Devânandâ, the real mother of Mahâvîra, and the Kshatriyânî Trisalâ; for the name of the alleged husband of the former, viz. Rishabhadatta, cannot be very old, because its Prâkrit form would in that case probably be Usabhadinna instead of Usabhadatta. Besides, the name is such as could be given to a Gaina only, not to a Brâhman. I therefore make no doubt that Rishabhadatta has been invented by the Gainas in order to provide Devânandâ with another husband. Now Siddhârtha was connected with persons of high rank and great influence through his marriage with Trisalâ. It was, therefore, probably thought more profitable to give out that Mahâvîra was the son, and not merely the step-son of Trisalâ, for this reason, that he should be entitled to the patronage of her relations. This story could all the more easily have gained credence as Mahâvîra's parents were dead many years when he came forward as a prophet. But as the real state of things could not totally have been erased from the memory of the people, the story of the transfer of the embryos was invented. The latter idea was not an original conception of the Gainas, but it is evidently borrowed from the Purânic story of the transfer of the embryo of Krishna from the womb of Devakî to that of Rohinî. The worship of Krishna seems to have been popular during the first centuries of the development of the Gaina creed; for the Gainas have reproduced the whole history of Krishna, with small alterations, in relating the life of the twenty-second Tîrthakara, Arishtanemi, who was a famous Yâdava.

proof for this theory a verse of Manu, VI, 97, as Professor Bühler informs me, was quoted. But not all commentators drew the same inference from that verse. Leaving aside this controverted point, it certainly became, in later times, the custom that a Brâhman, as a rule, passed through four, a nobleman through three, a citizen through two, a *S*ûdra through one of the four Â*s*ramas[1].

From all this it becomes probable that the non-Brahmanic ascetics even in early times were regarded as an order separate and distinguished from the Brahmanic ascetics. We can understand that this position of non-Brahmanic ascetics led to the formation of sects inclining to dissent. That the untrue ascetics had such an origin, may be collected from a remark of Vasish*th*a. It is known that the performance of religious ceremonies was discontinued by the ascetics, but some went beyond this and discontinued the recitation of the Veda. Against transgressors of this kind Vasish*th*a[2] has the following quotation: 'Let him discontinue the performance of all religious ceremonies, but let him never discontinue the recitation of the Veda. By neglecting the Veda he becomes a *S*ûdra; therefore he shall not neglect it.' An inhibition pronounced so emphatically presupposes the real occurrence of the practices forbidden. If therefore some ascetics already had ceased to recite the Veda, we may conclude that others began to disregard it as revelation and the highest authority. That those who were regarded as a sort of inferior ascetics, the non-Brahmanic ascetics, were most likely to make this step, is easy to imagine. We see thus that the germs of dissenting sects like those of the Buddhists and the *G*ainas were contained in the institute of the fourth Â*s*rama, and that the latter was the model of the heretical sects; therefore Buddhism and *G*ainism must be regarded as religions developed out of Brâhmanism not by a sudden reformation, but prepared by a religious movement going on for a long time.

[1] Max Müller, The Hibbert Lectures, p. 343.
[2] Chapter x, 4. Bühler's translation.

We have seen that neither the *G*aina legends about their last prophet, nor the ascetic life ordained for *G*aina monks, nor any other religious practices adhered to by the faithful, warrant our assuming that the *G*aina sect has developed, in one way or other, out of the Buddhistical church. It remains for me to show that the difference of both creeds as regards the principal tenets is such as not to admit a common origin. Whatever Buddha may have taught and thought about the state of Nirvâ*n*a, whether he went the length to identify it with absolute non-existence, or imagined it to be a sort of existence different from all we know or can conceive, it is beyond doubt, and a striking feature of Buddha's philosophy, that he combated the Brahmanic theory of the Âtman, as being the absolute and permanent soul, according to the pantheist as well as the monadic point of view. But the *G*ainas fully concur in the Brahmanic theory of the Âtman, with only this difference, that they ascribe to the Âtmans a limited space, while the Brâhmans of the Sâṅkhya, Nyâya, and Vai*s*eshika schools contend that the Âtmans are co-extensive with the universe. On the other hand, the Buddhistical theory of the five Skandhas with their numerous subdivisions have no counterpart in the psychology of the *G*ainas. A characteristic dogma of the *G*ainas which pervades their whole philosophical system and code of morals, is the hylozoistic theory that not only animals and plants, but also the smallest particles of the elements, earth, fire, water, and wind, are endowed with souls (*g*îva). No such dogma, on the other hand, is contained in the philosophy of the Buddhists. To Indian philosophers the various degrees of knowledge up to omniscience are matters of great moment. The *G*ainas have a theory of their own on this head, and a terminology which differs from that of the Brahmanic philosophers and of the Buddhists. Right knowledge, they say, is fivefold: (1) mati, right perception; (2) *s*ruta, clear knowledge based on mati; (3) avadhi, a sort of supernatural knowledge; (4) mana*h*-paryâya, clear knowledge of the thoughts of others; (5) kevala, the highest degree of knowledge, consisting in omniscience. This psychological theory is a fundamental one of the Gainas, as it is always before the mind of the authors of the sacred books when describing the spiritual career of the saints. But we search in vain for something analogous in the Buddhist scriptures. We could multiply the instances of difference between the fundamental tenets of both sects, but we abstain from it, fearing to tire the reader's patience with an enumeration of all such cases. Such tenets as the Gainas share with the Buddhists, both sects have in common with the Brahmanic philosophers, e. g. the belief in the regeneration of souls, the theory of the Karman, or merit and demerit resulting from former actions, which must take effect in this or another birth, the belief that by perfect knowledge and good conduct man can avoid the necessity of being born again and again, &c. Even the theory that from time immemorial prophets (Buddhas or Tîrthakaras) have proclaimed the same dogmas and renewed the sinking faith, has its Brahmanic counterpart in the Avatâras of Vish*n*u. Besides, such a theory is a necessary consequence both of the Buddhistical and Gaina creed. For what Buddha or Mahâvîra had revealed was, of course, regarded by the followers of either as truth and the only truth; this truth must have existed from the beginning of time, like the Veda of the Brâhmans; but could the truth have remained unknown during the infinite space of time elapsed before the appearance of the prophet? No, would answer the pious believer in Buddhism or Gainism, that was impossible; but the true faith was revealed in different periods by numberless prophets, and so it will be in the time to come. The theory of former prophets seems, therefore, to be a natural consequence of both religions; besides, it was not wholly unfounded on facts, at least as regards the Gainas. For the Nirgranthas are never spoken of in the Buddhist writings as a newly risen sect, nor Nâtaputta as their founder. Accordingly the Nirgranthas were probably an old sect at the time of Buddha, and Nâtaputta only the reformer of the Gaina church, which may have been founded by the twenty-third Tîrthakara, Pârsva. But what seems astonishing is the fact that the Gainas and Bauddhas have hit on nearly the same number of prophets believed to have risen since the creation of the present order of things, the former worshipping twenty-four Tîrthakaras, the latter twenty-five Buddhas. I do not deny that in developing this theory one sect was influenced by the other; but I firmly believe that it cannot be made out which of the two sects first invented, or borrowed from the Brâhmans, this theory. For if the twenty-five Buddhas were worshipped by the Buddhists of the first centuries after the Nirvâ*n*a, the belief in twenty-four Tîrthakaras is equally old, as it is common to the Digambaras and *S*vetâmbaras, who separated probably in the second century after the Nirvâ*n*a. However the decision of the question whether the Buddhists or the *G*ainas originally invented the theory of the succession of prophets, matters little; it cannot influence the result to which the previous discussion has led us, viz. (1) that *G*ainism had an origin independent from Buddhism, that it had a development of its own, and did not largely borrow from the rival sect; (2) that both *G*ainism and Buddhism owed to the Brâhmans, especially the Sa*m*nyâsins, the groundwork of their philosophy, ethics, and cosmogony.

Our discussion has as yet been conducted on the supposition that the tradition of the *G*ainas as contained in their sacred books may on the whole be credited. But the intrinsic value of this tradition has been called into question by a scholar of wide views and cautious judgment. Mr. Barth, in the Revue de l'Histoire des Religions, vol. iii, p. 90, admits that an historical personage is hidden under Nâtaputta, but he doubts that valid inferences may be drawn from the sacred books of the *G*ainas which, avowedly, have been reduced to writing in the fifth century A. D., or nearly a thousand years after the foundation of the sect. For, in his opinion, 'the self-conscient and continuous existence of the sect since that remote epoch, i. e. the direct tradition of peculiar doctrines and records, has not yet been demonstrated. During many centuries,' he says, 'the *G*ainas had not become distinct from the numerous groups of ascetics who could not boast of more than an obscure floating existence.' The tradition of the *G*ainas appears to Mr. Barth to have been formed of vague recollections in imitation of the Buddhist tradition.

Mr. Barth seems to base his theory on the assumption that the *G*ainas must have been careless in handing down their sacred lore, since they formed, for many centuries, but a small and unimportant sect. I cannot see the force of this argument of Mr. Barth's. Is it more likely that a sect of which the not very numerous followers are scattered over a large country, or a church which has to satisfy the religious wants of a great multitude, will better preserve its original tenets and traditions? It is impossible to decide this question on à priori grounds. The Jews and the Parsis may be adduced as instances in favour of the former view, the Roman Catholic church as one in favour of the latter. But we are not obliged to rely on such generalities in order to decide the question at issue with regard to the *G*ainas, for they were so far from having only dim notions of their own doctrines that they pronounced as founders of schisms those who differed from the great bulk of the faithful in comparatively unimportant details of belief. This fact is proved by the tradition about the seven sects of the *S*vetâmbaras made known by Dr. Leumann[1]. The Digambaras also, who separated from the *S*vetâmbaras probably in the second or third century after the Nirvâ*n*a, differ from their rivals but little with regard to philosophical tenets; yet they were nevertheless stigmatised by the latter as heretics on account of their rules of conduct. All these facts show that the *G*ainas, even previous to the redaction of their sacred books, had not a confused and undefined creed, which would have been liable to become altered and defiled by doctrines adopted from widely different religions, but one in which even the minutest details of belief were fixed.

What has been said about the religious doctrines of the *G*ainas can also be proved of their historical traditions. For the detailed lists of teachers handed down in the several Ga*kkh*as[2], and those incorporated in their sacred

[1] See Indische Studien, XVI. [2] See Dr. Klatt, Ind. Ant. XI.

books, show that the *G*ainas did possess an interest in the history of their church. I do not deny that a list of teachers may be invented, or an incomplete one filled up or made pakka, as the Hindus would say; the necessity of proving itself to be legitimately descended from a recognised authority may induce a sect to invent the names of a line of teachers. But what could have caused the *G*ainas to fabricate such a detailed list of teachers, *Ga*n*a*s, and *S*âkhâs as that in the Kalpa Sûtra? Of most of the details the *G*ainas of later times knew nothing beyond what they found in the Kalpa Sûtra itself,—and that is unfortunately very little,—nor did they pretend to anything more. For all practical purposes the short list of Sthaviras, as it stands in the Kalpa Sûtra, would have been sufficient; the preservation of the detailed list, containing so many bare names, proves that they must have had an interest for the members of the early church, though the more accurate knowledge of the times and events chronicled in that list was lost after some centuries.

However, it is not enough to have proved that the *G*ainas, even before the redaction of their sacred books, possessed the qualities necessary for continuing their creed and tradition, and preserving them from corruptions caused by large borrowings from other religious systems; we must also show that they did do what they were qualified to do. This leads us to a discussion of the age of the extant *G*aina literature. For if we succeed in proving that the *G*aina literature or at least some of its oldest works were composed many centuries before they were reduced to writing, we shall have reduced, if not closed, the gap separating the prophet of the *G*ainas from their oldest records.

The redaction of the *G*aina canon or the Siddhânta took place, according to the unanimous tradition, on the council of Valabhi, under the presidency of Devarddhi. The date of this event, 980 (or 993) A.V., corresponding to 454 (or 467) A.D.[1], is incorporated in the Kalpa Sûtra (§ 148). Devarddhi Ga*n*in, says the tradition, perceiving the Siddhânta in

[1] It is possible, but not probable, that the date of the redaction fell sixty years later, 514 (527) A.D.; see Kalpa Sûtra, introduction, p. 15.

danger of becoming extinct, caused it to be written in books. Before that time teachers made no use of written books when teaching the Siddhânta to novices, but after that time they did use books. The latter part of this statement is evidently true. For in olden times books were not used, it being the custom of the Brâhmans to rely rather on the memory than on the MSS., and in this they were, almost without doubt, followed by the *G*ainas and Buddhists. But now-a-days Yatis use MSS. when teaching the sacred lore to their novices. There is no reason why we should not credit the tradition that this change in the method of instruction was brought about by Devarddhi Ga*n*in; for the event was of too great importance not to be remembered. To provide every teacher or at least every Upâ*s*raya with copies of the sacred books, Devarddhi Ga*n*in must have issued a large edition of the Siddhânta. This is probably the meaning of the traditional record that Devarddhi caused the Siddhânta to be written in books, for it is hardly credible that the *G*aina monks should never before have attempted to write down what they had to commit to memory; the Brâhmans also have MSS. of their sacred books, though they do not use them in handing down the Veda. These MSS. were intended for private use, to aid the memory of the teacher. I make no doubt that the same practice was observed by the *G*aina monks, the more so as they were not, like the Brâhmans, influenced by any theory of their own not to trust to MSS., but were induced merely by the force of the prevalent custom to hand down their sacred lore by word of mouth. I do not maintain that the sacred books of the *G*ainas were originally written in books, for the same argument which has been brought forward to prove that the Buddhist monks could have had no MSS., as they are never mentioned in their sacred books, in which 'every movable thing, down to the smallest and least important domestic utensils, is in some way or other referred to[1],' the same argument, I say, holds good with regard to the *G*ainas as long as the

[1] Sacred Books of the East, vol. xiii, introduction, p. xxxiii.

monks led a wandering life; but when the monks were settled in Upâsrayas exclusively belonging to themselves, they may have kept there their MSS. as they do now-a-days.

Devarddhi's position relative to the sacred literature of the *G*ainas appears therefore to us in a different light from what it is generally believed to have been. He probably arranged the already existing MSS. in a canon, taking down from the mouth of learned theologians only such works of which MSS. were not available. Of this canon a great many copies were taken, in order to furnish every seminary with books which had become necessary by the newly introduced change in the method of religious instruction. Devarddhi's edition of the Siddhânta is therefore only a redaction of the sacred books which existed before his time in nearly the same form. Any single passage in a sacred text may have been introduced by the editor, but the bulk of the Siddhânta is certainly not of his making. The text of the sacred books, before the last redaction of the Siddhânta, did not exist in such a vague form as it would have been liable to if it were preserved only by the memory of the monks, but it was checked by MSS.

On this premise we now proceed to inquire into the date of the composition of the sacred books of the *G*ainas. Their own dogmatical theory that all sacred books were revealed by the first Tîrthakara, shall only be noticed to be dismissed. We must try to discover better grounds for fixing the age when the chief works of the Siddhânta were composed.

As single passages may have crept into the text at any time, we can draw no valid inferences from them, even if they be sanctioned by Devarddhi's receiving them into his revised text. I attach therefore no great weight to the lists of barbarous or un-Aryan tribes[1], nor to the mention of all seven schisms, the last of which occurred 584 A. V.[2] Nothing is more common than that such details should be

[1] Among the latter Ârava may denote the Arabs, as Weber thinks, or, as I prefer to think, the Tamils, whose language is called Aravamu by the Dravidians.

[2] See Weber, Indische Studien, XVI, p. 237.

added as a gloss, or be incorporated even in the text, by those who transmitted it either in writing or in instructing their pupils. But an argument of more weight is the fact that in the Siddhânta we find no traces of Greek astronomy. In fact the Gaina astronomy is a system of incredible absurdity, which would have been impossible, if its author had had the least knowledge of the Greek science. As the latter appears to have been introduced in India about the third or fourth century A. D., it follows that the sacred books of the Gainas were composed before that time.

Another argument which offers itself for fixing the period of the composition of the sacred books, is the language in which they are written. But, unfortunately, it is not at all clear whether the sacred books have been handed down in that language in which they were composed, or in that in which they were pronounced, and transcribed in later generations, according to the then current idiom, till Devarddhi's edition put an end to the modernising of the language of the sacred books. I am inclined to believe the latter view to be correct, and look upon the absence of a self-consistent orthography of the Gaina Prâkrit as the effect of the gradual change of the vernacular language in which the sacred books were recited. In all MSS. of Gaina texts, the same word is not always spelt in the same way. The differences of spelling refer chiefly to the retention, omission, or attenuation of single consonants between vowels, and the retention of the vowels e, o, before two consonants, or their change in i, u. It is hardly possible that the different spellings of a word should all correctly represent the pronunciation of that word at any given time, e.g. bhûta, bhûya; udaga, udaya, uaya; lobha, loha[1], &c.; but probably we must regard these methods of spelling as historical spellings, that is to say, that all different spellings presented in the MSS. which formed the materials for Devarddhi's edition of the Siddhânta, were looked upon as authentical and were preserved in all later copies of the sacred texts. If this assumption is correct, we

[1] I do not contend that no double forms of any word were current at any time, for there must have been a good many double forms, but I doubt that nearly every word should have existed in two or three forms.

must regard the most archaic spellings as representing the pronunciation at or shortly after the epoch of the composition of the sacred books, and the most modern one as representing the pronunciation at or shortly before the redaction of the Siddhânta[1]. Now on comparing the *G*aina Prâkrit especially in the oldest form attainable with the Pâli on one side, and the Prâkrit of Hâla, Setubandha, &c. on the other, it will appear to approach more the Pâli than the later Prâkrit. We may therefore conclude that chronologically also the sacred books of the *G*aina's stand nearer those of the Southern Buddhists than the works of later Prâkrit writers.

But we can fix the date of the *G*aina literature between still narrower limits by means of the metres employed in the sacred books. I am of opinion that the first book of the Â*k*ârâṅga Sûtra and that of the Sûtrak*ri*tâṅga Sûtra may be reckoned among the most ancient parts of the Siddhânta; the style of both works appears to me to prove the correctness of this assumption. Now a whole lesson of the Sûtrak*ri*tâṅga Sûtra is written in the Vaitâlîya metre. The same metre is used in the Dhammapadam and other sacred books of the Southern Buddhists. But the Pâli verses represent an older stage in the development of the Vaitâlîya than those in the Sûtrak*ri*tâṅga, as I shall prove in a paper on the post-Vedic metres soon to be published in the Journal of the German Oriental Society. Compared with the common Vaitâlîya verses of Sanskrit literature, a small number of which occur already in the Lalita Vistara, the Vaitâlîya of the Sûtrak*ri*tâṅga must be considered to represent an earlier form of the metre. Again, ancient Pâli works seem to contain no verses in the Aryâ metre; at least there is none in the Dhammapadam, nor have I found one in other works. But both the Â*k*ârâṅga and Sûtrak*ri*tâṅga

[1] It might be objected that archaic spellings are due to the influence of the knowledge of Sanskrit; but the *G*ainas must always have been so well acquainted with Prâkrit that they needed not any help from the Sanskrit to understand their sacred books. On the contrary, in their Sanskrit MSS. we frequently meet with words spelt like Prâkrit words. Besides, some spellings cannot be explained as Sanskriticisms, e.g. dâraga for dâraya, the Sanskrit prototype being dâraka.

contain each a whole lecture in Âryâ verses of a form which is decidedly older than, and probably the parent of the common Âryâ. The latter is found in the younger parts of the Siddhânta, in the Brahmanical literature, both in Prâkrit and in Sanskrit, and in the works of the Northern Buddhists, e.g the Lalita Vistara, &c. The form of the Trishtubh metre in ancient Gaina works is younger than that in the Pâli literature and older than that in the Lalita Vistara. Finally the great variety of artificial metres in which the greater number of the Gâthâs in the Lalita Vistara, &c., is composed and which are wanting in the Gaina Siddhânta, seems to prove that the literary taste of the Gainas was fixed before the composition of the latter works. From all these facts we must conclude that the chronological position of the oldest parts of the Gaina literature is intermediate between the Pâli literature and the composition of the Lalita Vistara. Now the Pâli Pitakas were written in books in the time of Vatta Gâmani, who began to reign 88 B.C. But they were in existence already some centuries before that time. Professor Max Müller sums up his discussion on that point by saying: 'We must be satisfied therefore, so far as I can see, at present with fixing the date, and the latest date, of a Buddhist canon at the time of the Second Council, 377 B.C.[1]' Additions and alterations may have been made in the sacred texts after that time; but as our argument is not based on a single passage, or even a part of the Dhammapada, but on the metrical laws of a variety of metres in this and other Pâli books, the admission of alterations and additions in these books will not materially influence our conclusion, viz. that the whole of the Gaina Siddhânta was composed after the fourth century B.C.

We have seen that the oldest works in the Gaina canon are older than the Gâthâs in the Lalita Vistara. As this work is said to have been translated into Chinese 65 A.D., we must place the origin of the extant Gaina literature before the beginning of our era. If we may judge about

[1] Sacred Books of the East, vol. x, p. xxxii.

the distance in time of the questionable date from either limit by the greater or less resemblance of the oldest *G*aina works in verse with such of the Southern and Northern Buddhists as regards metrical or stylistic peculiarities, we should place the beginning of the *G*aina literature nearer the time of the Pâli literature, rather than that of the Northern Buddhists. This result agrees pretty well with a tradition of the *S*vetâmbaras. For they say[1] that after the twelve years' famine, while Bhadrabâhu was the head of the church, the Aṅgas were brought together by the Saṅgha of Pâ*t*aliputra. Now Bhadrabâhu's death is placed 170 A.V. by the *S*vetâmbaras, and 162 A.V. by the Digambaras; he lived therefore, according to the former, under *K*andragupta, who is said to have ascended the throne 155 A.V. Professor Max Müller assigns to *K*andragupta the dates 315–291 B.C.; Westergaard prefers 320 B.C. as a more likely date for *K*andragupta, and so does Kern[2]. However this difference matters little: the date of the collection or, perhaps more correctly, the composition of the *G*aina canon would fall somewhere about the end of the fourth or the beginning of the third century B.C. It is worth noticing, that according to the above-cited tradition, the Saṅgha of Pâ*t*aliputra collected the eleven Aṅgas without the assistance of Bhadrabâhu. As the latter is claimed by the Digambaras for one of their teachers, and as the *S*vetâmbaras, though doing the same, still continue the list of Sthaviras from Sambhûtavi*g*aya, Bhadrabâhu's fellow Sthavira, not from Bhadrabâhu himself, it seems to follow that the Aṅgas, brought together by the Saṅgha of Pâ*t*aliputra, formed the canon of the *S*vetâmbaras only, not that of the whole *G*aina church. In that case we should not go wrong in placing the date of the canon somewhat later, under the patriarchate of Sthûlabhadra, i.e. in the first part of the third century B.C.

If the result of our preceding inquiry deserves credit—and I see no counter arguments entitling us to mistrust our conclusion—the origin of the extant *G*aina literature cannot be placed earlier than about 300 B.C., or two centuries after

[1] Parisish*t*a Parvan IX, 55 seqq.

[2] Geschiedenis van het Buddhisme in Indie, ii, p. 266 note.

the origin of the sect. But we are not from this fact obliged to assume that the Gainas in the time intermediate between their last prophet and the composition of their canon had to rely on nothing more solid than a religious and legendary tradition, never brought into a fixed form. In that case, Mr. Barth's objections to the trustworthiness of the Gaina tradition would, it is true, not be without ground. However, we are told by the Svetâmbaras, as well as the Digambaras, that besides the Aṅgas, there existed other and probably older works, called Pûrvas, of which there were originally fourteen. The knowledge of these Pûrvas was gradually lost, till at last it became totally extinct. The tradition of the Svetâmbaras about the fourteen Pûrvas is this: the fourteen Pûrvas had been incorporated in the twelfth Aṅga, the Drishtivâda, which was lost before 1000 A.V. But a detailed table of contents of it, and consequently of the Pûrvas, has survived in the fourth Aṅga, the Samavâyâṅga, and in the Nandî Sûtra[1]. Whether the Pûrvas, contained in the Drishtivâda, were the original ones, or, as I am inclined to believe, only abstracts of them, we cannot decide; at all events there has been a more detailed tradition about what they contained.

Now we should as a rule be careful in crediting any tradition about some lost book or books of great antiquity, because such a tradition is frequently invented by an author to furnish his doctrines with an authority from which they may be derived. But in our case, there are no grounds for suspecting the correctness of so general and old a tradition as that about the Pûrvas. For the Aṅgas do not derive their authority from the Pûrvas, but are believed to be coeval with the creation of the world. As a fraud, the tradition about the Pûrvas would therefore be unintelligible; but accepted as truth, it well falls in with our views about the development of the Gaina literature. The name itself testifies to the fact that the Pûrvas were superseded by a new canon, for pûrva means former,

[1] See Weber, Indische Studien, XVI, p. 341 seqq.

earlier[1]; and it is assuredly not by accident that the knowledge of the Pûrvas is said to have commenced to fade away at the same time when the Aṅgas were collected by the Saṅgha of Pâtaliputra. For after Bhadrabâhu, only ten out of the fourteen Pûrvas were known.

This then is the most natural interpretation we can place on the tradition about the fourteen Pûrvas, that they were the oldest sacred books, which however were superseded by a new canon. But as regards the cause of the abolition of the old canon and the composition of a new one, we are left to conjecture, and only as such I shall give my opinion. We know that the D*ri*sh*t*ivâda, which included the fourteen Pûrvas, dealt chiefly with the d*ri*sh*t*is or philosophical opinions of the *G*ainas and other sects. It may be thence inferred that the Pûrvas related controversies held between Mahâvîra and rival teachers. The title pravâda, which is added to the name of each Pûrva, seems to affirm this view. Besides, if Mahâvîra was not the founder of a new sect, but as I have tried to prove, the reformer of an old one, it is very likely that he should vigorously have combated the opinions of his opponents, and defended those he had accepted or improved. The founder of a religion has to establish his own system, he is not so much in danger to become a mere controversialist as a reformer. Now if the discourses of Mahâvîra, remembered and handed down by his disciples, were chiefly controversies, they must have lost their interest when the opponents of Mahâvîra had died and the sects headed by them had become extinct. Could such contentions about philosophical questions which were no more of any practical importance, and bickerings of divines all but forgotten, though these things were of paramount interest to the contemporary world, serve as a canon for later generations who lived in thoroughly changed circumstances? The want of a canon suiting the condition of the

---

[1] The *G*ainas explain the meaning of the word pûrva in the following way. The Tîrthakara himself taught the Pûrvas to his disciples, the Ga*n*adharas. The Ga*n*adharas then composed the Aṅgas. There is evidently some truth in this tradition, as it does not agree with the dogma of the Aṅgas, being taught already by the first Tîrthakara. See Weber, Indische Studien, XVI, p. 353.

community must have made itself felt, and it led, in my opinion, to the composition of a new canon and the neglect of the old one

Professor A. Weber[1] assigns as the probable cause of the D*ri*sh*t*ivâda being lost, that the development of the *S*vetâmbara sect had arrived at a point where the diversity of its tenets from those embodied in that book became too visible to be passed over. Therefore the D*ri*sh*t*ivâda, which contained the Pûrvas, fell into neglect. I cannot concur in Prof ssor Weber's opinion, seeing that the Digambaras also have lost the Pûrvas, and the Aṅgas to boot. It is not probable that the development of *G*ainism during the two first centuries after the Nirvâ*n*a should have gone on at so rapid a pace that its two principal sects should have been brought to the necessity of discarding their old canon. For, as stated above, after the splitting of the church in these two sects the philosophical system of the *G*ainas remained stationary, since it is nearly the same with both sects. As regards ethics, both sects, it is true, differ more. But as the extant canon of the *S*vetâmbaras is not falling into neglect, though many practices enjoined in it have long since been abandoned, it is not more probable that they should have been more sensible on the same score at the time when the Pûrvas formed their canon. Besides, some of the Pûrvas are said to have continued to be extant long after the time which we have assigned for the formation of the new canon. At last they disappeared, not by an intentional neglect, I presume, but because the new canon set into clearer light the *G*aina doctrines, and put them forward more systematically than had been done in the controversial literature of the Pûrvas.

Our discussion, which we here close, has, I hope, proved that the development of the *G*aina church has not been, at any time, violently interrupted by some very extraordinary events; that we can follow this development from its true beginning through its different stages, and that *G*ainism is as much independent from other sects, especially from

[1] Indische Studien, XVI, p. 248.

Buddhism, as can be expected from any sect. We must leave to future researches to work out the details, but I hope to have removed the doubts, entertained by some scholars, about the independence of the *G*aina religion and the value of its sacred books as trustworthy documents for the elucidation of its early history.

It remains for me to add a few remarks about the two works which have been translated in this book.

The Â*k*ârâṅga Sûtra, or, as it is sometimes called, the Sâmâyika[1], is the first of the eleven Aṅgas. It treats of the â*k*âra, or conduct, which falls under the last of the four heads, or anuyogas, into which the sacred lore is divided, viz. Dharmakathâ, Ga*n*ita, Dravya, and *K*ara*n*akara*n*a. The Âkârâṅga Sûtra contains two books, or *S*rutaskandhas, very different from each other in style and in the manner in which the subject is treated. The subdivisions of the second book being called *K*ûlâs, or appendices, it follows that only the first book is really old. That it was considered so even in later times, is apparent from a remark of *S*îlâṅka, who wrote the commentary, which is the oldest one extant[2]. For speaking of the maṅgala or auspicious sentence which, according to a current theory, must occur at the beginning, in the middle, and at the end of each work. *S*îlâṅka points out as such the first sentence of the first lesson of the first lecture, the first sentence of the fifth lesson of the fifth lecture, and the latter half of the 16th verse in the fourth lesson of the eighth lecture of the first book. It is evident that he regarded the Â*k*ârâṅga Sûtra as ending with the last-named passage, which is the last but one of the first book.

The first book, then, is the oldest part of the Â*k*ârâṅga Sûtra; it is probably the old Â*k*ârâṅga Sûtra itself to which other treatises have been added. For it is complete in

---

[1] See Professor Weber's remarks on the possible bearing of this name in the treatise I had so often occasion to quote, p. 243 seqq.

[2] It was not, however, the first commentary, for *S*îlâṅka mentions one by Gandhahastin.

itself; it describes in rather enigmatical language the progress of the faithful towards the highest perfection. The last lecture, a sort of popular ballad on the glorious suffering of the prophet, was perhaps added in later times, but as it stands now it serves well to illustrate and to set a high example of the true ascetic's life. But the greater part of the book is in prose of the most bewildering kind. Frequently we meet with fragments only of sentences, or with sentences which it is impossible to construe. This reminds us of the style of the Brahmânical Sûtras; but there is this difference, that in the last-named works the single aphorisms are the necessary links in the logical concatenation of ideas, while in our book the single sentences or parts of sentences do not seem to be connected with one another in order to carry on the illustration of an idea. They do not read like a logical discussion, but like a sermon made up by quotations from some then well-known sacred books. In fact the fragments of verses and whole verses which are liberally interspersed in the prose text go far to prove the correctness of my conjecture; for many of these 'disjecta membra' are very similar to verses or Pâdas of verses occurring in the Sûtrakritânga, Uttarâdhyayana, and Dasavaikâlika Sûtras. They must therefore be taken as allusions to standard authorities. The same must be assumed of at least some prose sentences, especially those which are incomplete in themselves. Other passages again seem to be added to those quotations in order to explain or to complete them. I shall give a few specimens. I, 4, 1, 3 we read, aho ya râo gatamânĕ dhîre; this is a Pâda of a Trishtubh, and accordingly a quotation. The words which follow, sayâ âgayapannane, explain the meaning of that quotation, aho ya râo = sayâ, gatamâne dhîre = âgayapannâne. The text continues pamatte bahiyâ pâsa. This is probably a Pâda of a Sloka; the rest of the sentence, appamatte sayâ parakkameggâ, is the moral application of the preceding one. We should therefore translate: 'Day and night exerting himself and steadfast,' i. e. always having ready wisdom. 'Look, the careless stand outside,' (therefore) being careful he should always exert himself. The commentator however does not separate the quotations from the glosses, but takes all these passages as parts of one sentence, which he interprets in the way that it has been rendered in the text of my translation, p. 37.

In this as in many other cases I have preferred to give in my translation the meaning which *S*îlâṅka has given in his commentary. For it is sometimes extremely difficult to separate the quotations from the remaining text. I have never dared to do so when they could not be proved to be parts of verses. I had therefore to leave unnoticed all such passages which, as the one quoted above, might be taken as a Pâda of a *S*loka; for in every prose work such passages occur, though they never were meant for verse. They may, therefore, only accidentally resemble parts of a *S*loka in our book too, though the great number of such passages is rather suspicious. The greatest difficulty however we should incur if we were to point out the prose quotations, though there are certainly such, e.g. I, 3, 1, 1, suttâ amu*n*î, mu*n*ino satata*m* *g*âgaranti. Such phrases differ in style from the rest of the prose part; but it would be impossible to draw the line between them and the work of the real author. From what has been said, it will appear how difficult it is to do justice to such a work as the first book of the Â*k*ârâṅga in the first attempt to translate it. In most cases I have contented myself with rendering the text according to the interpretation of the commentator. It must be left to future labours to come nearer the meaning of the author than it has been preserved by the tradition of the scholiasts.

Formerly the first book contained nine lectures instead of eight, one lecture, the Mahâparinnâ, being now lost. It was, according to some authorities, Samavâyâṅga, Nandî, Âva*s*yaka Niryukti, and Vidhiprabhâ [1], the ninth lecture; but according to the Niryukti of the Â*k*ârâṅga Sûtra, which contains a systematic exposition of the subjects treated in the single lectures and lessons of the Â*k*ârâṅga itself, and

[1] See Weber, Indische Studien, XVI, p. 251 seq.

to *S*îlâṅka and the other commentators, it was the eighth lecture. It contained seven lessons, and treated of some details of ascetic life[1]. The fact that the same subjects were treated in the second book probably occasioned the loss of the Mahâparinnâ, 'because it was superfluous[2].'

The second book consists of four parts (*K*ûlâ) or appendices. There were originally five *K*ûlâs, but the fifth, the Nisîhiya*gg*h*a*n*a*, is now reckoned as a separate work. The first and second parts lay down rules for conduct. Their style is very different from that of the first book, being rather cumbrous, and not at all aphoristical. The greatest difficulty in translating these parts is caused by the numerous technical terms, some of which remain obscure, notwithstanding the explanation of the commentary; others again are simply transcribed into Sanskrit by the scholiast, and seem to require no definition to be understood by the modern *G*ainas. But it is different with us, who are frequently reduced to guessing at the meaning of technicalities which a Yati could explain at once. It is therefore to be hoped that some scholars in India, who can avail themselves of the instruction of a Yati, will turn their attention to this subject, and get an authentic explanation of the many technical terms the meaning of which cannot be ascertained by a European scholar by the means of *G*aina works only.

The third and fourth *K*ûlâs have, according to the Parisish*t*a Parvan IX, been revealed to the eldest sister of Sthûlabhadra by Sîmandhara, a *G*ina living in Pûrvavideha, a mythical continent. This tradition is very remarkable, as it assigns what we should call the composition of the two last parts of the Âkârâṅga Sûtra to the same time when the Kalpa Sûtra, which treats of a similar subject, was composed.

The third part is of great interest, as it contains the materials from which the Life of Mahâvîra in the Kalpa Sûtra has been worked out. In fact most of the prose paragraphs occur with but small alterations in the Kalpa

[1] See Calcutta edition, I, p. 435 seq., vv. 251–268.

[2] Sâisayattane*n*a, Weber, l. c.

Sûtra. The latter work adds little that is material from an historical point of view, but a great deal of descriptions which have become typical and are to be found in other *G*aina works adapted to similar circumstances. The Â*k*â-rânga Sûtra contains, besides the above-mentioned paragraphs, some verses which are wanting in the Kalpa Sûtra. On comparing these verses with those in the eighth lecture of the first book, we become aware of the great difference which subsists between both portions of the Â*k*ârânga Sûtra, for in both, kindred subjects are treated in Âryâ verses, yet the difference in style and in the treatment of the metre is such as can only be explained by the assumption of a considerable distance of time.

The latter part of the third *K*ûlâ, which treats of the five great vows, with their twenty-five clauses, calls for no further remark; nor is anything more to be said about the twelve verses which make up the fourth *K*ûlâ, but that they are probably old, and have been added here for want of a better place.

The translation of the Â*k*ârânga Sûtra is based on my edition of the text in the Pâli Text Society[1], and the commentaries printed in the Calcutta edition of the Â*k*â-rânga Sûtra. They are:

1. *T*îkâ of *S*îlânka, also called Tattvâditya, said to have been finished in the *S*aka year 798 or 876 A.D., with the help of Vâhari Sâdhu.

2. Dîpikâ of *G*inaha*m*sa Sûri, a teacher of the B*ri*hat Kharatara Ga*kkh*a. The Dîpikâ is almost verbally copied from the *T*îkâ, which it pretends to reduce to a smaller compass. But the reduction consists almost entirely in the omission of *S*îlânka's comments on the Niryukti verses, which form his introduction to every lecture and lesson.

3. Pârsva*k*andra's Bâlâvabodha or Gugerati Gloss. In some parts of the second book, which are not explained in the older commentaries, this gloss was the only help I had. It generally closely follows the explanation of the older commentaries, more especially that of the Dîpikâ.

About the Kalpa Sûtra I have spoken at some length in

[1] The Âyârâ*m*ga Sutta of the *Ç*vetâmbara Jains, London, 1882.

the introduction to my edition of that work[1], to which I refer the reader for further particulars. Since that time Professor Weber has taken up the subject in his treatise on the Sacred Books of the *G*ainas and corrected some mistakes of mine. He ascertained that the whole Kalpa Sûtra is incorporated as the eighth lecture in the Da*s*â-*s*rutaskandha, the fourth *Kh*eda Sûtra. Professor Weber concurs in my opinion that the 'Rules for Yatis' may be the work of Bhadrabâhu[2], and that the 'List of Sthaviras' probably has been added by Devarddhi, the editor of the Siddhânta. I do not think, however, that Devarddhi was the author of the Life of Mahâvîra also, as Professor Weber suggests. For if it were the work of so well known a man, tradition would certainly not have allowed such a fact to become forgotten. It was a different thing with the List of Sthaviras, which consists of four or five distinct treatises only put together and added to the Lives of the *G*inas by the editor of the work. We cannot argue from the style of the Lives of the *G*inas that that part must be younger than the Rules for Yatis; for the same difference of style occasioned by the diversity of the matter exists between the third *K*ûlâ of the Â*k*ârâṅga Sûtra and the two preceding ones. Nor can the meagreness of the contents be adduced as an argument against the antiquity of the Lives of the *G*inas, since they were probably not intended for biographical treatises, but served a liturgical purpose; for when the images of the Tîrthakaras are worshipped in the temples they are addressed with hymns, one of which sums up the Kalyâ*n*akas or auspicious moments[3]. It is

[1] The Kalpa Sûtra of Bhadrabâhu, Leipzig, 1879. Abhandlungen für die Kunde des Morgenlandes, VII, 1.

[2] That the 'Rules for Yatis' must have been composed at least six generations after Mahâvîra is evident from §§ 3–8, but probably the work is still younger. For in § 6 the Sthaviras, who come immediately after the disciples of the Ga*n*adharas, are spoken of in some contrast to the '*S*rama*n*as Nirgranthas of the present time.' Yet the work cannot be comparatively young, because it appears from §§ 28–30 that the *G*inakalpa had not yet fallen into disuse, as it had done in later times.

[3] The rites are described and the hymns given in a modern work called *K*aturvi*m*satitîrthaṅkarâ*n*âm pûgâ, a MS. of which belongs to the Deccan College.

with these Kalyâ*n*akas that the Lives of the *G*inas are chiefly concerned, and this fact seems to prove that the custom of mentioning the Kalyâ*n*akas in the worship of the Tîrthakaras is a very old one; for otherwise it would be impossible to conceive what could have induced an author to treat so largely of so barren a subject as has been done in the Kalpa Sûtra. But whatever may be the age of the several parts of the Kalpa Sûtra, it is certain that this work has been held in high esteem by the *G*ainas for more than a thousand years. It therefore deserves a place in this collection of translations from the Sacred Books of the East. I could only have wished to make my translation more worthy of the place where it is to make its appearance; but if I have somewhat fallen short in my performance, I hope it will be accepted as an excuse that I had to translate into a language which is not my own, works of a literature which, notwithstanding all that has been done for it, still is all but virgin soil to us.

HERMANN JACOBI.

MÜNSTER, WESTPHALIA,
June, 1884.

ÂKÂRÂṄGA SÛTRA.

ÂKÂRÂṄGA SÛTRA.

FIRST BOOK[1].

FIRST LECTURE[2],

CALLED

KNOWLEDGE OF THE WEAPON.

First Lesson[3].

O long-lived (Gambûsvâmin[4])! I (Sudharman) have heard the following discourse from the venerable (Mahâvîra): (1)

Here many do not remember whether they have descended in an eastern direction (when they were born in this world), or in a southern, or in a western, or in a northern direction, or in the direction from above, or in the direction from below, or in a direction intermediate (between the cardinal points), or in a direction intermediate between these (and the

---

[1] Suyakkhamdha, srutaskandha.

[2] Agghayana, adhyayana. The first lecture is called satthaparinnâ (sastra-parigñâ), 'knowledge of the weapon.' Weapons are divided into material weapon and weapon consisting in a state (bhâva). The latter is explained to be non-control (asamyama) or the wrong use of mind, speech, and body. Knowledge (parigñâ) is twofold: comprehension and renunciation. The subject of the first lecture is, therefore, the comprehension and renunciation of everything that hurts other beings.

[3] Uddesaya, uddesaka.

[4] Gambûsvâmin was the disciple of Sudharman, one of the eleven chief disciples (ganadhara) of Mahâvîra.

cardinal points). (2) Similarly, some do not know whether their soul is born again and again or not; nor what they were formerly, nor what they will become after having died and left this world. (3) Now this is what one should know, either by one's own knowledge or through the instruction of the highest (i. e. a Tîrthakara), or having heard it from others: that he descended in an eastern direction, or in any other direction (particularised above). Similarly, some know that their soul is born again and again, that it arrives in this or that direction, whatever direction that may be. (4) He believes in soul [1], believes in the world [2], believes in reward [3], believes in action (acknowledged to be our own doing in such judgments as these): 'I did it;' 'I shall cause another to do it;' 'I shall allow another to do it [4].' In the world, these are all the causes of sin [5], which must be comprehended and renounced. (5) A man that does not comprehend and renounce the causes of sin, descends in a cardinal or intermediate direction, wanders to all cardinal or intermediate directions, is born again and again in manifold births, experiences all painful feelings. (6) About this the Revered One has taught

[1] I. e. in a permanent soul, different from the body. This is said against the *K*ârvâkas.

[2] I. e. the plurality of souls, not in one all-soul, as the Vedântins.

[3] Kamma (karma) is that which darkens our intellect, &c. Its result is the suffering condition of men, its cause is action (kiriyâ, kriyâ).

[4] The different tenses employed in these sentences imply, according to the commentators, the acknowledgment of the reality of time, as past, present, future.

[5] Kamma-samâra*m*bha. Kamma has been explained above. Samâra*m*bha, a special action (kriyâ), is the engaging in something blamable (sâvadyânush*th*âna).

the truth (comprehension and renunciation). For the sake of the splendour, honour, and glory of this life, for the sake of birth, death, and final liberation, for the removal of pain, all these causes of sin are at work, which are to be comprehended and renounced in this world. He who, in the world, comprehends and renounces these causes of sin, is called a reward-knowing sage (mu*n*i). Thus I say[1]. (7)

SECOND LESSON[2].

The (living) world is afflicted, miserable, difficult to instruct, and without discrimination. In this world full of pain, suffering by their different acts, see the benighted ones cause great pain. (1) See! there are beings individually embodied (in earth; not one all-soul). See! there are men who

[1] These words (tti bemi) stand at the end of every lesson. The commentators supply them also for the beginning of each lesson.

[2] After the chief tenets of *G*ainism with regard to soul and actions have briefly been stated in the first lesson, the six remaining lessons of the first lecture treat of the actions which injure the six classes of lives or souls. The *G*ainas seem to have arrived at their concept of soul, not through the search after the Self, the self-existing unchangeable principle in the ever-changing world of phenomena, but through the perception of life. For the most general *G*aina term for soul is life (*g*îva), which is identical with self (âyâ, âtman). There are numberless lives or souls, not only embodied in animals, men, gods, hell-beings (tasa, trasa), and plants (va*n*assaî, vanaspati), but also in the four elements—earth, water, fire, wind. Earth, &c., regarded as the abode of lives is called earth-body, &c. These bodies are only perceptible when an infinite number of them is united in one place. The earth-lives, &c., possess only one organ, that of feeling; they have undeveloped (avyakta) intellect and feelings (vedanâ), but no limbs, &c. The doctrines about these elementary lives are laid down in Bhadrabâhu's Niryukti of our Sûtra, and are commented upon in *S*îlâṅka's great commentary of it. They are very abstruse, and deal in the most minute distinctions, which baffle our comprehension.

control themselves, (whilst others only) pretend to be houseless (i.e. monks, such as the Bauddhas, whose conduct differs not from that of householders), because one destroys this (earth-body) by bad and injurious doings, and many other beings, besides, which he hurts by means of earth, through his doing acts relating to earth. (2) About this the Revered One has taught the truth: for the sake of the splendour, honour, and glory of this life, for the sake of birth, death, and final liberation, for the removal of pain, man acts sinfully towards earth, or causes others to act so, or allows others to act so. This deprives him of happiness and perfect wisdom. About this he is informed when he has understood or heard, either from the Revered One or from the monks, the faith to be coveted. (3) There are some who, of a truth, know this (i.e. injuring) to be the bondage, the delusion, the death, the hell. For this[1] a man is longing when he destroys this (earth-body) by bad, injurious doings, and many other beings, besides, which he hurts by means of earth, through his doing acts relating to earth. Thus I say. (4)

As somebody may cut or strike a blind man (who cannot see the wound), as somebody may cut or strike the foot, the ankle, the knee, the thigh, the hip, the navel, the belly, the flank, the back, the bosom, the heart, the breast, the neck, the arm, the finger, the nail, the eye, the brow, the forehead, the head, as some kill (openly), as some extirpate

[1] Ikk' attham. The commentators think this to be a reference to the sentence, For the sake of the splendour, &c. It would be more natural to connect it with the foregoing sentence; the meaning is, For bondage, &c., men commit violence, though they believe it to be for the happiness of this life.

(secretly), (thus the earth-bodies are cut, struck, and killed though their feeling is not manifest). (5)

He who injures these (earth-bodies) does not comprehend and renounce the sinful acts; he who does not injure these, comprehends and renounces the sinful acts. Knowing them, a wise man should not act sinfully towards earth, nor cause others to act so, nor allow others to act so. He who knows these causes of sin relating to earth, is called a reward-knowing sage. Thus I say. (6)

Third Lesson[1].

(Thus I say): He who acts rightly, who does pious work, who practises no deceit, is called houseless. (1) One should, conquering the world, persevere in that (vigour of) faith which one had on the entrance in the order; the heroes (of faith), humbly bent, (should retain their belief in) the illustrious road (to final liberation) and in the world (of water-bodies); having rightly comprehended them through the instruction (of Mahâvîra), (they should retain) that which causes no danger (i.e. self-control). Thus I say. (2) A man should not (himself) deny the world of (water-bodies), nor should he deny the self. He who denies the world (of water-bodies), denies the self; and he who denies the self, denies the world of (water-bodies). (3)

See! there are men who control themselves;

[1] The water-lives which are treated of in this lesson are, as is the case with all elementary lives, divided into three classes: the sentient, the senseless, and the mixed. Only that water which is the abode of senseless water-lives may be used. Therefore water is to be strained before use, because the senseless lives only are believed to remain in water after that process.

others pretend only to be houseless; for one destroys this (water-body) by bad, injurious doings, and many other beings, besides, which he hurts by means of water, through his doing acts relating to water. (4) About this the Revered One has taught the truth: for the sake of the splendour, honour, and glory of this life, for the sake of birth, death, and final liberation, for the removal of pain, man acts sinfully towards water, or causes others to act so, or allows others to act so. (5) This deprives him of happiness and perfect wisdom. About this he is informed when he has understood and heard from the Revered One, or from the monks, the faith to be coveted. There are some who, of a truth, know this (i.e. injuring) to be the bondage, the delusion, the death, the hell. For this a man is longing when he destroys this (water-body) by bad and injurious doings, and many other beings, besides, which he hurts by means of water, through his doing acts relating to water. Thus I say. (6)

There are beings living in water, many lives; of a truth, to the monks water has been declared to be living matter. See! considering the injuries (done to water-bodies), those acts (which are injuries, but must be done before the use of water, e.g. straining) have been distinctly declared. Moreover he (who uses water which is not strained) takes away what has not been given (i.e. the bodies of water-lives). (A Bauddha will object): 'We have permission, we have permission to drink it, or (to take it) for toilet purposes.' Thus they destroy by various injuries (the water-bodies). But in this their doctrine is of no authority.

He who injures these (water-bodies) does not

comprehend and renounce the sinful acts; he who does not injure these, comprehends and renounces the sinful acts. (7) Knowing them, a wise man should not act sinfully towards water, nor cause others to act so, nor allow others to act so. He who knows these causes of sin relating to water, is called a reward-knowing sage. Thus I say. (8)

FOURTH LESSON.

(Thus I say): A man should not, of his own accord, deny the world (of fire-bodies), nor should he deny the self. He who denies the world (of fire-bodies), denies the self; and he who denies the self, denies the world (of fire-bodies). (1) He who knows that (viz. fire) through which injury is done to the long-living bodies (i.e. plants)[1], knows also that which does no injury (i.e. control); and he who knows that which does no injury, knows also that through which no injury is done to the long-living bodies. (2) This has been seen by the heroes (of faith) who conquered ignorance; for they control themselves, always exert themselves, always mind their duty. He who is unmindful of duty, and desiring of the qualities (i.e. of the pleasure and profit which may be derived from the elements) is called the torment[2] (of living beings). Knowing this, a wise man (resolves): 'Now (I shall do) no more what I used to do wantonly before.' (3) See! there are men who control themselves; others pretend only to be houseless; for one destroys this (fire-body) by bad and injurious doings, and many

[1] The fire-bodies live not longer than three days.

[2] Da*m*d*a.

other beings, besides, which he hurts by means of fire, through his doing acts relating to fire. About this the Revered One has taught the truth: for the sake of the splendour, honour, and glory of this life, for the sake of birth, death, and final liberation, for the removal of pain, man acts sinfully towards fire, or causes others to act so, or allows others to act so. (4) This deprives him of happiness and perfect wisdom. About this he is informed when he has understood, or heard from the Revered One or from the monks, the faith to be coveted. There are some who, of a truth, know this (i.e. injuring) to be the bondage, the delusion, the death, the hell. For this a man is longing, when he destroys this (fire-body) by bad and injurious doings, and many other beings, besides, which he hurts by means of fire, through his doing acts relating to fire. Thus I say. (5)

There are beings living in the earth, living in grass, living on leaves, living in wood, living in cowdung, living in dust-heaps, jumping beings which coming near (fire) fall into it. Some, certainly, touched by fire, shrivel up; those which shrivel up there, lose their sense there; those which lose their sense there, die there. (6)

He who injures these (fire-bodies) does not comprehend and renounce the sinful acts; he who does not injure these, comprehends and renounces the sinful acts. Knowing them, a wise man should not act sinfully towards fire, nor cause others to act so, nor allow others to act so. He who knows the causes of sin relating to fire, is called a reward-knowing sage. Thus I say. (7)

Fifth Lesson[1].

'I shall not do (acts relating to plants) after having entered the order, having recognised (the truth about these acts), and having conceived that which is free from danger (i.e. control).'

He who does no acts (relating to plants), has ceased from works; he who has ceased from them is called 'houseless.' (1) Quality is the whirlpool (âva*tt*a = sa*m*sâra), and the whirlpool is quality. Looking up, down, aside, eastward, he sees colours, hearing he hears sounds; (2) longing upwards, down, aside, eastward, he becomes attached to colours and sounds. That is called the world; not guarded against it, not obeying the law (of the Tîrthakaras), relishing the qualities, conducting himself wrongly, he will wantonly live in a house (i.e. belong to the world). (3)

See! there are men who control themselves; others pretend only to be houseless, for one destroys this (body of a plant) by bad and injurious doings, and many other

[1] The discussion of the 'wind-bodies,' which should follow that of the fire-bodies, is postponed for two lessons in which the vegetable and animal world is treated of. The reason for this interruption of the line of exposition is, as the commentators state, that the nature of wind, because of its invisibleness, is open to doubts, whilst plants and animals are admitted by all to be living beings, and are, therefore, the best support of the hylozoistical theory. That wind was not readily admitted by the ancient Indians to be a peculiar substance may still be recognised in the philosophical Sûtras of the Brahmans. For there it was thought necessary to discuss at length the proofs for the existence of a peculiar substance, wind. It should be remarked that wind was never identified with air, and that the *G*ainas had not yet separated air from space.

beings, besides, which he hurts by means of plants, through his doing acts relating to plants. (4) About this the Revered One has taught the truth: for the sake of the splendour, honour, and glory of this life, for the sake of birth, death, and final liberation, for the removal of pain, man acts sinfully towards plants, or causes others to act so, or allows others to act so. This deprives him of happiness and perfect wisdom. About this he is informed when he has understood, or heard from the Revered One or from the monks, the faith to be coveted. There are some who, of a truth, know this (i.e. injuring) to be the bondage, the delusion, the death, the hell. For this a man is longing when he destroys this (body of a plant) by bad and injurious doings, and many other beings, besides, which he hurts by means of plants, through his doing acts relating to plants. Thus I say. (5)

As the nature of this (i.e. men) is to be born and to grow old, so is the nature of that (i.e. plants) to be born and to grow old; as this has reason, so that has reason[1]; as this falls sick when cut, so that falls sick when cut; as this needs food, so that needs food; as this will decay, so that will decay; as this is not eternal, so that is not eternal; as this takes increment, so that takes increment; as this is changing, so that is changing. (6) He who injures these (plants) does not comprehend and renounce the sinful

[1] The plants know the seasons, for they sprout at the proper time, the Asoka buds and blooms when touched by the foot of a well-attired girl, and the Vakula when watered with wine; the seed grows always upwards: all this would not happen if the plants had no knowledge of the circumstances about them. Such is the reasoning of the commentators.

acts; he who does not injure these, comprehends and renounces the sinful acts. Knowing them, a wise man should not act sinfully towards plants, nor cause others to act so, nor allow others to act so. He who knows these causes of sin relating to plants, is called a reward-knowing sage. Thus I say. (7)

Sixth Lesson.

Thus I say: There are beings called the animate, viz. those who are produced 1. from eggs (birds, &c.), 2. from a fetus (as elephants, &c.), 3. from a fetus with an enveloping membrane (as cows, buffaloes, &c.), 4. from fluids (as worms, &c.), 5. from sweat (as bugs, lice, &c.), 6. by coagulation (as locusts, ants, &c.), 7. from sprouts (as butterflies, wagtails, &c.), 8. by regeneration (men, gods, hell-beings). This is called the Sa*m*sâra (1) for the slow, for the ignorant. Having well considered it, having well looked at it, I say thus: all beings, those with two, three, four senses, plants, those with five senses, and the rest of creation, (experience) individually pleasure or displeasure, pain, great terror, and unhappiness. Beings are filled with alarm from all directions and in all directions. See! there the benighted ones cause great pain. See! there are beings individually embodied. (2)

See! there are men who control themselves; others pretend only to be houseless, for one destroys this (body of an animal) by bad and injurious doings, and many other beings, besides, which he hurts by means of animals, through his doing acts relating to animals. (3) About this the Revered One has taught the truth: for the sake of the splendour, honour, and glory of this life, for the sake of birth, death, and final liberation, for the removal of pain, man acts sinfully towards animals, or causes others to act so, or allows others to act so. This deprives him of happiness and perfect wisdom. About this he is informed, when he has understood, or heard from the Revered One or from the monks, the faith to be coveted. There are some who, of a truth, know this (i.e. injuring) to be the bondage, the delusion, the death, the hell. For this a man is longing, when he injures this (body of an animal) by bad and injurious doings, and many other beings, besides, which he hurts by means of animals, through acts relating to animals. Thus I say. (4)

Some slay (animals) for sacrificial purposes, some kill (animals) for the sake of their skin, some kill (them) for the sake of their flesh, some kill them for the sake of their blood; thus for the sake of their heart, their bile, the feathers of their tail, their tail, their big or small horns, their teeth, their tusks, their nails, their sinews, their bones[1]; with a purpose or without a purpose. Some kill animals because they have been wounded by them, or are wounded, or will be wounded. (5)

He who injures these (animals) does not comprehend and renounce the sinful acts; he who does not injure these, comprehends and renounces the sinful acts. Knowing them, a wise man should not act sinfully towards animals, nor cause others to act so, nor allow others to act so. He who knows

[1] The word after bones (a*tth*îe) is a*tth*imi*mg*âe, for which buffaloes, boars, &c. are killed, as the commentator states. I do not know the meaning of this word which is rendered asthimi*ñg*â.

these causes of sin relating to animals, is called a reward-knowing sage. Thus I say. (6)

SEVENTH LESSON.

He who is averse from (all actions relating to) wind, knows affliction. Knowing what is bad, he who knows it with regard to himself, knows it with regard to (the world) outside; and he who knows it with regard to (the world) outside, knows it with regard to himself: this reciprocity (between himself and) others (one should mind). Those who are appeased, who are free from passion, do not desire to live. (1)

See! there are men who control themselves; others pretend only to be houseless, for one destroys this (wind-body) by bad and injurious doings, and many other beings, besides, which he hurts by means of wind, through his doing acts relating to wind. (2) About this the Revered One has taught the truth: for the sake of the splendour, honour, and glory of this life, for the sake of birth, death, and final liberation, for the removal of pain, man acts sinfully towards wind, or causes others to act so, or allows others to act so. This deprives him of happiness and perfect wisdom. About this he is informed when he has understood, or heard from the Revered One or from the monks, the faith to be coveted. There are some who, of a truth, know this to be the bondage, the delusion, the death, the hell. For this a man is longing when he destroys this (wind-body) by bad and injurious acts, and many other beings, besides, which he hurts by means of wind, through his doing acts relating to wind. Thus I say. (3)

There are jumping beings which, coming near wind, fall into it. Some, certainly, touched by wind, shrivel up; those which shrivel up there, lose their sense there; those which lose their sense there, die there. (4)

He who injures these (wind-bodies) does not comprehend and renounce the sinful acts; he who does not injure these, comprehends and renounces the sinful acts. Knowing them, a wise man should not act sinfully towards wind, nor cause others to act so, nor allow others to act so. He who knows these causes of sin relating to wind, is called a reward-knowing sage. Thus I say. (5)

Be aware that about this (wind-body) too those are involved in sin who delight not in the right conduct, and, though doing acts, talk about religious discipline, who conducting themselves according to their own will, pursuing sensual pleasures, and engaging in acts, are addicted to worldliness. He who has the true knowledge about all things, will commit no sinful act, nor cause others to do so, &c. (6) Knowing them, a wise man should not act sinfully towards the aggregate of six (kinds of) lives, nor cause others to act so, nor allow others to act so. He who knows these causes of sin relating to the aggregate of the six (kinds of) lives, is called a reward-knowing sage. Thus I say. (7)

End of the First Lecture, called Knowledge of the Weapon.

SECOND LECTURE,

CALLED

CONQUEST OF THE WORLD.

First Lesson.

Quality is the seat of the root, and the seat of the root is quality[1]. He who longs for the qualities, is overcome by great pain, and he is careless[2]. (For he thinks) I have to provide for a mother, for a father, for a sister, for a wife, for sons, for daughters, for a daughter-in-law, for my friends, for near and remote relations, for my acquaintances[3], for different kinds of property, profit, meals, and clothes. Longing for these objects, people are careless, suffer day and night, work in the right and the wrong time, desire wealth and treasures, commit injuries and violent acts, direct the mind, again and again, upon these injurious doings (described in the preceding lecture). (1) (Doing so), the life of some mortals (which by destiny would have been long) is shortened. For when with the deterioration of the perceptions of the ear, eye, organs of smelling, tasting, touching, a man becomes aware of the decline of life, they[4] after a time

[1] I. e. in the qualities of the external things lies the primary cause of the Samsâra, viz. sin; the qualities produce sin, and sinfulness makes us apt to enjoy the qualities.

[2] I. e. gives way to love, hate, &c.

[3] Samthuya. The commentators explain this word acquaintance or one who is recommended to me.

[4] I. e. these failing perceptions.

produce dotage. Or his kinsmen with whom he lives together will, after a time, first grumble at him, and he will afterwards grumble at them. They cannot help thee or protect thee, nor canst thou help them or protect them. (2) He is not fit for hilarity, playing, pleasure, show. Therefore, ah! proceeding to pilgrimage, and thinking that the present moment is favourable (for such intentions[1]), he should be steadfast and not, even for an hour, carelessly conduct himself. His youth, his age, his life fade away.

A man who carelessly conducts himself, who killing, cutting, striking, destroying, chasing away, frightening (living beings) resolves to do what has not been done (by any one)—him his relations with whom he lived together, will first cherish, and he will afterwards cherish them. But they cannot help thee or protect thee, nor canst thou help them or protect them. (3)

Or he heaps up treasures for the benefit of some spendthrifts, by pinching himself. Then, after a time, he falls in sickness; those with whom he lives together will first leave him, and he will afterwards leave them. They cannot help thee or protect thee, nor canst thou help them or protect them. (4)

Knowing pain and pleasure in all their variety[2], and seeing his life not yet decline, a wise man should know that to be the proper moment (for entering a religious life); while the perceptions of his ear, eye, organs of smelling, tasting, touching are not

[1] I.e. his present life; for the birth in âryakshetra and in a noble family is difficult to obtain in this Sa*m*sâra.

[2] Patteya*m*, singly, with regard to the living beings.

yet deteriorated, while all these perceptions are not yet deteriorated, man should prosecute [1] the real end of his soul [2]. Thus I say. (5)

SECOND LESSON.

A wise man should remove any aversion (to control [3]); he will be liberated in the proper time. Some, following wrong instruction, turn away (from control). They are dull, wrapped in delusion. While they imitate the life of monks, (saying), 'We shall be free from attachment,' they enjoy the pleasures that offer themselves [4]. Through wrong instruction the (would-be) sages trouble themselves (for pleasures); thus they sink deeper and deeper in delusion, (and cannot get) to this, nor to the opposite shore [5]. Those who are freed (from attachment to the world and its pleasures), reach the opposite shore [6]. Subduing desire by desirelessness, he does not enjoy the pleasures that offer themselves. Desireless, giving up the world, and ceasing to act, he knows, and sees, and has no wishes because of his discernment [7]; he is called houseless. (1)

[1] Samanuvâseggâsi (tti bemi) is taken by the commentators for the second person, which always occurs before tti bemi, but nowhere else. I think si belongs to tti bemi, and stands for se = asau.

[2] Viz. control.

[3] Arati is usually dislike, âuttai exercise; but, according to the commentators, these words here mean samyamârati and nivartayati.

[4] E. g. the Buddhists, &c., Sâkyâdayah.

[5] I. e. they are neither householders nor houseless monks.

[6] I. e. moksha, final liberation.

[7] Viz. between good and bad, or of the results of desire.

(But on the contrary) he suffers day and night, works in the right and the wrong time, desires wealth and treasures, commits injuries and violent acts, again and again directs his mind upon these injurious doings[1]; for his own sake, to support or to be supported by his relations, friends, the ancestors, gods, the king, thieves, guests, paupers, *S*rama*n*as. (2)

Thus violence is done by these various acts, deliberately, out of fear, because they think 'it is for the expiation of sins[2],' or for some other hope. Knowing this, a wise man should neither himself commit violence by such acts, nor order others to commit violence by such acts, nor consent to the violence done by somebody else.

This road (to happiness) has been declared by the noble ones, that a clever man should not be defiled (by sin). Thus I say. (3)

THIRD LESSON.

'Frequently (I have been born) in a high family, frequently in a low one; I am not mean, nor noble, nor do I desire (social preferment).' Thus reflecting, who would brag about his family or about his glory, or for what should he long? (1)

Therefore a wise man should neither be glad nor angry (about his lot): thou shouldst know and consider the happiness of living creatures. Carefully conducting himself, he should mind this: blindness, deafness, dumbness, one-eyedness, hunchbacked-

[1] See I, 2, 1, § 1.

[2] The sacrificial rites of the Brâhma*n*as are meant.

ness[1], blackness, variety of colour (he will always experience); because of his carelessness he is born in many births, he experiences various feelings. (2)

Not enlightened (about the cause of these ills) he is afflicted (by them), always turns round (in the whirl of) birth and death. Life is dear to many who own fields and houses. Having acquired dyed and coloured (clothes), jewels, earrings, gold, and women, they become attached to these things. And a fool who longs for life, and worldly-minded[2], laments that (for these worldly goods) penance, self-restraint, and control do not avail, will ignorantly come to grief. (3)

Those who are of a steady conduct do not desire this (wealth). Knowing birth and death, one should firmly walk the path (i.e. right conduct), (and not wait for old age to commence a religious life),

For there is nothing inaccessible for death. All beings are fond of life[3], like pleasure, hate pain, shun destruction, like life, long to live. To all life is dear[4]. (4)

Having acquired it (i.e. wealth), employing bipeds and quadrupeds, gathering riches in the three ways[5],

---

[1] Hereafter va*d*abhatta*m* explained by vinirgatap*ri*thivî va*d*abha-laksha*n*a*m*.

[2] Sa*m*pu*nn*a*m*=sampûr*n*a*m*, lit. complete, i.e. the complete end of human existence is enjoyment of the world.

[3] Another reading mentioned by the commentator is piyâyayâ, fond of themselves.

[4] The original of this paragraph reads partly metrical; after the verse marked in my edition there follow three final pâdas of a *s*loka.

[5] According to the commentators, the three modes of activity (yoga), action, order, consent, or the three organs of activity (kara*n*a), mind, speech, body, are meant.

whatever his portion will be, small or great, he will desire to enjoy it. Then at one time, his manifold savings are a large treasure. Then at another time, his heirs divide it, or those who are without a living steal it, or the king takes it away, or it is ruined in some way or other, or it is consumed by the conflagration of the house. Thus a fool doing cruel deeds which benefit another, will ignorantly come thereby to grief. (5)

This certainly has been declared by the sage[1]. They do not cross the flood[2], nor can they cross it; they do not go to the next shore, nor can they go to it; they do not go to the opposite shore, nor can they go to it.

And though hearing the doctrine, he does not stand in the right place; but the clever one who adopts the true (faith), stands in the right place (i.e. control)[3].

He who sees by himself, needs no instruction. But the miserable, afflicted fool who delights in pleasures, and whose miseries do not cease, is turned round in the whirl of pains. Thus I say. (6)

---

[1] I.e. the Tîrthakara.

[2] I.e. the Samsâra, represented under the idea of a lake or slough, in the mud of which the worldly are sinking without being able to reach the shore.

[3] Âyâniggam *k*a âdâya tammi *th*â*n*e na *ki*t*th*ai | avitaha*m* pappa kheyanne tammi *th*â*n*ammi *ki*t*th*ai || These words form a regular *s*loka, which has not been noticed by any commentator. *S*îlâṅka seems to have read vitaha*m* pappa akheyanne, but I consider the reading of our MSS. better, for if we adopt it, *th*â*n*a retains the same meaning (viz. control) in both parts of the couplet, while if we adopt *S*îlâṅka's reading, *th*â*n*a must in the one place denote the contrary of what it means in the other; âdânîya, doctrine, lit. to be adopted.

Fourth Lesson.

Then, after a time, he falls in sickness: those with whom he lives together, first grumble at him, and he afterwards grumbles at them. But they cannot help thee or protect thee, nor canst thou help them or protect them. (1)

Knowing pleasure and pain separately[1], they trouble themselves about the enjoyment (of the external objects). For some men in this world have (such a character that) they will desire to enjoy their portion, whether it be large or small, in the three ways[2]. Then, at one time, it will be sufficiently large, with many resources. Then, at another time, his heirs divide it, or those who have no living steal it, or the king takes it away, or it is ruined in some way or other, or it is consumed by the conflagration of the house. Thus a fool, doing cruel acts, comes ignorantly to grief. (2)

Wisely reject hope and desire[3], and extracting that thorn (i.e. pleasure) thou (shouldst act rightly). People who are enveloped by delusion do not understand this: he who (gathers wealth) will, perhaps, not have the benefit of it.

The world is greatly troubled by women. They (viz. men) forsooth say, 'These are the vessels (of happiness).' But this leads them to pain, to delusion,

[1] The meaning seems to be: If people do not know that pleasure and pain are the result of their own works, &c.

[2] The commentators give no explanation of what is meant by 'the three ways,' yet cf. 3, § 5.

[3] The words âsa*m* *k*a *kham*da*m* *k*a vigi*mk*a dhîre form a trish*t*ubh pâda.

to death, to hell, to birth as hell-beings or brute beasts. The fool never knows the law. (3)

Thus spake the hero[1]: 'Be careful against this great delusion; the clever one should have done with carelessness by considering death in tranquillity, and that, the nature of which is decay (viz. the body); these (pleasures), look! will not satisfy (thee). Therefore have done with them! Sage, look! this is the great danger, it should overcome none whomsoever. He is called a hero who is not vexed by (the hardships caused) by control. He should not be angry because the (householder) gives him little. If turned off, he should go. Thou shouldst conform to the conduct of the sages.' Thus I say. (4)

Fifth Lesson.

That for this (viz. pleasure) the wants of the world should be supplied by bad injurious doings: for one's own sons, daughters, daughters-in-law, kinsmen, nurses, kings, male and female slaves, male and female servants, for the sake of hospitality, of supper and breakfast, the accumulation of wealth is effected. (1)

(This is) here for the enjoyment of some men. (But a wise man) exerting himself, houseless, noble, of noble intellect, of noble perception recognises the proper moment (for all actions). He should not accept, nor cause others to accept, or permit them

---

[1] The MSS. have udâhu dhîre. The last word is a frequent mistake for vîre, which is adopted by the commentators. They explain udâhu by ud-âha=uktavân.

to accept anything unclean[1]. Free from uncleanliness he should wander about. (2)

Being not seen in buying and selling, he should not buy, nor cause others to buy, nor consent to the buying of others. This mendicant who knows the time, the strength (of himself), the measure (of all things), the practice[2], the occasion (for begging, &c.), the conduct, the religious precepts[3], the true condition (of the donor or hearer), who disowns all things not requisite for religious purposes[4], who is under no obligations, he proceeds securely (on the road to final liberation) after having cut off both (love and hate). Clothes, alms-bowls, blankets, brooms, property[5], straw mats, with regard to these things he should know (what is unclean). When he receives food he should know the quantity required. This has been declared by the Revered One: he should not rejoice in the receipt of a gift, nor be sorry when he gets nothing. Having got much, one should not store it away; one should abstain from things not requisite for religious purposes. With a mind different (from that of common people) a seer abandons (these things). This is the road taught by the noble ones, well acquainted with which one should not be defiled (by sin). Thus I say. (3)

---

[1] Âmagandha, unclean, is also a Buddhist term; see Rhys Davids' Buddhism, pp. 131, 181.

[2] Kheda = abhyâsa, or the pain of worldly existence.

[3] Samaya.

[4] Pariggaha; it might also be translated, who disowns attachment.

[5] Oggaha = avagraha property e.g. the ground or space which the householder allows the mendicant who stays in his house.

Pleasures are difficult to reject, life is difficult to prolong. That man, certainly, who loves pleasures, is afflicted (by their loss), is sorry in his heart, leaves his usual ways, is troubled, suffers pain. The far-sighted one who knows the world, knows its inferior part (hell), its upper part (heaven), its side-long part (the state of brute beasts). He who knows the relation (of human affairs, viz.) that he who desires for the world is always turned round (in the sa*m*sâra), is called among mortals a hero, who liberates those who are fettered. (4)

As the interior (of the body is loathsome), so is the exterior; as the exterior, so is the interior. In the interior of the body he perceives the foul interior humours, he observes their several courses (or eruptions). A well-informed man knowing (and renouncing the body and pleasures), should not eat (his saliva[1]); he should not oppose himself to the (current of knowledge). Certainly, that man who engages in worldly affairs, who practises many tricks, who is bewildered by his own doings, acts again and again on that desire which increases his unrighteousness[2]. Hence the above has been said for the increase of this (life)[3]. (A man addicted to pleasures) acts as if immortal, and puts great faith (in pleasure); but when he perceives that this body sustains pains, he cries in his ignorance. Therefore keep in your mind what I say. (5)

---

[1] I.e. what he has thrown away, vomited, as it were; pleasures.

[2] Vera*m* va*ddh*ei appa*n*o, apparently the close of a *s*loka; see I, 3, 2, 3.

[3] The commentators supply *s*arîrasya, the body. For sinful acts injure the bodies of living beings; therefore they are increased by our abstaining from sin.

A heretic[1] professes to cure (the love of pleasure), while he kills, cuts, strikes, destroys, chases away, resolves to do what has not been done before. To whom he applies the cure—enough of that fool's affection[2]; or he who has (the cure) applied, is a fool. This does not apply to the houseless. Thus I say. (6)

SIXTH LESSON.

He who perfectly understands (what has been said in the preceding lesson) and follows the (faith) to be coveted, should therefore do no sinful act, nor cause others to do one. Perchance he meditates a sin (by an act against only) one (of the six aggregates of lives); but he will be guilty (of sin against) every one of the six. Desiring happiness and bewailing much, he comes ignorantly to grief through his own misfortune. (1) Through his own carelessness every one produces that phase of life in which the vital spirits are pained. Observing (the pain of mundane existence, one should) not (act) with violence. This is called the true knowledge (and renunciation). He who ceasing from acts relinquishes the idea of property, relinquishes property itself. That sage has seen the path (to final liberation) for whom there exists no property. Knowing this, a wise man, who knows the world and has cast off the idea of the world,

[1] Pa*m*d*i*te=pa*n*d*i*ta*m*mânî, who believes or pretends to be a learned man.

[2] Ala*m* bâlassa sa*m*ge*n*a, a pâda of *s*loka; followed by the words in note 2, p. 24, it forms the hemistich of verse 3 in the Second Lesson of the next Chapter.

should prudently conquer[1] the obstructions to righteousness. Thus I say. (2)

The hero does not tolerate discontent,

The hero does not tolerate lust.

Because the hero is not careless,

The hero is not attached (to the objects of the senses).

Being indifferent against sounds (and the other) perceptions, detest the comfort of this life.

A sage adopting a life of wisdom, should treat his gross body roughly.

The heroes who have right intuition, use mean and rough food[2].

Such a man is said to have crossed the flood (of life), to be a sage, to have passed over (the sa*m*sâra), to be liberated, to have ceased (from all activity). Thus I say. (3)

A sage is called unfit who does not follow the law and fails in his office. (But on the contrary) he is praised as a hero, he overcomes the connection with the world, he is called the guide (or the right way). What has been declared to be here the unhappiness of mortals, of that unhappiness the clever ones propound the knowledge. (4)

Thus understanding (and renouncing) acts, a man who recognises the truth, delights in nothing else; and he who delights only in the truth, recognises nothing else. As (the law) has been revealed for the full one, so for the empty one; as for the empty

[1] See p. 17, note 1.

[2] These words apparently form a *s*loka, though the third pâda is too short by one syllable; but this fault can easily be corrected by inserting *k*a: pa*m*ta*m* lûha*m* *k*a sevanti. The commentators treat the passage as prose.

one, so for the full one[1]. But he (to whom the faith is preached) will perhaps disrespectfully beat (the preacher). Yet know, there is no good in this (indiscriminate preaching). (But ascertain before) what sort of man he is, and whom he worships. He is called a hero who liberates the bound, above, below, and in the sideward directions. He always conforms to all knowledge (and renunciation); the hero is not polluted by the sin of killing. He is a wise man who perfectly knows the non-killing[2], who searches after the liberation of the bound. The clever one is neither bound nor liberated; he should do or leave undone (what the hero does or does not do); he should not do what (the hero) leaves undone:

Knowing (and renouncing) murder of any kind and worldly ideas in all respects[3].

He who sees himself, needs no instruction. But the miserable and afflicted fool who delights in pleasures and whose miseries do not cease, is turned round in the whirl of pains[4]. Thus I say. (5)

End of the Second Lecture, called Conquest of the World.

---

[1] The full and the empty designate those who adopt the true faith, and those who do not.

[2] A*n*ugghâya*n*a. According to the commentator, the destruction of karman.

[3] This is again a stray half *s*loka. The text abounds in minor fragments of verses, trish*t*ubhs, or *s*lokas.

[4] See the end of the Third Lesson.

THIRD LECTURE,

CALLED

HOT AND COLD.

First Lesson.

The unwise sleep, the sages always wake. Know, that in this world the (cause of) misery[1] brings forth evil consequences! Knowing the course of the world[2], one should cease from violent acts. He who correctly possesses[3] these (sensual perceptions), viz. sounds, and colours, and smells, and tastes, and touches (1), who self-possessed, wise, just, chaste, with right comprehension understands the world, he is to be called a sage, one who knows the law, and righteous. He knows the connection of the whirl (of births) and the current (of sensation with love and hate). Not minding heat and cold, equanimous against pleasure and pain, the Nirgrantha does not feel the austerity of penance. Waking and free from hostility, a wise man, thou liberatest (thyself and others) from the miseries. (2)

But a man always benighted, subject to old age and death, does not know the law. Seeing living beings suffering, earnestly enter a religious life[4]. Considering this, O prudent one, look!

Knowing the misery that results from action,
The deluded and careless one returns to life;

[1] I. e. ignorance and delusion.

[2] Regarding the evil-doer.

[3] And renounces.

[4] Again a half sloka, unnoticed as such by the commentators.

Disregarding sounds and colours, upright,
Avoiding Mâra one is liberated from death[1].

Carefully abstaining from pleasures and ceasing from bad works he is a hero, guarding himself, who is grounded in knowledge[2]. (3) He who knows the violence done for the sake of special objects, knows what is free from violence[3]; he who knows what is free from violence, knows the violence done for special objects. For him who is without karman, there is no appellation[4]. The condition of living beings arises from karman.

Examining karman and the root of karman, viz. killing[5], examining (it) and adopting its contrary[6], he is not seen by both ends[7]. Knowing this, a wise man who knows the world and has cast off the idea of the world, should prudently conquer the obstructions to righteousness[8]. Thus I say. (4)

SECOND LESSON.

Look, Sir, at birth and old age here,
Examine and know the happiness of the living,
Thence the most learned, knowing (what is called)
the highest good,
He who has right intuition, commits no sin. (1)

---

[1] A trish*t*ubh unnoticed by the commentators.

[2] Kheyanna=khedag*ñ*a nipu*n*a. I think the Sanskrit would rather be kshetrag*ñ*a.

[3] I. e. control.

[4] As man, god, hell-being, young, old, &c.

[5] See p. 28, note 4.

[6] Literally, the left side (savyam); control is intended.

[7] I. e. he is not touched by love and hate, which cause death.

[8] See I, 2, 6 (2).

Undo the bond with mortals here;
He who lives by sins, is subject to both[1],
Desirous of pleasures they heap up karman,
Influenced by it they are born again. (2)
Killing (animals) he thinks good sport, and derives mirth from it:
Away with that fool's company, he increases his own unrighteousness. (3)
Thence the most learned, knowing (what is called) the highest good,
Aware of the punishment, commits no sin;
Wisely avoid the top and the root[2]!
Cutting them off, he knows himself free from karman. (4)

That man will be liberated from death; he is a sage who sees the danger[3], knowing the highest good in this world, leading a circumspect life, calm, guarded, endowed (with knowledge, &c.), always restrained, longing for death, he should lead a religious life. Manifold, indeed, appear sinful actions; therefore prove constant to truth! Delighting in it[4], a wise man destroys all karman. (1)

Many, indeed, are the plans of this man (of the world); he will satisfy his desires; he (thereby causes) the slaughter of others, the pain of others, the punishment of others, the slaughter, the blame,

[1] Literally, sees both, i.e. experiences bodily and mental (agonies), those of this world and of the next.

[2] The root means delusion, the top the rest of the sins.

[3] Arising from worldliness. The same words occur in 2, 6, § 2; but bhae (bhaya) stands here instead of pahe, road. Bhae occurs also in the former place in some MSS.

[4] Ettho 'varae is usually 'ceasing from it, i.e. activity.' But here the commentators explain it as translated above.

the punishment of a whole province. Doing such things, some have exerted themselves [1]. (2)

Therefore the second (i.e. the wrong creed) is not adhered to. The knowing one seeing the vanity (of the world) [knowing the rise and fall of the souls [2]], the Brahman follows the unrivalled (control of the *G*ainas). He should not kill, nor cause others to kill, nor consent to the killing of others. 'Avoid gaiety, not delighting in creatures (i.e. women), having the highest intuition,' keeping off from sinful acts. (3)

And the hero should conquer wrath and pride,
Look at the great hell (as the place) for greed.
Therefore the hero abstaining from killing,
Should destroy sorrow, going the road of easiness [3].

Here now the hero, knowing the bondage,
Knowing sorrow, should restrain himself.
Having risen to birth among men,
He should not take the life of living beings.

THIRD LESSON.

'Knowing the connection of the world, (carelessness is not for his benefit [4]).'. 'Look at the exterior

---

[1] Samu*tth*iyâ is commonly used in the sense of right effort, and thus explained by the commentators in this place, though we should expect the contrary.

[2] The words in brackets [] are a gloss upon the preceding sentence. If we leave them out, the rest forms half a *s*loka.

[3] Laghubhûya, i. e. nirvâ*n*a.

[4] This is a very difficult passage. Connection (sandhi) is explained in different ways, as karmavivara, samyag*gñ*ânâvâpti, and the state of the soul, which has only temporarily and not thoroughly come to rest. To complete the sentence the commentators add pramâdo na *s*reyase. As the words of the text form the pâda of a *s*loka, it is probable that something like pamâo neva se*gg*ase

(world from analogy with thy own) self; [then] thou wilt neither kill nor destroy (living beings);' viz. out of reciprocal regard [well examining] he does no sinful act. What is the characteristic of a sage? 'Recognising the equality (of all living beings), he appeases hisself.' (1)

Knowing the highest good, one should never be careless;
Guarding one's self, always prudent, one should pass life on the right road.

'One should acquire disregard of sensual enjoyment, being with a great one (i.e. a god) or the small ones (men).' When one knows whence men come and where they go, and when both ends are out of sight[1], one is not cut, nor slit, nor burnt, nor struck[2] (2) by any one in the whole world[3].

Some do not remember what preceded the present: 'what has been his past? what will be his future?' Some men here say: 'what has been his past, that will be his future[4].'

There is no past thing, nor is there a future one;
So opine the Tathâgatas.

He whose karman has ceased and conduct is right,

concluded the hemistich. The meaning is, 'Make good use of any opening to get out of worldly troubles.'

[1] See 1, lesson 4.

[2] The reading of the Nâgârgunîyas, according to the commentary, was, 'Knowing well and essentially the five (perceptions) in the object and the three degrees (i.e. good, middle, bad), in the twofold (i.e. what is to be avoided and to be adopted), one is not marred by either (love and hate).' These words form a sloka.

[3] The commentary connects these words with the preceding sentence, saying that the accusative stands for the instrumental by any one.

[4] The words of the original read like a trishtubh in disorder; the same is the case with a different reading quoted by the commentator.

who recognises the truth (stated above) and destroys sinfulness (thinks):

What is discontent and what is pleasure? not subject to either, one should live;

Giving up all gaiety, circumspect and restrained, one should lead a religious life. (3)

Man! Thou art thy own friend; why wishest thou for a friend beyond thyself? Whom he knows as a dweller on high[1], him he should know as a dweller far (from sin); and whom he knows as a dweller far (from sin), him he should know as a dweller on high. Man! restraining thyself (from the outward world) 'thou wilt get free from pain.' Man, understand well the truth! exerting himself in the rule of truth a wise man overcomes Mâra. (4)

'The gifted man[2], following the law, sees well his true interest.' In a twofold way[3], for the sake of life's splendour, honour and glory (some men exert themselves), wherein they go astray. The gifted[2], touched by calamity, are not confounded. 'Mind this! the worthy one, in this world, gets out of the creation[4].' Thus I say. (5)

Fourth Lesson.

That man (i.e. the liberated) conquers wrath, pride, deceit, and greed. This is the doctrine of the Seer who does not injure living beings and has put an end (to acts and to sa*m*sâra). Preventing

---

[1] There is apparently a pun in the text: u*kk*âlaiya*m* is explained by u*kk*âlayitâram = remover (of sins), but as contrasted with dûrâlaiya it has the meaning we have adopted above.

[2] With knowledge, &c.

[3] For the sake of love and hate, or worldly and heavenly bliss.

[4] If loyâloya is omitted, the last words form the half of a *s*loka.

propensity to sin destroys former actions. He who knows one thing, knows all things; and he who knows all things, knows one thing[1]. He who is careless in all respects, is in danger[2]; he who is not careless in all respects, is free from danger. (1)

He who conquers one (passion), conquers many; and he who conquers many, conquers one. 'Knowing the misery of the world' rejecting the connection with the world, 'the heroes go on the great journey,' they rise gradually; 'they do not desire life.' (2)

He who avoids one (passion), avoids (them all) severally; and he who avoids them severally, avoids one. Faithful according to the commandment (of the Tîrthakaras), wise, and understanding the world according to the commandment—such a man is without danger[2] from anywhere. There are degrees in injurious acts, but there are no degrees in control. (3)

He who knows[3] wrath, knows pride; he who knows pride, knows deceit; he who knows deceit, knows greed; he who knows greed, knows love; he who knows love, knows hate; he who knows hate, knows delusion; he who knows delusion, knows conception; he who knows conception, knows birth; he who knows birth, knows death; he who knows death, knows hell; he who knows hell, knows animal existence; he who knows animal existence, knows pain.

Therefore, a wise man should avoid wrath, pride, deceit, greed, love, hate, delusion, conception, birth, death, hell, animal existence, and pain.

---

[1] Because true knowledge of one thing is inseparable from true knowledge of all things.

[2] I. e. he heaps up karman.

[3] And accordingly avoids wrath.

This is the doctrine of the Seer, who does not injure living beings and has put an end (to acts and to samsâra). Preventing the propensity to sin destroys former actions. Is there any worldly weakness in the Seer? There exists none, there is none. Thus I say. (4)

End of the Third Lecture, called Hot and Cold.

FOURTH LECTURE,

CALLED

RIGHTEOUSNESS.

First Lesson.

The Arhats and Bhagavats of the past, present, and future, all say thus, speak thus, declare thus, explain thus: all breathing, existing, living, sentient creatures[1] should not be slain, nor treated with violence, nor abused, nor tormented, nor driven away. (1)

This is the pure, unchangeable, eternal law, which the clever ones, who understand the world, have declared: among the zealous and the not zealous, among the faithful and the not faithful, among the not cruel and the cruel, among those who have worldly weakness and those who have not, among those who like social bonds and those who do not: 'that is the truth, that is so, that is proclaimed in this (creed).' (2)

Having adopted (the law), one should not hide it, nor forsake it. Correctly understanding the law, one should arrive at indifference for the impressions of the senses[2], and 'not act on the motives of the world.' 'He who is not of this mind[3], how should he come to the other[4]?'

[1] Pâ*n*â bhûyâ *g*îvâ sattâ. In the sequel we translate these words, all sorts of living beings.

[2] Literally, what one sees.

[3] Who acts not on worldly motives.

[4] Sinfulness.

What has been said here, has been seen (by the omniscient ones), heard (by the believers), acknowledged (by the faithful), and thoroughly understood by them. Those who acquiesce and indulge (in worldly pleasures), are born again and again. 'Day and night exerting thyself, steadfast,' always having ready wisdom, perceive that the careless (stand) outside (of salvation); if careful, thou wilt always conquer. Thus I say. (3)

SECOND LESSON.

There are as many âsravas[1] as there are parisravas, and there are as many parisravas as there are âsravas. There are as many anâsravas as there are aparisravas, and there are as many aparisravas as there are anâsravas. He who well understands these words and regards the world according to the instruction (and understands), that which has been distinctly declared, that 'wise man proclaims (the truth) here to men,' who still belong to the sa*m*sâra, who are awakened, and have reached discrimination. (1)

'Those also who are afflicted and careless' (will be instructed). I say this as a truth. There is nothing secure from the mouth of death. Those who are led by their desires, who are the tabernacle of fraud, 'who seized by Time dwell in the heap (of karman),' are born again and again. [Many who are again and again (immersed) in delusion, (will

[1] Âsrava is that by means of which karman takes effect upon the soul, parisrava that (nir*g*arâ, &c.) by which the influence of karman is counteracted. Anâsrava is that by which âsrava is avoided (religious vows), and aparisrava that by which karman is acquired.

often renew) their acquaintance with the places of pain; they experience the pains inherent in regeneration. He who often does cruel acts, often undergoes (punishment in hell, &c.) He who seldom does cruel acts, seldom undergoes (punishment).][1] (2)

Some say thus, also the wise ones; the wise ones say thus, also some others[2]. Many and several in this world, Brâhma*n*as or *S*rama*n*as, raise this discussion: We have seen, heard, acknowledged, thoroughly understood, in the upper, nether, and sidelong directions, and in all ways examined it: all sorts of living beings may be slain, or treated with violence, or abused, or tormented, or driven away. Know about this: there is no wrong in it. (3)

That is a doctrine of the unworthy. But those who are teachers, have said: You have wrongly seen, wrongly heard, wrongly acknowledged, wrongly understood, in the upper, nether, and sidelong directions, in all ways wrongly examined it, when you say thus, speak thus, declare thus, explain thus: All sorts of living beings may be slain, or treated with violence, or abused, or tormented, or driven away. Know about this: there is no wrong in it. That is a doctrine of the unworthy. (4) But we say thus, speak thus, declare thus, explain thus:

---

[1] The passage in brackets is introduced by the words pâ*th*ântara*m* vâ, 'various reading.' It occurs in all MSS. I have consulted, and is commented upon by the commentaries as belonging to the text.

[2] By some is meant the highest class of sages. The meaning is that all professors, high or low, say the same, agree in the doctrine of ahi*m*sâ.

All sorts of living beings should not be slain, nor treated with violence, nor abused, nor tormented, nor driven away. Know about this, there is no wrong in it. This is the doctrine of the teachers. (5)

First the persuasion of every one should be ascertained, and then we will ask them severally: Ye professors! is pain pleasant to you, or unpleasant? If they give the right answer, reply: For all sorts of living beings pain is unpleasant, disagreeable, and greatly feared. Thus I say. (6)

THIRD LESSON.

'Reflect and observe that whether you go to this world or to that beyond, in the whole world those who are discerning beings, who abstain from cruelty[1], relinquish karman. They are flesh-subduing, called duty-knowing, upright men, aware that pain results from actions.' Thus say those who have right intuition. (1)

All the professors, conversant with pain, preach renunciation. Thus thoroughly knowing karman, observing the commandment, wise, unattached (to the world), recognising thy Self as one[2], subdue the body, chastise thyself, weaken thyself: 'just as fire consumes old wood!' Thus with a composed mind, unattached, 'unhesitatingly avoid wrath!' Considering the shortness of life 'know pain, or what will come[3];' one shall feel the several feelings; and perceive the world suffering under them. (2)

[1] Nikkhittada*nd*â, literally, those who have laid down the rod.
[2] I. e. as separate and different from the world.
[3] According to the commentators the present and future pains.

Those who are free from sinful acts are called anidâna[1]. Hence a very wise man should not be inflamed (by wrath). Thus I say. (3)

FOURTH LESSON.

One should mortify (one's flesh) in a low, high, and highest degree, quitting one's former connections, and entering tranquillity. Therefore a hero is careful, a person of pith[2], guarded, endowed (with knowledge, &c.), and always restrained. Difficult to go is the road of the heroes, who go whence there is no return (final liberation). Subdue blood and flesh. (1)

That man is called a worthy one, a hero, one to be followed, who living in chastity [guarding his eyes] shakes off the aggregate[3].

He who desires the current of karman, is a fool who has not cut off the fetters of, nor conquered the connection with, (the world.) For such as dwell in darkness, and are without knowledge, there is no success in faith. Thus I say. (2)

'Whence should he have it[4], who does not get it

[1] If we read nivvu*d*â pâvakammehi*m* a*n*iyâ*n*â viyâhiyâ, we have a hemistich of a *s*loka.

[2] Sârae. The commentators translate it with svârata = su + â (â *g*îvanamaryâdâyâ) + rata (sa*m*yamânush*th*âne), for ever delighting in the exercise of control. I think the Sanskrit prototype of sârae is sâraka.

[3] These words seem to have formed a *s*loka, which could easily be restored if we read: purise davie vîre âyâ*n*ig*g*e viyâhie | vâsittâ ba*m*bha*k*era*m*si *g*e dhu*n*âi samussaya*m* || The aggregate is either that of the constituent parts of the body, i. e. the body itself, or that of karman, i. e. the sum of karman.

[4] Success in faith.

early, late, or in the middle of life?' But the discerning one is awakened, and ceases to act. See that it is good to be so! Cutting off that 'whence bondage, cruel death, and dreadful pain,' 'and the (desire for) external (objects) flow, he who among mortals knows freedom from acts,' 'seeing that acts will bear fruit, the knower of the sacred lore, parts from (karman).' (3)

There are those who have established themselves in the truth, who (were, are, or will be) heroes, endowed (with knowledge), always exerting themselves, full of equanimity[1], valuing the world (as it deserves) in the east, west, south, north. We shall tell the knowledge of them who (were, &c.) heroes, endowed (with knowledge), always exerting themselves, full of equanimity, valuing the world (as it deserves).

Is there any worldly weakness in the Seer? There exists none, there is none. Thus I say. (4)

End of the Fourth Lecture, called Righteousness.

---

[1] Sa*m*gha*d*ada*m*si*n*o: nirantaradar*s*ina*h* *s*ubhâ*s*ubhasya.

FIFTH LECTURE,

CALLED

ESSENCE OF THE WORLD.

First Lesson.

Many entertain cruel thoughts against the world with a motive or without one; they entertain cruel thoughts against these (six classes of living beings). To him[1] pleasures are dear. Therefore he is near death. Because he is near death, he is far (from liberation). But he who is neither near (death) nor far (from liberation), considers the life of a slow and ignorant fool as similar to a dewdrop trembling on the sharp point of the blade of Kusa grass which falls down when shaken by the wind. A fool, doing cruel acts, comes thereby ignorantly to grief. 'Through delusion he is born, dies, &c.' Being conversant with the deliberation about this delusion, one is conversant with the samsâra; being not conversant with that deliberation, one is not conversant with the samsâra. He who is clever, should not seek after sexual intercourse. But having done so, (it would be) a second folly of the weak-minded not to own it. Repenting and excluding (from the mind) the begotten pleasures, one should instruct others to follow the commandment. Thus I say. (1)

See! many who desire colours, are led around

[1] The change of number here and in the analogous passages at the beginning of the second and third lessons is one of the grammatical irregularities in which our text abounds.

(in the sa*m*sâra), they (experience) here again and again feelings (i.e. punishment)[1]. Many live by injurious deeds against the world, they live by injurious deeds against these (living beings)[2]. Also the fool, suffering (for his passions), delights in bad acts here, mistaking that for salvation which is none. Many (heretics) lead the life of a hermit (in order to avoid worldly sorrows and pains). (2)

Such a man has much wrath, much pride, much conceit, much greed; he delights in many (works), acts frequently like a stage-player or a rogue, forms many plans, gives way to his impulses, is influenced by his acts though he pretends to be awakened: (thinking) that nobody will see him. Through the influence of ignorance and carelessness the fool never knows the law. Men! unhappy creatures, world-wise are those who, not freeing themselves from ignorance, talk about final liberation: they turn round and round in the whirlpool (of births). Thus I say. (3)

SECOND LESSON.

Many do not live by injurious deeds against the world, they do not live by injurious deeds against

[1] This interpretation of the scholiast can scarcely be correct. Probably the same ideas which are introduced in the last paragraph with the words, Being conversant with, &c., are to be repeated here. For this passage is similar to the commencement of that in § 1, or identical if we adopt the pâ*th*ântaram.

[2] This passage is perfectly analogous to that in the beginning of the lesson. But the scholiast explains the locatives which we have, according to his explanation in the former place, translated against the world, against these, here and in the similar passages which occur in this lecture, by, in the world, amongst these, viz. householders.

these (living beings). Ceasing from them, making an end of them, he perceives: this is a favourable opportunity[1]; he who searches for[2] the right moment for this body (should never be careless). This is the road taught by the noble ones. (1)

When he has become zealous for the law, he should never be careless, knowing pain and pleasure in their various forms. Men act here on their own motives; it has been declared that they suffer for their own sins. Neither killing nor lying, he should (patiently) bear (all unpleasant) feelings when affected by them. That man is called a true monk. (2)

Those who are not given to sinful acts are (nevertheless) attacked by calamities; but then the steadfast will bear them. (He has to bear) them afterwards as (he has done) before (his conversion). (The body) is of a fragile, decaying nature, (it is) unstable, transient, uneternal, increasing and decreasing, of a changeable nature. Perceive this as its true character. For him who well understands this, who delights in the unique refuge[3], for the liberated and inactive there is no passage (from birth to birth). Thus I say. (3)

Many are attached to something in the world—be it little or much, small or great, sentient or non-sentient—they are attached to it (here) amongst these (householders). Thus some incur great danger. For him who contemplates the course of the world and does not acknowledge these attachments (there

---

[1] For adopting the right conduct.

[2] Annesî = anveshin. I think that annesî may be an aorist of *gñâ*, knew.

[3] Âyata*n*a, i.e. the triad: right knowledge, right intuition, right conduct.

is no such danger). Knowing that that which is well understood is well practised, man! with thy eyes on the highest good, be victorious (in control). Among such men only is real Brahmanhood. Thus I say. (4)

I have heard this, and it is in my innermost heart; and the freedom from bonds is in your innermost heart. He who has ceased (to have worldly attachments), the houseless, suffers with patience a long time.

The careless stand outside, the careful lead a religious life.
Maintain rightly this state of a sage. Thus I say. (5)

Third Lesson.

Many are not attached to something in this world, they are not attached to it among these (householders). He is a wise man who has heard and understood the word of the learned ones. Without partiality the law has been declared by the noble ones. As I have destroyed here[1] the connection with the world, so is the connection elsewhere difficult to destroy. Therefore I say: One should not abandon firmness. (1) Some who early exert themselves, do not afterwards slide back; some who early exert themselves, afterwards slide back; those who do not early exert themselves, (can of course) not slide back. That man also is of this description[2], who knowing the world (as worthless nevertheless) follows its ways. 'Knowing this, it has been declared by the sage.' Here the follower of the com-

[1] 'Here' and 'elsewhere' mean, in the church of Mahâvîra, and in that of the Tîrthikas.

[2] Belongs to the last category, to which belong the *S*âkyas, &c.

mandment, the wise, the passionless, he who exerts himself before morning and after evening[1], always contemplating virtue[2] and hearing (the merit of it) will become free from love and delusion. 'Fight with this (your body)! why should you fight with anything else?' Difficult to attain is this (human body) which is worth the fight. For the clever ones have praised the discernment of wisdom; the fool who falls from it, is liable to birth, &c. (2) In this (religion of the *G*ainas the cause of the fool's fall) has been declared (to depend) on colour[3] and killing. But a sage who walks the beaten track (to liberation), regards the world in a different way. 'Knowing thus (the nature of) acts in all regards, he does not kill,' he controls himself, he is not overbearing. (3)

Comprehending that pleasure (and pain) are individual, advising kindness, he will not engage in any work in the whole world: keeping before him the one (great aim, liberation), and not turning aside, 'living humbly, unattached to any creature.' The rich (in control) who with a mind endowed with all penetration (recognises) that a bad deed should not be done, will not go after it. What you acknowledge as righteousness, that you acknowledge as sagedom (mauna); what you acknowledge as sagedom, that you acknowledge as righteousness. It is

[1] Puvvâvararâyam, the first and the last wake (yâma) of the night; the intermediate time is allowed for sleep.

[2] Sîla is either samyama, control with its 18,000 subdivisions, or it consists of (1) the five great vows, (2) the three guptis, (3) the restraint of the senses, (4) the avoidance of sin (kashâya).

[3] Colour stands for all perceptions of the senses. Of course, the attachment to sensual pleasures is meant.

inconsistent with weak, sinning, sensual, ill-conducted house-inhabiting men. (4) 'A sage, acquiring sagedom, should subdue his body.' 'The heroes who look at everything with indifference, use mean and rough (food, &c.)' Such a man is said to have crossed the flood (of life), to be a sage, to have passed over (the sa*m*sâra), to be liberated, to have ceased (from acts). Thus I say. (5)

FOURTH LESSON.

For a monk who has not yet reached discrimination[1], it is bad going and difficult proceeding when he wanders (alone) from village to village. Some men (when going wrong) will become angry when exhorted with speech. And a man with wary pride is embarrassed with great delusion[2]. (1) There are many obstacles which are very difficult to overcome for the ignorant and the blinded. Let that not be your case! That is the doctrine of the clever one (Mahavîra). Adopting the (â*k*ârya's) views, imitating his indifference (for the outer world), making him the guide and adviser (in all one's matters), sharing his abode, living carefully, acting according to his mind, examining one's way[3], not coming too near (the â*k*ârya), minding living beings, one should go (on one's business). (2)

[1] Avyakta, either with regard to *s*ruta, sacred knowledge, or to his age.

[2] The result will be that he thinks himself above the admonition of the spiritual head (â*k*ârya) of the chapter (ga*kkh*a), and leaves the chapter, living as a ga*kkh*anirgata.

[3] The monk must closely inspect everything with which he comes in contact in order to avoid killing animals; this holds good with regard to walking, sitting, sleeping, eating, drinking, &c.

(A monk should according to the âkârya's order) go and return, contract or stretch (his limbs), thoroughly clean (what ought to be cleaned). Sometimes, though a monk be endowed with virtue and walks in righteousness, living beings, coming in contact with his body, will be killed. (If this happens through mere carelessness) then he will get his punishment in this life; but if it was done contrary to the rules[1], he should repent of it and do penance for it[2]. Thus he who knows the sacred lore[3], recommends penance combined with carefulness. (3)

(When a monk) with fully developed intuition and knowledge, calm, guarded, endowed (with knowledge), always restrained, perceives (a woman tempting him), he should consider within himself: what will this person do? The greatest temptation in this world are women. This has been declared by the sage. (4)

When strongly vexed by the influence of the senses, he should eat bad food, mortify himself, stand upright, wander from village to village, take no food at all, withdraw his mind from women. First troubles, then pleasures; first pleasures, then troubles[4]: thus they are the cause of quarrels. Considering this and well understanding it, one should teach oneself not to cultivate (sensuality). Thus I say. He should not speak of women, nor look at them, nor converse with them, nor claim them as his own, nor do their work. Careful in his speech and

[1] Âuttîkammam=âkuttikarman.

[2] Vivega=viveka, explained as prâyaskittam. [3] Vedavid.

[4] In order to attain pleasure, one has to work for the means; after the enjoyment of the pleasures one has to undergo punishment in hell, &c.

guarding his mind, he should always avoid sin. He should maintain this sagedom. Thus I say. (5)

FIFTH LESSON.

Thus I say: a lake is full of water, it is in an even plain, it is free from dust, it harbours (many fish)[1]. Look! he (the teacher) stands in the stream (of knowledge) and is guarded in all directions. Look! there are great Seers in the world, wise, awakened, free from acts. Perceive the truth: from a desire of (a pious) end they chose a religious life. Thus I say. (1)

He whose mind is always wavering, does not reach abstract contemplation[2]. Some, bound (by worldly ties), are followers (i. e. understand the truth); some who are not bound, are followers. How should he not despond who amongst followers is a non-follower? 'But that is truth beyond doubt, what has been declared by the *G*inas.' (2)

Whatever[3] a faithful, well-disposed man, on entering the order, thought to be true, that may afterwards appear to him true; what he thought to be true, that may afterwards appear to him untrue; what he thought to be untrue, that may afterwards appear to him true; what he thought to be untrue, that may afterwards appear to him true. What he thinks to be true, that may, on consideration, appear to him true, whether it be true or untrue. What he thinks to be untrue, that may, on consideration, appear to him untrue, whether it be true or untrue. But he

[1] Like unto it is a teacher who is full of wisdom, who lives in a quiet country, is free from passion, and protects living beings.

[2] Samâdhi, the means of a religious death.

[3] Any article of the *G*aina faith.

who reflects should say unto him who does not reflect: Consider it to be true. Thus the connection (i. e. the continuity of sins) is broken. (3)

Regard this as the course of the zealous one, who stands (in obedience to the spiritual guide). In this point do not show yourself a fool[1]!

As it would be unto thee, so it is with him whom thou intendest to kill. As it would be unto thee, so it is with him whom thou intendest to tyrannise over. As it would be unto thee, so it is with him whom thou intendest to torment. In the same way (it is with him) whom thou intendest to punish, and to drive away. The righteous man who lives up to these sentiments, does therefore neither kill nor cause others to kill (living beings). He should not intentionally cause the same punishment for himself[2]. (4)

The Self is the knower (or experiencer), and the knower is the Self. That through which one knows, is the Self. With regard to this (to know) it (the Self) is established[3]. Such is he who maintains the right doctrine of Self. This subject has truly been explained. Thus I say. (5)

Sixth Lesson.

Some not instructed (in the true law) make (only a show) of good conduct; some, though instructed,

---

[1] Fool, bâla; the scholiast explains bâla as *S*âkya or Pâr*s*vastha, an outsider, or a follower of Pâr*s*va (?).

[2] For the same pain he has caused to others in this life, he will suffer in the life hereafter.

[3] This means that knowledge is a modification (pari*n*âma) of the Self, and therefore one with it, but not as a quality or action of the Self different from it.

have no good conduct. Let that not be your case! That is the doctrine of the clever one. Adopting the (â*k*ârya's) views, imitating his indifference (for the outer world), making him the guide and adviser (in all one's matters), sharing his abode, conquering (sinfulness), one sees the truth; unconquered one should be one's own master, having no reliance on anything (in the world). He who is great and withdraws his mind from the outer world, should learn the teaching (of the Tîrthakaras) through the teaching (of the â*k*ârya); by his own innate knowledge, or through the instruction of the highest [1], or having heard it from others. A wise man should not break the commandment. Examining all (wrong) doctrines from all sides and in all respects, one should clearly understand (and reject) them. 'Knowing the delight of this world [2], circumspect and restrained, one should lead the life of an ascetic.' Desiring liberation [3], a hero should, through the sacred lore, ever be victorious. Thus I say. (1)

The current (of sin) [4] is said to come from above, from below, and from the sides; these have been declared to be the currents through which, look, there is sinfulness.

'Examining the whirlpool [5], a man, versed in the sacred lore, should keep off from it.' Leaving the world to avert the current (of sin), such a great

[1] I. e. the Tîrthakaras. [2] I. e. self-control.

[3] The original has ni*tth*iya = nish*th*ita.

[4] It is called the door of âsrava. The three directions mentioned in the text, are the three divisions of the universe. Objects of desire in each induce men to sin. The original is a *s*loka, noticed as such by the scholiast.

[5] Of worldly desires and their objects.

man, free from acts, knows and sees the truth; examining (pleasures) he does not desire them. (2) Knowing whence we come and whither we go, he leaves the road to birth and death, rejoicing in the glorious (liberation). 'All sounds recoil thence, where speculation has no room,' nor does the mind penetrate there[1]. The saint[2] knows well that which is without support[3]. (3)

(The liberated) is not long nor small nor round nor triangular nor quadrangular nor circular; he is not black nor blue nor red nor green nor white; neither of good nor bad smell; not bitter nor pungent nor astringent nor sweet; neither rough nor soft; neither heavy nor light; neither cold nor hot; neither harsh nor smooth; he is without body, without resurrection, without contact (of matter), he is not feminine nor masculine nor neuter; he perceives, he knows, but there is no analogy (whereby to know the nature of the liberated soul); its essence is without form; there is no condition of the unconditioned. There is no sound, no colour, no smell, no taste, no touch—nothing of that kind. Thus I say. (4)

End of the Fifth Lecture, called Essence of the World.

[1] It is impossible to express the nature of liberation in words, since it cannot be reached even by the mind.

[2] Oe=oga, he who is free from love and hate.

[3] I.e. liberation, or the state of the liberated. Support, patiṭṭhâna, is the body or karman.

SIXTH LECTURE,

CALLED

THE CLEANING[1].

FIRST LESSON.

He who is awakened amongst men, preaches; the man to whom all these classes of lives are well known, preaches the unparalleled wisdom. He praises the road to liberation for those who well exert themselves, who have forsworn cruelty, are zealous and endowed with knowledge. Thus some great heroes are victorious; but, look, some others who are wanting in control do not understand (the welfare of) their souls. Thus I say. (1)

As in a lake a greedy leaf-covered tortoise cannot rise up; as the trees do not leave their place (though shaken by storms, &c.): thus men, born in various families, cry bitterly because they are attached to the objects of the senses[2]; on account of their sinfulness they do not reach liberation[3]. (2)

Now look at those who are born in these families to reap the fruit of their own acts[4]:

Boils and leprosy, consumption, falling sickness, blindness and stiffness, lameness and humpbackedness, 1

[1] Dhuta, literally, shaken. Compare the dhutaṅgas of the Buddhists. Childers' Pâli Dict. s. v.

[2] Literally, the colours.

[3] This paragraph reads like prose mixed with parts of verses. But it is not possible to restore one complete verse.

[4] 'To reap the fruit of their own acts' is, according to the commentary, the meaning of âyattâe=âtmatvâya.

Dropsy and dumbness, look! apoplexy(?) and eye-disease, trembling and crippledness, elephantiasis and diabetes, 2

These are the sixteen diseases enumerated in due order; besides them many illnesses and wounds occur. 3

Contemplating their (i. e. the creatures') death, knowing their births in higher and lower regions, contemplating the fruit (of their acts), hear about this according to truth. 4

There are said to be blind beings dwelling in darkness; once or frequently meeting this lot, they experience pleasant and unpleasant feelings. This has been declared by the awakened ones. (3) There are beings endowed with voice, with taste, water-beings dwelling in water, beings living in the air: 'beings torment beings. See the great danger in this world[1];' many pains (are the lot) of the creatures. Men who are given to their lusts, come to destruction through their weak, frail body. 'The fool works hard, thinking' that the unhappy one suffers many pains. 'Knowing that these diseases are many, should the afflicted search after (remedies)?' See! they are of no avail, have done with them! Sage! see this great danger! Do not hurt anybody! Contemplate. Be attentive! I shall proclaim the doctrine of renunciation[2]. (4)

To reap the fruit of their acts they are born in these various families, they increase, are born, grow up, become awakened, and leave the world in due order as great sages. The lamenting parents say to them who proceed on the glorious road: 'Do not

[1] The result of former acts.

[2] Dhûtavâda.

leave us!' (5) Consulting their own pleasure, indulging their passions, 'making a noise[1], the parents cry:' No man who leaves his parents is (fit to become) a flood-crossing sage! (The ascetic) does not take refuge there (in his family); for what could attract him there?

He should always maintain this knowledge! Thus I say. (6)

SECOND LESSON.

Though some know the misery of the world, have relinquished their former connections, have given up ease, live in chastity, and, whether monk or layman, thoroughly understand the law, they are not able (to persevere in a religious life). The ill-disposed, giving up the robe, alms-bowl, blanket, and broom, do not bear the continuous hardships that are difficult to bear. He who prefers pleasures will, now or after an hour[2], be deprived (of the body[3], not to recover it) for an infinite space of time. And thus they do not cross (the samsâra), for the sake of these pleasures which entail evil consequences and are associated with others of their kind. (1)

But some who embrace the law, will practise it, being careful about its outward signs; not giving way to worldliness, but being firm. Knowing (and renouncing) all lust, a devout man becomes a great sage when he breaks all bonds, thinking: Nothing

[1] The commentator explains this passage: 'We do your will, we depend on you (?),' so shouting they cry, &c.

[2] I.e. after a short time.

[3] The body with five organs, in which alone liberation can be realised.

belongs to me. A man who, thinking, I am I[1], exerts himself for this (creed), ceases (to act), is houseless, walks about bald-headed. The naked, fasting (monk), who combats the flesh, will be abused, or struck, or hurt[2]; he will be upbraided with his former trade, or reviled with untrue reproaches. Accounting (for this treatment) by his former sins, knowing pleasant and unpleasant occurrences, he should patiently wander about. Quitting all worldliness[3] one should bear all (disagreeable) feelings, being possessed of the right view[4]. (2)

Those are called naked, who in this world, never returning (to a worldly state), (follow) my religion according to the commandment. This highest doctrine has here been declared for men. Delighted with this, destroying that (i.e. the effect of works), he will successively[5] give up sinfulness[6], after having come to a knowledge of it. Here (in our religion) some live as single mendicants. Therefore a wise man should lead the life of an ascetic by collecting pure alms or any alms in all sorts of families. 'If (the food) be of good or bad smell, or if dreadful beasts inflict pain on (other) beings'—

---

[1] I have nothing to do with anybody else.

[2] Lûsie. The commentator translates it by lu*n*kita, to tear out the hair. This would be a rather difficult operation on the bald head of a *G*aina monk. Lûsiya is, of course, the Sanskrit lûshita, hurt.

[3] Visottiya*m*. Sanskrit vi*s*rotasikâ (?) = *s*ankâ.

[4] Samiyada*m*sa*n*e. The commentator explains it by samitadar*s*ana. I think it corresponds to samyagdar*s*ana.

[5] Pariyâe*n*a*m* = paryâya. The commentator interprets it by *s*râma*n*ya.

[6] Âdâ*n*iggam = âdânîya. It means usually faith; but I have here translated it according to the commentary.

all that happens to you, you will firmly bear it. Thus I say. (3)

Third Lesson.

A sage who is well instructed in the law and leads a life of abstinence, is always a destroyer of the effects of works[1]. To a mendicant who is little clothed[2] and firm in control, it will not occur (to think): My clothes are torn, I shall beg for (new) clothes; I shall beg for thread; I shall beg for a needle; I shall mend (my clothes); I shall darn them; I shall repair them; I shall put them on; I shall wrap myself in them. (1)

The unclothed one, who excels in this (abstinence), will often be molested by (sharp blades of) grass, by cold, heat, gnats, and mosquitoes. The unclothed one, who effects scarcity (of his wants or of his karman), bears these and various other hardships. He is fit for penance, as has been declared by the Revered One. Understanding this in all respects and with his whole mind, he should perfectly know righteousness. The great heroes (i.e. the Tîrthakaras) who for a long time[3] walked

---

[1] Âdânam explained as implements which are not requisite for the law.

[2] A*k*ela, literally, unclothed. But it has that meaning only when it is applied to a *g*inakalpika. A *g*inakalpika is a monk who wears no clothes and uses the hollow of the hand for an alms-bowl. The only implements he has are the broom (ra*g*ohara*n*am) and the piece of cloth which the monk places before the mouth while speaking, in order to prevent insects from getting into his mouth (mukhavastrikâ).

[3] *K*irarâta, literally, long night. Compare dîrgharâtra, which the Bauddhas and *G*ainas employ in the sense we have given to *k*irarâtam in the text.

in the former years[1], the worthy ones bore the troubles (mentioned above); endowed with perfect knowledge they had lean arms and very little flesh and blood. He who discontinues (to sin) and is enlightened, is said to have crossed (the samsâra), to be liberated, and to have ceased (to act). Thus I say. (2)

But can discontent lay hold of a mendicant, who has ceased to act and leads a religious life, for a long time controlling himself? He advances in his spiritual career and exerts himself. As an island which is never covered with water, so is the law taught by the noble ones (a safe refuge for those in danger). They are free from desires, free from murder, beloved, wise, learned. For their benefit has been the exertion of the Revered One; as birds (feed) their young ones, so are the disciples regularly to be instructed day and night. Thus I say. (3)

FOURTH LESSON.

The disciples are thus regularly instructed, day and night, by the knowledge-endowed great heroes, receiving knowledge from them. Some, being seduced from the calmness of the mind, adopt rough manners. Some, living in chastity, dispute the authority (of the teacher), others hear and understand his words; they intend to lead a godly life, but having left the world[2], they are not qualified (for a religious life). Others, being incensed by lusts,

---

[1] **Puvvâim vâsâim**, the former years are those long periods by which the length of the early Tîrthakaras' life is measured. Walked means walked in righteousness.

[2] Or obedience to their teacher?

greedy, sensual, 'do not care for abstract meditation and religious instruction:- these men speak harshly unto the teacher.' It is a second folly of the slow-minded to call virtuous, calm, religiously living men worthless.

Some, turning from (control), assign its difficulty as their reason (for doing so)[1]; others, falling from the pure knowledge and defiling the creed, though not without devotion, for the love of life change (their vows). 'When they feel the hardships (of a religious life) they slide back, for their love of life.' Their leaving the world is a bad leaving. (1)

Those who deserve to be called fools, are born again and again. Standing low (in learning or control) they will exalt themselves (and say) in their pride: I am learned. They speak harshly unto the passionless; they upbraid them with their former trades, or revile them with untrue reproaches[2]. The wise, therefore, should know the law. Thou lovest unrighteousness, because thou art young, and lovest acts, and sayest: 'Kill beings;' thou killest them or consentest to their being killed by others. (Such a man) thinks contemptuously: A very severe religion has been proclaimed. Sinking in opposition to the law, he is called murderer. Thus I say. (2)

Some think: What have I to do with this or that man? Thus they leave father and mother, kith and kin, like heroes exerting themselves, free from murder. Look! the pious and calm become

---

[1] They do not upbraid their teachers, and hence are not guilty of the second folly.

[2] Compare second lesson, § 3. Paliya, which we have here as in the passage above translated 'former trade,' is here explained by anush*th*âna, exertion.

desponding; the rising, cast down. Those troubled with sensuality, the cowardly men become perverters of the faith[1]. Therefore the reputation of some becomes bad. He is an apostate ascetic! He is an apostate ascetic! (3)

Look! Some, though living with religious, pious, calm, and worthy (monks), are not religious, nor pious, nor calm, nor worthy. Knowing them, the learned, the wise, the steadfast hero will always be victorious through the right faith. Thus I say. (4)

Fifth Lesson.

Staying in or between houses, in or between villages, in or between towns, in or between counties, a monk is attacked by murderers, or is subject to the hardships (of a mendicant's life). A hero should bear these hardships. (1)

A saint[2], with right intuition, who cherishes compassion for the world, in the east, west, south, and north, should preach, spread, and praise (the faith), knowing the sacred lore[3]. He should proclaim it among those who exert themselves, and those who do not[4], among those who are willing to hear (the word). (2)

Not neglecting tranquillity, indifference, patience, liberation, purity, uprightness, gentleness, and freedom from worldly cares[5], one should, with due consideration, preach the law of the mendicants to all sorts of creatures. (3)

[1] Or breakers of vows.

[2] Oya, see note 2, p. 52.

[3] Veyavî=vedavid.

[4] This is equivalent either to believers and heretics, or to clerical and lay men.

[5] Lâghaviya, lightness, explained, freedom from bonds.

With due consideration preaching the law of the mendicants, one should do no injury to one's self, nor to anybody else, nor to any of the four kinds of living beings. But a great sage, neither injuring nor injured, becomes a shelter for all sorts of afflicted creatures, even as an island, which is never covered with water. (4)

Thus a man who exerts himself, and is of a steady mind, without attachment, unmoved (by passion) but restless (in wandering about), having no worldly desires, should lead the life of an ascetic.

Having contemplated the beautiful law, the discerning one is liberated.

Therefore look at worldliness, ye men, fettered in fetters!

Those whom lust conquers, sink; therefore do not shrink from the hard (control)! He who knows (and renounces) perfectly and thoroughly these injurious acts, from whom the injurers do not shrink[1], 'who has shaken off wrath, pride,' delusion, and greed, 'he is called a removed one.' Thus I say. (5)

On the decay of the body (he does not despond, but deserves) his appellation, 'the leader of the battle.' The sage who has reached the other side, unafflicted and unmoved like a beam, being in the power of death, desires death as the dissolution of the body. Thus I say. (6)

End of the Sixth Lecture, called the Cleaning.

---

[1] One expects, who does not shrink from the injurers.

SEVENTH LECTURE,

CALLED

LIBERATION.

First Lesson.

I say: To friendly or hostile (heretics) one should not give food, drink, dainties and spices, clothes, alms-bowls, and brooms; nor exhort these persons to give (such things), nor do them service, always showing the highest respect. Thus I say[1]. (1)

(A heretic may say): Know this for certain: having or not having received food, &c. (down to) brooms, having or not having eaten (come to our house), even turning from your way or passing (other houses; we shall supply your wants). Confessing an individual creed, coming and going, he may give, or exhort to give, or do service (but one should not accept anything from him), showing not the slightest respect. Thus I say. (2)

Some here are not well instructed as regards the subject of conduct; for desirous of acts, they say: 'Kill creatures;' they themselves kill or consent to the killing of others; or they take what has not been given; or they pronounce opinions, e.g. the world exists, the world does not exist, the world is

[1] This and the following paragraph are extremely difficult to translate. I have translated the words according to the scholiast, and supplied what he supplies; but his interpretation can scarcely be reconciled with the text.

unchangeable, the world is ever changing; the world has a beginning, the world has no beginning; the world has an end, the world has no end; (or with regard to the self and actions): this is well done, this is badly done; this is merit, this is demerit; he is a good man, he is not a good man; there is beatitude, there is no beatitude; there is a hell, there is no hell. When they thus differ (in their opinions) and profess their individual persuasion, know (that this is all) without reason[1]. Thus they are not well taught, not well instructed in the religion such as it has been declared by the Revered One, who knows and sees with quick discernment. (One should either instruct the opponent in the true faith) or observe abstinence as regards speech. Thus I say. (3)

Everywhere[2] sins are admitted; but to avoid them is called my distinction. For ye who live in a village or in the forest, or not in a village and not in the forest, know the law as it has been declared. 'By the Brahman, the wise (Mahâvîra), three[3] vows have been enjoined.' Noble and tranquil men who are enlightened and exert themselves in these (precepts), are called free from sinful acts. (4)

Knowing (and renouncing) severally and singly

---

[1] The *G*ainas do not espouse one of the alternative solutions of the metaphysical and ethical questions; but they are enabled by the syâdvâda to believe in the co-existence of contrary qualities in one and the same thing.

[2] In all other religious sects.

[3] *G*âma = yâma. These are, (1) to kill no living being, (2) to speak no untruth, (3) to abstain from forbidden things (theft and sexual pleasures). Or the three ages of man are intended by *g*âma, which we have rendered vows.

the actions against living beings, in the regions above, below, and on the surface, everywhere and in all ways—a wise man neither gives pain to these bodies, nor orders others to do so, nor assents to their doing so. Nay, we abhor those who give pain to these bodies. Knowing this, a wise man should not cause this or any other pain (to any creatures). Thus I say. (5)

SECOND LESSON.

A mendicant may exert himself, or stand or sit or lie in a burying-place or in an empty house or in a mountain cave or in a potter's workshop. A householder may approach a mendicant who stays in any of these places, and say unto him: O long-lived *S*rama*n*a! I shall give you what I have bought or stolen or taken, though it was not to be taken, nor given, but was taken by force, viz. food, drink, dainties and spices, clothes, an alms-bowl, a plaid, a broom—by acting sinfully against all sorts of living beings; or I shall prepare you snug lodgings; eat (the offered food), dwell (in the prepared house[1]). (1)

O long-lived *S*rama*n*a! A mendicant should thus refuse a householder of good sense and ripe age: O long-lived householder! I do not approve of thy words, I do not accept thy words, that, for my sake, thou givest unto me what thou hast bought or stolen or taken, though it was not to be taken, nor given, but was taken by force, viz. food, drink, dainties and spices, clothes, an alms-bowl, a plaid, a broom—by

[1] Later on in the commentary (beginning of the sixth lesson) this is called udgamotpâdanaishanâ.

acting sinfully against all sorts of living beings; or that thou preparest pleasant lodgings for me. O long-lived householder! I have given up this, because it is not to be done. (2) A mendicant may exert himself, &c. (first sentence of § 1). A householder, without betraying his intention, may approach him who stays in some one of the above-mentioned places, and give unto him what has been taken, &c. (all as above, down to) or prepare pleasant lodgings, and accommodate the mendicant with food (and lodging). A mendicant should know it by his own innate intelligence, or through the instruction of the highest (i. e. the Tîrthakaras), or having heard it from others: This householder, forsooth, for my sake injures all sorts of living beings, to give me food, &c., clothes, &c., or to prepare pleasant lodgings. A mendicant should well observe and understand this, that he may order (the householder) not to show such obsequiousness. Thus I say. (3)

Those who having, with or without the mendicant's knowledge, brought together fetters[1], become angry (on the monk's refusal) and will strike him, saying: Beat, kill, cut, burn, roast, tear, rob, despatch, torture him! But the hero, come to such a lot, will bravely bear it, or tell him the code of conduct, considering that he is of a different habit; or by guarding his speech he should in due order examine the subject, guarding himself.

This has been declared by the awakened ones: The faithful should not give to dissenters food, &c., clothes, &c., nor should they exhort them (to give),

[1] The above-detailed benefactions.

nor do them service, always showing the highest respect. Thus I say. (4)

Know the law declared by the wise Brâhma*n*a: one should give to one of the same faith food, &c., clothes, &c., and one should exhort him (to give) or do him service, always showing the highest respect. Thus I say. (5)

Third Lesson.

Some are awakened as middle-aged men and exert themselves well, having, as clever men, heard and received the word of the learned[1]. The noble ones have impartially preached the law. Those who are awakened, should not wish for pleasure, nor do harm, nor desire (any forbidden things). A person who is without desires and does no harm unto any living beings in the whole world, is called by me 'unfettered.' (1)

One free from passions understands perfectly the bright one[2], knowing birth in the upper and nether regions.

'Bodies increase through nourishment, they are frail in hardships.' See some whose organs are failing (give way to weakness).

A person who has no desires, cherishes pity. He who understands the doctrine of sin, is a mendicant who knows the time, the strength, the measure, the occasion, the conduct, the religious precept; he disowns all things not requisite for religious purposes,

[1] The scholiast says that there are three classes of the awakened: the Svayambuddha, the Pratyekabuddha, and the Buddhabodhita. The last only is treated of in the text.

[2] I. e. self-control.

in time exerts himself, is under no obligations; he proceeds securely (on the road to final liberation) after having cut off both (love and hate)[1]. (2)

A householder approaching a mendicant whose limbs tremble for cold, may say:

O long-lived *S*rama*n*a! are you not subject to the influences of your senses?

O long-lived householder! I am not subject to the influences of my senses. But I cannot sustain the feeling of cold. Yet it does not become me to kindle or light a fire[2], that I may warm or heat myself; nor (to procure that comfort) through the order of others.

Perhaps after the mendicant has spoken thus, the other kindles or lights a fire that he may warm or heat himself. But the mendicant should well observe and understand this, that he may order him to show no such obsequiousness. Thus I say. (3)

Fourth Lesson.

A mendicant who is fitted out with three robes[3], and a bowl as fourth (article), will not think: I shall beg

[1] The latter part of this paragraph is nearly identical with lecture 2, lesson 5, § 3, to which we refer the reader for the explanation of the dark phrases.

[2] The original has fire-body, which the faithful are enjoined not to injure; see lecture 2, lesson 4.

[3] The three robes allowed to a *G*aina monk are two linen under garments (kshaumikakalpa) and one woollen upper garment (aur*n*ikakalpa). Besides these (kalpatraya), the monk possesses, 2. an alms-bowl (pâtra) with six things belonging to it, 3. a broom (ragohara*n*a), 4. a veil for the mouth (mukhavastrikâ). The alms-bowl and the articles belonging to it are specialised in the following gâthâ: patta*m* pattâba*m*dho pâya*tth*ava*n*a*m* *k*a pâyakesariyâ ı pa*d*alâi rayattâ*n*a*m* *k*a go*kkh*ao pâyaniggogo ıı

for a fourth robe. He should beg for (clothes) which he wants, and which are permitted by the religious code[1]; he should wear the clothes in the same state in which they are given him; he should neither wash nor dye them, nor should he wear washed or dyed clothes, nor (should he) hide (his garments when passing) through other villages, being careless of dress. This is the whole duty[2] of one who wears clothes. But know further, that, after winter is gone and the hot season has come, one should leave off the used-up (garment of the three), being clad with an upper and under garment, or with the undermost garment, or with one gown, or with no clothes—aspiring to freedom from bonds[3] Penance suits him. Knowing what the Revered One has declared, one should thoroughly and in all respects conform to it. (1)

When it occurs to a blessed[4] mendicant that he suffers pain, and cannot bear the influence of cold, he should not try to obviate these trials, but stand fast in his own self which is endowed with all knowledge[5]. 'For it is better for an ascetic that he should take poison.' Even thus he will in due time put an end to existence. This (way to escape trials) has been adopted by many who were

[1] Things, &c.: this is the meaning of the technical term ahesa*n*igga yathaisha*n*îya, allowed objects of begging.

[2] Literally, outfit. Cf. II, 5, 2, § 1.

[3] I. e. freedom from worldly cares and interest.

[4] Vasuma*m*: rich (in control).

[5] But he should not, in order to escape these trials, commit such suicide as is only permitted to ascetics who have reached the highest degree of perfection, when they are ripe for Nirvâ*n*a. Suicide only puts off the last struggle for Nirvâ*n*a; but it is better than breaking the vow.

free from delusion; it is good, wholesome, proper, beatifying, meritorious. Thus I say. (2)

FIFTH LESSON.

A mendicant who is fitted out with two robes, and a bowl as third (article), will not think: I shall beg for a third robe. He should beg for robes which are allowed to be begged for; he should wear the clothes, &c. &c.[1] This is the whole outfit of one who wears clothes. But know further, that after the winter is gone and the hot season has come, one should leave off the used-up garments; having left off the used-up garments, (one should) be clad with the undermost garment, with a gown[2], or with no clothes at all—aspiring to freedom from bonds. Penance suits him. Knowing what the Revered One has declared, one should thoroughly and in all respects conform to it. (1)

When the thought occurs to a mendicant that through illness he is too weak, and not able to beg from house to house—and on his thus complaining a householder brings food, &c., obtained (without injuring life[3]), and gives it him—then he should, after deliberation, say[4]: O long-lived householder! it does not become me to eat or drink this[3] food, &c., or (accept) anything else of the same kind. (2)

---

[1] See lesson 4, § 1.

[2] The MSS. are at variance with each other in adapting the words of the former lesson to the present case. As the commentaries are no check, and do not explain our passage, I have selected what seemed to me to be the most likely reading.

[3] Abhiha*d*a=abhyâh*ri*ta: it is a typical attribute of objectionable things. The commentator explains it here by *g*îvopamardani*vri*tta.

[4] The original has only âloe*gg*â, he should examine whether

A mendicant who has resolved, that he will, when sick, accept the assistance of fellow-ascetics [1] in good health, when they offer (assistance) without being asked, and that vice versa he, when in health, will give assistance to sick fellow-ascetics, offering it without being asked—(he should not deviate from his resolution though he die for want of help). (3)

Taking the vow to beg (food, &c.) for another (who is sick), and to eat (when sick) what is brought by another; taking the vow to beg, &c., and not to eat what is brought; taking the vow not to beg, &c., but to eat what is brought; taking the vow neither to beg, &c., nor to eat what is brought—(one should adhere to that vow). Practising thus the law as it has been declared, one becomes tranquil, averted from sin, guarded against the allurements of the senses. Even thus (though sick) he will in due time put an end to existence [2]. This (method) has been adopted by many who were free from delusion; it is good, wholesome, proper, beatifying, meritorious. Thus I say. (4)

---

the food &c. is acceptable or not. This is called the grahanaishanâ.

[1] Sâhammiya=sâdharmika, one who follows the same rule in cases where different rules are left to the option of the mendicants. The word abhikamkha=abhikâṅkshya is not translated, the commentator makes it out to mean, wishing for freedom from sinful acts.

[2] As in the preceding lesson a man who cannot conquer his sensuality, is permitted to commit suicide (by hanging himself, &c.), in order to put an end to his trials and temptations, so in this lesson a man whose sickness prevents him from persevering in a life of austerities, is permitted to commit suicide by rejecting food and drink. This is called bhaktapânapratyâkhyânamukti. It seems therefore to have been regarded as leading to final liberation (mukti).

Sixth Lesson.

A mendicant who is fitted out with one robe, and a bowl as second (article), will not think: I shall beg for a second robe. He should beg for such a robe only as is allowed to be begged for, and he should wear it in the same state as he receives it. This is, &c. (see lesson 4, § 1).

But when the hot season has come, one should leave off the used-up clothes; one should be clad with one or no garment—aspiring to freedom from bonds. Knowing what the Revered One, &c. (see lesson 5, § 1).

When the thought occurs to a mendicant: 'I am myself, alone; I have nobody belonging to me, nor do I belong to anybody,' then he should thoroughly know himself as standing alone—aspiring to freedom from bonds. Penance suits him. Knowing what the Revered One has declared, one should thoroughly and in all respects conform to it. (1)

A male or female mendicant eating food &c. should not shift (the morsel) from the left jaw to the right jaw, nor from the right jaw to the left jaw, to get a fuller taste of it, not caring for the taste (of it)—aspiring to freedom from bonds. Penance suits him. Knowing what the Revered One has declared, one should thoroughly and in all respects conform to it. (2)

If this thought occurs to a monk: 'I am sick and not able, at this time, to regularly mortify the flesh,' that monk should regularly reduce his food; regularly reducing his food, and diminishing his sins, 'he should take proper care of his body, being immovable like a beam; exerting himself he dissolves his body[1].' (3)

Entering a village, or a scot-free town, or a town with an earth-wall, or a town with a small wall, or an isolated town, or a large town, or a sea-town, or a mine, or a hermitage, or the halting-places of processions, or caravans, or a capital[2]—a monk should beg for straw; having begged for straw he should retire with it to a secluded spot. After having repeatedly examined and cleaned the ground, where there are no eggs, nor living beings, nor seeds, nor sprouts, nor dew, nor water, nor ants, nor mildew, nor waterdrops, nor mud, nor cobwebs—he should spread the straw on it. Then he should there and then effect (the religious death called) itvara[3]. (4)

---

[1] There is no finite verb in this sentence, nor any word which could supply its place. The old *G*aina authors were so accustomed to surround their meaning with exclusions and exceptions, and to fortify it with a maze of parentheses, that they sometimes apparently forgot to express the verb, especially when they made use of fragments of old verses, as in the present case.

[2] This is one of the most frequent gamas or identical passages which form a rather questionable ornament of the Sûtra style. The gamas are usually abbreviated, e.g. villages, &c., all down to capital, or eggs, &c., all down to cobwebs, which we shall presently meet with.

[3] Itvara or iṅgitamara*n*a consists in starving oneself, while keeping within a limited space. A religious death is usually permitted only to those who have during twelve years undergone preparatory penance, consisting chiefly in protracted periods of fasting. The scholiast says that in our case the itvara is not enjoined for sick persons who can no longer sustain austerities; but they should act as if they were to commit the itvara suicide, hoping that in five or six days the sickness would leave them, in which case they are to return to their former life. But if they should not get better but die, it is all for the best.

This is the truth: speaking truth, free from passion, crossing (the samsâra), abating irresoluteness, knowing all truth and not being known, leaving this frail body, overcoming all sorts of pains and troubles through trust in this (religion), he accomplishes this fearful (religious death). Even thus he will in due time put an end to existence. This has been adopted by many who were free from delusion; it is good, wholesome, proper, beatifying, meritorious. Thus I say. (5)

SEVENTH LESSON.

To a naked[1] monk the thought occurs: I can bear the pricking of grass, the influence of cold and heat, the stinging of flies and mosquitos; these and other various painful feelings I can sustain, but I cannot leave off the covering of the privities. Then he may cover his privities with a piece of cloth[2].

A naked monk who perseveres in this conduct, sustains repeatedly these and other various painful feelings: the grass pricks him, heat and cold attack him, flies and mosquitos sting him. A naked monk (should be) aspiring to freedom from bonds. Penance suits him. Knowing what the Revered One has declared, one should thoroughly and in all respects conform to it. (1)

A monk who has come to any of the following resolutions,—having collected food, &c., I shall give of it to other monks, and I shall eat (what they have) brought; (or) having collected food, &c., I shall give of it to other monks, but I shall not eat

[1] Akela.

[2] This is the katibandhana or kolapattaka; it should be four fingers broad and one hasta long.

(what they have) brought; (or) having collected food, &c., I shall not give of it to other monks, but I shall eat (what they have) brought; (or) having collected food, &c., I shall not give of it to other monks, nor eat (what they have) brought; (2) (or) I shall assist a fellow-ascetic with the remnants of my dinner, which is acceptable[1] and remained in the same state in which it was received[2], and I shall accept the assistance of fellow-ascetics as regards the remnants of their dinner, which is acceptable and remained in the same state in which it was received;—(that monk should keep these vows even if he should run the risk of his life) (3)—aspiring to freedom from bonds. Penance suits him. Knowing what the Revered One has declared, one should thoroughly conform to it. (4)

(The last two paragraphs of the last lesson are to be reproduced here.)

Thus I say. (5)

Eighth Lesson.

The wise ones who attain in due order[3] to one of the unerring states (in which suicide is prescribed), those who are rich in control and endowed with knowledge, knowing the incomparable (religious death, should continue their contemplation). (1)

---

[1] Ahesa*n*igg*a*: it had those qualities which are required of a thing the mendicant may accept.

[2] Ahâpariggahiya=ahâparig*ri*hîta.

[3] The preceding lessons treated of suicide conceded to sick persons as a means of entering Nirvâ*n*a. The eighth lesson, which is written in *s*lokas, describes the different kinds of religious deaths which form the end of a twelve-years' mortification of the flesh (sa*m*lekhanâ). But the ascetic must ask and get the permission of his Guru, before he commits suicide.

Knowing the twofold (obstacles, i. e. bodily and mental), the wise ones, having thoroughly learned the law, perceiving in due order (that the time for their death has come), get rid of karman. (2)

Subduing the passions and living on little food[1], he should endure (hardships). If a mendicant falls sick, let him again take food. (3)

He should not long for life, nor wish for death; he should yearn after neither, life or death. (4)

He who is indifferent and wishes for the destruction of karman, should continue his contemplation. Becoming unattached internally and externally, he should strive after absolute purity. (5)

Whatever means one knows for calming one's own life[2], that a wise man should learn (i. e. practise) in order to gain time (for continuing penance). (6)

In a village or in a forest, examining the ground and recognising it as free from living beings, the sage should spread the straw[3]. (7)

Without food he should lie down and bear the pains which attack him. He should not for too long time give way to worldly feelings which overcome him. (8)

When crawling animals or such as live on high or below, feed on his flesh and blood, he should neither kill them nor rub (the wound). (9)

Though these animals destroy the body, he should not stir from his position.

---

[1] Compare lecture 7, lesson 6, § 3.

[2] I. e. for preserving the life, when too severe penance brings on sickness and the probability of instant death.

[3] Here commences the description of the bhaktapratyâkhyânamara*n*a, suicide by rejecting food.

After the âsravas have ceased, he should bear (pains) as if he rejoiced in them. (10)

When the bonds fall off, then he has accomplished his life.

(We shall now describe) a more exalted (method[1]) for a well-controlled and instructed monk. (11)

This other law has been proclaimed by *Gñâtri*-putra:

He should give up all motions except his own in the thrice-threefold way[2]. (12)

He should not lie on sprouts of grass, but inspecting the bare ground he should lie on it.

Without any comfort and food, he should there bear pain. (13)

When the sage becomes weak in his limbs, he should strive after calmness[3].

For he is blameless, who is well fixed and immovable (in his intention to die). (14)

He should move to and fro (on his ground), contract and stretch (his limbs) for the benefit of the whole body; or (he should remain quiet as if he were) lifeless. (15)

He should walk about, when tired of (lying), or stand with passive limbs; when tired of standing, he should sit down. (16)

Intent on such an uncommon death, he should regulate the motions of his organs.

---

[1] Viz. the iṅgitamarana, which differs from the preceding one by the restriction of the motions of the candidate for suicide to a limited space.

[2] I. e. of body, speech, and mind; doing, or causing, or allowing to be done.

[3] He should not give way to melancholy thoughts.

Having attained a place swarming with insects, he should search for a clean spot. (17)

He should not remain there whence sin would rise.

He should raise himself above (sinfulness), and bear all pains. (18)

And this is a still more difficult method [1], when one lives according to it: not to stir from one's place, while checking all motions of the body. (19)

This is the highest law, exalted above the preceding method:

Having examined a spot of bare ground he should remain there; stay O Brâhma*n*a! (20)

Having attained a place free from living beings, he should there fix himself.

He should thoroughly mortify his flesh, thinking: There are no obstacles in my body. (21)

Knowing as long as he lives the dangers and troubles, the wise and restrained (ascetic) should bear them as being instrumental to the dissolution of the body. (22)

He should not be attached to the transitory pleasures, nor to the greater ones; he should not nourish desire and greed, looking only for eternal praise. (23)

He should be enlightened with eternal objects [2], and not trust in the delusive power of the gods;

[1] It is called pâovagama*n*a, translated by the commentators pâdapopagamana, remaining motionless like a felled tree. This etymology, which is generally adopted by the *G*ainas, is evidently wrong; for the Sanskrit prototype is the Brahmanical prâyopagamana.

[2] This is the scholiast's interpretation of nima*m*te*gg*â nimantrayet.

a Brâhma*n*a should know of this and cast off all inferiority[1]. (24)

Not devoted to any of the external objects he reaches the end of his life; thinking that patience is the highest good, he (should choose) one of (the described three) good methods of entering Nirvâ*n*a. (25) Thus I say.

End of the Seventh Lecture, called Liberation.

---

[1] Nûmam karma mâyâ vâ.

EIGHTH LECTURE,

(CALLED)

THE PILLOW OF RIGHTEOUSNESS.

First Lesson.

As I have heard it, I shall tell how the Venerable Ascetic, exerting himself and meditating, after having entered the order in that winter, wandered about[1],

'I shall not cover myself with that robe[2],' only in that winter (he used it). He had crossed (the *sam*sâra) for the rest of his life. This (refusing of dress) is in accordance with his doctrine. (1)

More than four months many sorts of living beings gathered on his body, crawled about it, and caused pain there. (2)

For a year and a month he did not leave off his robe. Since that time the Venerable One, giving up his robe, was a naked, world-relinquishing, houseless (sage)[3]. (3)

Then he meditated (walking) with his eye fixed on a square space before him of the length of a

[1] The commentators call this passage a *s*loka, though only the beginning of it looks like a pâda, the rest showing no metrical law. The beginning of the last passage looks also like the first pâda of a *s*loka; but the rest requires some violent alterations to answer the metrical laws of a *s*loka.

[2] The divine robe given him by Indra.

[3] The commentator says that this happened at the Suvar*n*abâlukâ river.

man[1]. Many people assembled, shocked at the sight; they struck him and cried. (4)

Knowing (and renouncing) the female sex in mixed gathering places[2], he meditated, finding his way himself: I do not lead a worldly life. (5)

Giving up the company[3] of all householders whomsoever, he meditated. Asked, he gave no answer; he went, and did not transgress the right path. (6)

For some it is not easy (to do what he did), not to answer those who salute; he was beaten with sticks, and struck by sinful people. (7)

Disregarding slights difficult to bear, the Sage wandered about, (not attracted) by story-tellers, pantomimes, songs, fights at quarter-staff, and boxing-matches. (8)

At that time the son of *Gñâtri* saw without sorrow (or pleasure) people in mutual conversation. *Gñâtri*putra obtained oblivion of these exquisite sorrows. (9)

For more than a couple of years he led a religious life without using cold water; he realised singleness, guarded his body, had got intuition, and was calm. (10)

Thoroughly knowing the earth-bodies and water-bodies and fire-bodies and wind-bodies, the lichens, seeds, and sprouts, (11)

He comprehended that they are, if narrowly

---

[1] Tiriyabhittim is left out in the translation. I cannot make out the exact meaning of it, perhaps: 'so that he was a wall for the animals.'

[2] Sayanehim in the original.

[3] Literally, the mixed state.

inspected, imbued with life, and avoided to injure them; he, the great Hero. (12)

The immovable (beings) are changed to movable ones, and the movable beings to immovable ones; beings which are born in all states become individually sinners[1] by their actions. (13)

The Venerable One understands thus: he who is under the conditions (of existence)[2], that fool suffers pain. Thoroughly knowing (karman), the Venerable One avoids sin. (14)

The sage, perceiving the double (karman)[3], proclaims the incomparable activity[4], he, the knowing one; knowing the current of worldliness, the current of sinfulness, and the impulse, (15)

Practising the sinless abstinence from killing, he did no acts, neither himself nor with the assistance of others; he to whom women were known as the causes of all sinful acts, he saw (the true state of the world). (16)

He did not use what had expressly been prepared for him[5]; he well saw (that bondage comes) through action. Whatever is sinful, the Venerable One left that undone: he consumed clean food. (17)

He did not use another's robe, nor does he eat out of another's vessel. Disregarding contempt, he went with indifference to places where food was prepared. (18)

Knowing measure in eating and drinking, he was not desirous of delicious food, nor had he a longing for it. A sage should not rub his eyes nor scratch his body. (19)

[1] Or sinful? bâlâ.

[2] Upadhi.

[3] Present and future.

[4] I. e. religious life.

[5] Âhâka*d*am: yathâ yena prakâre*n*a p*r*ish*t*vâ ap*r*ish*t*vâ vâ k*r*ita*m* yathâk*r*itam âdhâkarmâdinâ.

Looking a little sideward, looking a little behind, answering little when spoken to, he should walk attentively looking on his path. (20)

When the cold season has half-way advanced, the houseless, leaving off his robe and stretching out his arms, should wander about, not leaning against a trunk. (21)

This is the rule which has often been followed by the wise Brâhma*n*a, the Venerable One, who is free from attachment: thus proceed (the monks).

Thus I say. (22)

SECOND LESSON.

Whatever different seats and couches have been told, whatever have been used by the great Hero, these resting-places are thus detailed[1]. (1)

He sometimes lodged in workshops, assembling-places, wells, or shops; sometimes in manufactories or under a shed of straw. (2)

He sometimes lodged in travellers' halls, garden-houses, or towns; sometimes on a burying-ground, in relinquished houses, or at the foot of a tree. (3)

In these places was the wise *S*rama*n*a for thirteen long years; he meditated day and night, exerting himself, undisturbed, strenuously. (4)

The Venerable One, exerting himself, did not seek

[1] *S*îlâṅka remarks: 'This verse has not been explained by the author of the old *T*îkâ. Why? Either because it offers no difficulty, or because it was wanting. Yet it is found in the MSS. of the text alone. We do not exactly know the reason.' Which old *T*îkâ is meant by *S*îlâṅka we cannot tell with certainty. It scarcely can be the *K*ûr*n*i, for in the Bombay MS. of it the text of the verse in question is given, but no explanation beyond the words: esâ pu*kkh*â, this is (given as an answer to) a question.

sleep for the sake of pleasure; he waked up himself, and slept only a little, free from desires. (5)

Waking up again, the Venerable One lay down, exerting himself; going outside for once in a night, he walked about for an hour. (6)

In his resting-places he sustained fearful and manifold calamities; crawling or flying animals attack him. (7)

Bad people, the guard of the village, or lance-bearers attack him; or there were domestic temptations, single women or men; (8)

Fearful and manifold (calamities) of this and the next world; pleasant and unpleasant smells, and manifold sounds: (9)

Always well controlled, he bore the different sorts of feelings; overcoming carelessness and pleasure, the Brâhma*n*a wandered about, speaking but little. (10)

In the resting-places there once, in a night, the single wanderers asked him (who he was, and why he was there); as he did not answer, they treated him badly; but he persevered in his meditations, free from resentment. (11)

(Sometimes to avoid greater troubles when asked), 'Who is there within?' he answered, 'It is I, a mendicant.' But this is the best law: silently to meditate, even if badly treated. (12)

When a cold wind blows, in which some feel pain, then some houseless monks in the cold rain seek a place sheltered from the wind. (13)

(Some heretical monks say), 'We shall put on more clothes; kindling wood or (well) covered, we shall be able (to bear) the very painful influence of the cold.' (14)

But the Venerable One desired nothing of the kind;

strong in control, he suffered, despising all shelter. Going outside once of a night, the Venerable One was able (to endure all hardships) in calmness. (15)

This is the rule which has often been followed by the wise Brâhma*n*a, the Venerable One, who is free from attachment: thus proceed (the monks).

Thus I say. (16)

Third Lesson.

Always well guarded, he bore the pains (caused by) grass, cold, fire, flies, and gnats; manifold pains. (1)

He travelled in the pathless country of the Lâ*dh*as, in Va*gg*abhûmi and Subbhabhûmi[1]; he used there miserable beds and miserable seats. (2)

In Lâ*dh*a (happened) to him many dangers. Many natives attacked him. Even in the faithful part of the rough country[2] the dogs bit him, ran at him. (3)

Few people kept off the attacking, biting dogs. Striking the monk, they cried '*Kh*u*kkh*û,' and made the dogs bite him. (4)

Such were the inhabitants. Many other mendicants, eating rough food in Va*gg*abhûmi, and carrying about a strong pole or a stalk (to keep off the dogs), lived there. (5)

Even thus armed they were bitten by the dogs, torn by the dogs. It is difficult to travel in Lâ*dh*a. (6)

---

[1] Va*g*rabhûmi and *S*ubhrabhûmi (or *S*vabhrabhûmi) are, according to the commentaries, the two divisions of Lâ*dh*a. I think that Lâ*dh*a may be identical with the classical Râ*dh*â or western Bengal and the Lâla of the Buddhists, the native country of Vi*g*aya, the legendary conqueror of Ceylon. Subbhabhûmi is probably the country of the Suhmas, who are also identified with the Râ*dh*as.

[2] The commentator seems to understand the words lukkhadesie bhatte in the sense: There the living also was rough; for they used clothes of grass instead of cotton.

Ceasing to use the stick (i. e. cruelty) against living beings, abandoning the care of the body, the houseless (Mahâvîra), the Venerable One, endures the thorns of the villages (i.e. the abusive language of the peasants), (being) perfectly enlightened. (7)

As an elephant at the head of the battle, so was Mahâvîra there victorious. Sometimes he did not reach a village there in Lâ*dh*a. (8)

When he who is free from desires approached the village, the inhabitants met him on the outside, and attacked him, saying, 'Get away from here.' (9)

He was struck with a stick, the fist, a lance, hit with a fruit, a clod, a potsherd. Beating him again and again, many cried. (10)

When he once (sat) without moving his body, they cut his flesh[1], tore his hair under pains, or covered him with dust. (11)

Throwing him up, they let him fall, or disturbed him in his religious postures; abandoning the care of his body, the Venerable One humbled himself and bore pain, free from desire. (12)

As a hero at the head of the battle is surrounded on all sides[2], so was there Mahâvîra. Bearing all hardships, the Venerable One, undisturbed, proceeded (on the road to Nirvâ*n*a). (13)

This is the rule which has often been followed, &c.

FOURTH LESSON.

The Venerable One was able to abstain from indulgence of the flesh[3], though never attacked by

---

[1] Or his mustaches.
[2] Or is on his guard.
[3] Omodariya.

diseases. Whether wounded or not wounded, he desired not medical treatment. (1)

Purgatives and emetics, anointing of the body and bathing, shampooing and cleansing of the teeth do not behove him, after he learned (that the body is something unclean). (2)

Being averse from the impressions of the senses[1], the Brâhma*n*a wandered about, speaking but little. Sometimes in the cold season the Venerable One was meditating in the shade. (3)

In summer he exposes himself to the heat, he sits squatting in the sun; he lives on rough (food): rice, pounded jujube, and beans. (4)

Using these three, the Venerable One sustained himself eight months. Sometimes the Venerable One did not drink for half a month or even for a month. (5)

Or he did not drink for more than two months, or even six months, day and night, without desire (for drink). Sometimes he ate stale food. (6)

Sometimes he ate only the sixth meal, or the eighth, the tenth, the twelfth; without desires, persevering in meditation. (7)

Having wisdom, Mahâvîra committed no sin himself, nor did he induce others to do so, nor did he consent to the sins of others. (8)

Having entered a village or a town, he begged for food which had been prepared for somebody else. Having got clean[2] food, he used it, restraining the impulses. (9)

When there were hungry crows, or thirsty beings stood in his way, where he begged, or when he saw them flying repeatedly down, (10)

[1] Gâmadhamma.

[2] I. e. free from faults.

When a Brâhma*n*a or *S*rama*n*a, a beggar or guest, a *K*â*nd*âla[1], a cat, or a dog stood in his way, (11)

Without ceasing in his reflections, and avoiding to overlook them[2], the Venerable One slowly wandered about, and, killing no creatures, he begged for his food. (12)

Moist or dry or cold food, old beans, old pap, or bad grain, whether he did or did not get such food, he was rich (in control). (13)

And Mahâvîra meditated (persevering) in some posture, without the smallest motion; he meditated in mental concentration on (the things) above, below, beside, free from desires. (14)

He meditated free from sin and desire, not attached to sounds or colours; though still an erring mortal (*kh*admastha), he wandered about, and never acted carelessly. (15)

Himself understanding the truth and restraining the impulses for the purification of the soul, finally liberated, and free from delusion, the Venerable One was well guarded during his whole life. (16)

This is the rule which has been followed, &c.

End of the Ninth Lecture, called the Pillow of Righteousness.

End of the First Book.

---

[1] *S*vapâka.

[2] Tassa appattiya*m* parihara*m*to, avoiding the non-perception of it, i. e. the interruption of his reflections.

SECOND BOOK

FIRST PART[1].

FIRST LECTURE,

CALLED

BEGGING OF FOOD[2].

FIRST LESSON.

WHEN a male or a female mendicant, having entered the abode of a householder with the intention of collecting alms, recognises[3] food, drink, dainties, and spices as affected by, or mixed up with, living beings, mildew, seeds or sprouts, or wet with water, or covered with dust—either in the hand or the pot of another[4]—they should not, even if they can get it, accept of such food, thinking that it is impure and unacceptable[5]. (1)

But if perchance they accept of such food, under pressing circumstances[6], they should go to a secluded spot, a garden, or a monk's hall—where there are no

---

[1] *K*û*d*â. [2] Pi*nd*aisha*n*â.

[3] This is the typical beginning of most precepts or sûtras in this *k*û*d*â: se bhikkhû vâ bhikkhu*n*î vâ gâhâvaikula*m* pi*m*davâyapa*d*iyâe a*n*upavi*tth*e samâ*n*e se *ggam* pu*n*a *g*â*n*e*gg*â. In the sequel I have shortened this rather lengthy preamble.

[4] By the other is meant the householder or the giver (dâ*tri*).

[5] This is the typical conclusion of all prohibitions: aphâsuya*m* a*n*esa*n*i*gg*a*m* ti mannamâ*n*e lâbhe sa*m*te no pa*d*iggâhe*gg*â. In the translation the plural is used throughout, in order to avoid the necessity of always repeating 'he or she.'

[6] As e. g. total want of another opportunity to get suitable food during famine and sickness.

eggs, nor living beings, nor sprouts, nor dew, nor water, nor ants, nor mildew, nor drops (of water), nor mud, nor cobwebs---and rejecting (that which is affected by), and cleaning that which is mixed up (with living beings, &c.), they should circumspectly eat or drink it. But with what they cannot eat or drink, they should resort to a secluded spot, and leave it there on a heap of ashes or bones, or rusty things, or chaff, or cowdung, or on any such-like place which they have repeatedly examined and cleaned. (2)

A monk or a nun on a begging-tour should not accept as alms whatever herbs they recognise, on examining them, as still whole, containing their source of life, not split longwise or broadwise, and still alive, fresh beans, living and not broken; for such food is impure and unacceptable. (3)

But when they recognise after examination that those herbs are no more whole, do not contain their source of life, are split longwise or broadwise, and no more alive, fresh beans, lifeless and broken, then they may accept them, if they get them; for they are pure and acceptable. (4)

A monk or nun on a begging-tour should not accept as alms whatever flattened grains, grains containing much chaff, or half-roasted spikes of wheat, &c., or flour of wheat, &c., or rice or flour of rice, they recognise as only once worked[1]; for such food is impure and unacceptable. (5)

But when they recognise these things as more than once worked, as twice, thrice worked, then they may accept them, if they get them; for they are pure and acceptable. (6)

---

[1] Pounded or cooked or roasted, &c., because after only one operation sperms of life might still be left.

A monk or a nun desiring to enter the abode of a householder for collecting alms, should not enter or leave it together with a heretic or a householder; or a monk who avoids all forbidden food, &c., together with one who does not. (7)

A monk or a nun entering or leaving the out-of-door places for religious practices or for study[1] should not do so together with a heretic or a householder; or a monk who avoids all forbidden food, together with one who does not. (8)

A monk or a nun wandering from village to village should not do so together with a heretic or a householder; or a monk who avoids all forbidden food, together with one who does not. (9)

A monk or a nun on a begging-tour should not give, immediately or mediately, food, &c., to a heretic or a householder; or a monk who avoids all forbidden food, to one who does not. (10)

A monk or a nun on a begging-tour should not accept food, &c., from a householder whom they know to give out of respect for a Nirgrantha, in behalf of a fellow-ascetic, food, &c., which he has bought or stolen or taken, though it was not to be taken nor given, but was taken by force, by acting sinfully towards all sorts of living beings; for such-like food, &c., prepared by another man[2] or by the giver himself, brought out of the house or not brought out of the house, belonging to the giver or not belonging to him, partaken or tasted of, or not partaken or tasted of, is impure and unacceptable.

---

[1] These are the vi*k*ârabhûmi and vihârabhûmi.

[2] Purisa*m*taraka*d*a. I have rendered this word according to the interpretation of the commentators; but in a similar passage, 8, 3, §§ 2 and 3, they understand the word to mean appropriated by another person.

In this precept substitute for 'on behalf of one fellow-ascetic,' (2) on behalf of many fellow-ascetics, (3) on behalf of one female fellow-ascetic, (4) on behalf of many female fellow-ascetics; so that there will be four analogous precepts. (11)

A monk or a nun should not accept of food, &c., which they know has been prepared by the householder for the sake of many *S*rama*n*as and Brâhma*n*as, guests, paupers, and beggars, after he has counted them, acting sinfully towards all sorts of living beings; for such food, whether it be tasted of or not, is impure and unacceptable. (12)

A monk or a nun should not accept of food, &c., procured in the way described in § 11 for the sake of the persons mentioned in § 12, if the said food, &c., has been prepared by the giver himself, has been brought out of the house, does not belong to the giver, has not been partaken or tasted of; for such food, &c., is impure and unacceptable; but if the food, &c., has been prepared by another person, has been brought out of the house, belongs to the giver, has been partaken or tasted of, one may accept it; for it is pure and acceptable. (13)

A monk or a nun wishing to enter the abode of a householder with the intention of collecting alms, should not, for the sake of food or drink, enter or leave such always liberal, always open houses, where they always give a morsel, always the best morsel, always a part of the meal, always nearly the half of it.

This certainly is the whole duty of a monk or a nun in which one should, instructed in all its meanings and endowed with bliss, always exert oneself.

Thus I say. (14)

SECOND LESSON.

A monk or a nun on a begging-tour should not accept food, &c., in the following case: when, on the eighth or paushadha day, on the beginning of a fortnight, of a month, of two, three, four, five, or six months, or on the days of the seasons, of the junction of the seasons, of the intervals of the seasons, many *S*ramaṇas and Brâhmaṇas, guests, paupers, and beggars are entertained with food, &c., out of one or two or three or four vessels, pots, baskets, or heaps of food; such-like food which has been prepared by the giver, &c., (all down to) not tasted of, is impure and unacceptable. But if it is prepared by another person, &c. (see first lesson, § 13), one may accept it; for it is pure and acceptable. (1)

A monk or a nun on a begging-tour may accept food, &c., from unblamed, uncensured families, to wit, noble families, distinguished families, royal families, families belonging to the line of Ikshvâku, of Hari, cowherds' families, Vai*s*ya families, barbers' families, carpenters' families, *t*akurs' families, weavers' families; for such food, &c., is pure and acceptable. (2)

A monk or a nun on a begging-tour should not accept food, &c., in the following case: when in assemblies, or during offerings to the manes, or on a festival of Indra or Skanda or Rudra or Mukunda or demons or Yakshas or the snakes, or on a festival in honour of a tomb, or a shrine, or a tree, or a hill, or a cave, or a well, or a tank, or a pond, or a river, or a lake, or the sea, or a mine—when on such-like various festivals many *S*ramaṇas and Brâhmaṇas, guests, paupers, and beggars are entertained with food, &c. (all as in § 1, down to) acceptable. (3)

But when he perceives that all have received their due share, and are enjoying their meal, he should address[1] the householder's wife or sister or daughter-in-law or nurse or male or female servant or slave and say: 'O long-lived one! (or, O sister!) will you give me something to eat?' After these words of the mendicant, the other may bring forth food, &c., and give it him. Such food, &c., whether he beg for it or the other give it, he may accept; for it is pure and acceptable. (4)

When a monk or a nun knows that at a distance of more than half a yo*g*ana a festive entertainment[2] is going on, they should not resolve to go there for the sake of the festive entertainment. (5)

When a monk hears that the entertainment is given in an eastern or western or southern or northern place, he should go respectively to the west or east or north or south, being quite indifferent (about the feast); wherever there is a festive entertainment, in a village or scot-free town, &c. (see I, 7, 6, § 4), he should not go there for the sake of the festive entertainment.

The Kevalin assigns as the reason for this precept, that if the monk eats food, &c., which has been given him on such an occasion, he will incur the sin of one

---

[1] Puvvâm eva âloe*gg*â, he should first look at him or her (and then say).

[2] Sa*m*kha*d*i, somewhere explained odanapâka, cooking of rice; in the commentary the following etymology is given: sa*m*-kha*nd*yante virâdhyante prâ*n*ino yatra sâ sa*m*kha*d*i. But the Guzerati commentator explains it: *g*ihâ*m* gha*n*â *g*a*n* nimitti âhâra kelvivâ bha*n*â.

who uses what[1] has been prepared for him, or is mixed up with living beings, or has been bought or stolen or taken, though it was not to be taken, nor was it given, but taken by force. (6)

A layman[2] might, for the sake of a mendicant, make small doors large, or large ones small; put beds[3] from a level position into a sloping one, or from a sloping position into a level one; place the beds[3] out of the draught or in the draught; cutting and clipping the grass outside or within the upâsraya, spread a couch for him, (thinking that) this mendicant is without means for a bed[3]. Therefore should a well-controlled Nirgrantha not resolve to go to any festival which is preceded or followed by a feast.

This certainly is the whole duty, &c. (see end of lesson 1).

Thus I say. (7)

Third Lesson.

When he has eaten or drunk at a festive entertainment, he might vomit (what he has eaten), or not well digest it; or some other bad disease or sickness might befall him. (1)

The Kevalin says this is the reason:

A mendicant, having drunk various liquors, together with the householder or his wife, monks or nuns, might not find the (promised) resting-place on leaving the scene of entertainment and looking

[1] This stands for âhâkammiya and uddesiya, pure and impure food prepared for a mendicant.

[2] Asa*mg*ae, the uncontrolled one; it denotes a layman or a householder.

[3] Se*gg*â=*s*ayyâ, bed; but the scholiast explains it by vasati, dwelling, lodging.

out for it; or in the resting-place he may get into mixed company; in the absence of his mind or in his drunkenness he may lust after a woman or a eunuch; approaching the mendicant (they will say): 'O long-lived *S*rama*n*a! (let us meet) in the garden, or in the sleeping-place, in the night or in the twilight.' Luring him thus by his sensuality (she says): 'Let us proceed to enjoy the pleasures of love.' He might go to her, though he knows that it should not be done.

These are the causes to sin, they multiply continuously. Therefore should a well-controlled Nirgrantha not resolve to go to any festival which is preceded or followed by a feast. (2)

A monk or a nun, hearing or being told of some festivity, might hasten there, rejoicing inwardly: 'There will be an entertainment, sure enough!' It is impossible to get there from other families alms which are acceptable and given out of respect for the cloth[1], and to eat the meal. As this would lead to sin, they should not do it[2]. But they should enter there, and getting from other families their alms, should eat their meal. (3)

A monk or a nun, knowing that in a village or a scot-free town, &c. (see I, 7, 6, § 4), an entertainment will be given, should not resolve to go to that village, &c., for the sake of the entertainment. The Kevalin assigns as the reason herefore: When a man goes to

[1] Esiya*m* vesiya*m*. The latter word is explained by ragohara*n*âdiveshâl labdham, what one gets for the sake of one's apparel, the broom, &c.

[2] Mâi*tth*â*n*am sa*m*phâse, no eva*m* kare*gg*â, i. e. mât*ri*sthâna*m* samsp*ri*set, na eva*m* kuryât: mât*ri*sthâna is somewhere explained karmopadânasthâna.

a much-frequented and vulgar entertainment somebody's foot treads on his foot, somebody's hand moves his hand, somebody's bowl clashes against his bowl, somebody's head comes in collision with his head, somebody's body pushes his body, or somebody beats him with a stick or a bone or a fist or a clod, or sprinkles him with cold water, or covers him with dust; or he eats unacceptable food, or he receives what should be given to others. Therefore should a well-controlled Nirgrantha not resolve to go to a much-frequented and vulgar entertainment to partake of it. (4)

A monk or a nun on a begging-tour should not accept such food, &c., about the acceptability or unacceptability of which his (or her) mind has some doubts or misgivings; for such food, &c. (5)

When a monk or a nun wishes to enter the abode of a householder, they should do so with the complete outfit[1]. (6)

A monk or a nun entering or leaving the out-of-door places for religious practices or study, should do so with the complete outfit. (7)

A monk or a nun wandering from village to village should do so with the complete outfit[2]. (8)

A monk or a nun should not, with the complete outfit, enter or leave the abode of a householder to collect alms, or the out-of-door places for religious practices and study, or wander from village to village on perceiving that a strong and widely-spread rain pours down, or a strong and widely-spread mist is

[1] See I, 7, 4, note 1.

[2] These Sûtras are perfectly analogous with §§ 7, 8 of the first lesson.

coming on, or a high wind raises much dust, or many flying insects are scattered about and fall down. (9)

A monk or a nun on a begging-tour should not accept food, &c., in the houses of Kshatriyas, kings, messengers, and relations of kings, whether they are inside or outside, or invite them; for such food, &c., is impure and unacceptable. Thus I say. (10)

Fourth Lesson.

A monk or a nun on a begging-tour should not resolve to go to a festival, preceded or followed by an entertainment, to partake of it, when they know that there will be served up chiefly meat or fish or roasted slices of meat or fish; nor to a wedding breakfast in the husband's house or in that of the bride's father; nor to a funeral dinner or to a family dinner where something is served up,—if on their way there, there are many living beings, many seeds, many sprouts, much dew, much water, much mildew, many drops (of water), much dust, and many cobwebs; or if there have arrived or will arrive many *S*rama*n*as and Brâhma*n*as, guests, paupers, and beggars, and if it will be a crowded assembly, so that a wise man may not enter or leave it, or learn there the sacred texts, to question about them, to repeat them, to consider them, to think about the substance of the law. (1)

A monk or a nun may go to such an entertainment (as described in the preceding Sûtra), provided that on their way there, there are few living beings, few seeds, &c.; that no *S*rama*n*as and Brâhma*n*as, &c., have arrived or will arrive; that it is not a crowded assembly, so that a wise man may enter or leave, &c.[1] (2)

A monk or a nun desirous to enter the abode of a householder, should not do so, when they see that the milch cows are being milked, or the food, &c., is being cooked, and that it is not yet distributed. Perceiving this, they should step apart and stay where no people pass or see them. But when they conceive that the milch cows are milked, the dinner prepared and distributed, then they may circumspectly enter or leave the householder's abode for the sake of alms. (3)

Some of the mendicants say to those who follow the same rules of conduct, live (in the same place), or wander from village to village: 'This is indeed a small village, it is too populous, nor is it large; reverend gentlemen, go to the outlying villages to beg alms[2].'

Some mendicant may have there kinsmen or relations, e.g. a householder or his wife, or daughters, or daughters-in-law, or nurses, or male and female slaves or servants. Such families with which he is connected by kindred or through marriage, he intends to visit before (the time of begging): 'I shall get there (he thinks) food or dainties or milk or thick sour milk or fresh butter or ghee or sugar or oil or honey or meat or liquor, a sesamum dish[3], or raw sugar, or a meal of parched wheat[4], or a meal of curds and sugar with spices[5]; after having eaten and drunk, and having cleaned and rubbed the alms-bowl, I shall,

[1] This precept applies, according to the commentator, only to sick monks, or such as can get nothing elsewhere.

[2] The just arrived monks should do as they are bidden.

[3] Sa*m*kuli. [4] Pûya. [5] *S*ikhari*n*î.

together with other mendicants, enter or leave the abode of a householder to collect alms.' As this would be sinful, he should not do so. (4)

But, at the proper time, entering there with the other mendicants, he may there in these or other families accept alms which are acceptable and given out of respect for his cloth, and eat his meal.

This certainly is the whole duty, &c. (see end of lesson 1).

Thus I say. (5)

FIFTH LESSON.

When a monk or a nun on entering the abode of a householder sees that the first portion of the meal is being thrown away[1] or thrown down, or taken away, or distributed, or eaten, or put off, or has already been eaten or removed; that already other *S*rama*n*as and Brâhma*n*as, guests, paupers, and beggars go there in great haste; (they might think), 'Hallo! I too shall go there in haste.' As this would be sinful, they should not do so. (1)

When a monk or a nun on a begging-tour comes upon walls or gates, or bolts or holes to fit them, they should, in case there be a byway, avoid those (obstacles), and not go on straight.

The Kevalin says: This is the reason: Walking there, he might stumble or fall down; when he stumbles or falls down, his body might become contaminated with fæces, urine, phlegmatic humour, mucus, saliva, bile, matter, semen, or blood. And if his body has become soiled, he should not wipe or

[1] In honour of the gods.

rub or scratch or clean[1] or warm or dry it on the bare ground or wet earth [or dusty earth[2]] on a rock or a piece of clay containing life, or timber inhabited by worms, or anything containing eggs, living beings, &c. (down to) cobwebs; but he should first beg for some straw or leaves, wood or a potsherd, which must be free from dust, resort with it to a secluded spot, and on a heap of ashes or bones, &c. (see II, 1, 1, § 2), which he has repeatedly examined and cleaned, he should circumspectly wipe or rub, warm or dry (his body). (2)

When a monk or a nun on a begging-tour perceives a vicious cow coming towards them, or a vicious buffalo coming towards them, or a vicious man, horse, elephant, lion, tiger, wolf, panther, bear, hyena, *s*arabha, shakal, cat, dog, boar, fox, leopard coming towards them, they should, in case there be a byway, circumspectly avoid them, and not walk on straight. (3)

When a monk or a nun on a begging-tour comes on their way upon a pit, pillar, thorns, or unsafe, marshy or uneven ground, or mud, they should, in case there be a byway, avoid these (obstacles), and not walk on straight.

When a monk or a nun on a begging-tour perceives that the entrance of a householder's abode is secured by a branch of a thorn bush, they should not, without having previously got the (owner's) permission, and having examined and swept (the entrance), make it passable or enter and leave (the

[1] This stands for uvvale*gg*a vâ uvva*ll*e*gg*â vâ (udvaled vâ udvarted vâ), for which words, denoting some rather indistinct varieties of rubbing, I know no adequate English words.

[2] The words in brackets are the translation of varia lectio.

house). But they may circumspectly do so, after having got the (owner's) permission, and having examined and swept it. (4)

When a monk or a nun on a begging-tour knows that a *S*rama*n*a or a Brâhma*n*a, a guest, pauper or beggar has already entered (the house), they should not stand in their sight or opposite the door[1].

The Kevalin[2] says: This is the reason: Another, on seeing him, might procure and give him food, &c. Therefore it has been declared to the mendicants: This is the statement, this is the reason, this is the order, that he should not stand in the other mendicants' sight or opposite the door.

Knowing this, he should go apart and stay where no people pass or see him. Another man may bring and give him food, &c., while he stays where no people pass or see him, and say unto him: 'O long-lived *S*rama*n*a! this food, &c., has been given for the sake of all of you; eat it or divide it among you.' Having silently accepted the gift, he might think: 'Well, this is just (enough) for me!' As this would be sinful, he should not do so.

Knowing this, he should join the other beggars, and after consideration say unto them[3]: 'O long-lived *S*rama*n*as! this food, &c., is given for the sake of all of you; eat it or divide it among you.' After these words another might answer him: 'O long-lived

[1] This might also be translated: at an opposite door.

[2] The following passage is not explained in the commentaries, and is wanting in the oldest MS., though supplied on the margin. It may therefore be concluded that the whole passage, the greater part of which is typical, is a later addition.

[3] Âloe*gg*â. The scholiast explains it here by dar*s*ayet, he should show the food, &c. Professor Oldenberg has identified this word with the Pâli âro*k*eti.

*S*rama*n*a! distribute it yourself.' Dividing the food, &c., he should not (select) for himself too great a portion, or the vegetables, or the conspicuous things, or the savoury things, or the delicious things, or the nice things, or the big things; but he should impartially divide it, not being eager or desirous or greedy or covetous (of anything). When he thus makes the division, another might say: 'O long-lived *S*rama*n*a! do not divide (the food); but let us, all together, eat and drink.' When he thus eats, he should not select for himself too great a portion, &c.; but should eat and drink alike with all, not being desirous, &c.[1] (5)

When a monk or a nun on a begging-tour perceives that a *S*rama*n*a or Brâhma*n*a, a beggar or guest has already entered the house, they should not overtake them and address (the householder) first. Knowing this, they should go apart and stay where no people pass or see them. But when they perceive that the other has been sent away or received alms, and has returned, they may circumspectly enter the house and address the householder.

This certainly is the whole duty, &c.

Thus I say. (6)

SIXTH LESSON.

When a monk or a nun on a begging-tour perceives that many hungry animals have met and come together in search of food, e.g. those of the chicken-kind or those of the pig-kind, or that crows

[1] The scholiast says that the way to procure food, &c., as described in this paragraph, should only be resorted to under pressing circumstances.

have met and come together, where an offering is thrown on the ground, they should, in case there be a byway, avoid them and not go on straight. (1)

A monk or a nun on a begging-tour should not stand leaning against the door-post of the householder's abode, or his sink or spitting-pot, nor in sight of, or opposite to his bathroom or privy; nor should they contemplate a loophole or a mended spot or a fissure (of the house) or the bathing-house, showing in that direction with an arm or pointing with a finger, bowing up and down. (2)

Nor should they beg, pointing with a finger at the householder, or moving him with a finger, or threatening him with a finger, or scratching him with a finger, or praising him, or using coarse language. (3)

If he sees somebody eating, e.g. the householder or his wife, &c., he should after consideration say: 'O long-lived one! (or, O sister!) will you give me some of that food?' After these words the other might wash or wipe his hand or pot or spoon or plate with cold or hot water[1]. He should after consideration say: 'O long-lived one! (or, O sister!) do not wash or wipe your hand or pot or spoon or plate! If you want to give me something, give it as it is!' After these words the other might give him a share, having washed or wiped his hand, &c., with cold or hot water. But he should not accept anything out of such a hand, &c., which has been before treated thus; for it is impure and unacceptable. (4)

It is also to be known that food, &c., is impure

[1] Sîodagavigada, usinodagavigada. Vigada, Sanskrit vikata, is explained apkâya. It is therefore cold or hot water which is to be considered as containing life.

and unacceptable, which is given with a wet hand, though the hand be not purposely wetted. (5)

The same rule holds good with regard to a moistened hand, &c., and a dusty hand, &c., and a hand which is soiled with clay, dew, orpiment, vermilion, realgar, collyrium, white chalk, alum, rice-flour, kukkusa, ground drugs. (6)

It is also to be known that he may accept such food, &c., which is given with a soiled hand, &c., to one similarly soiled (i. e. with what one is to receive), or to one unsoiled, with hand similarly soiled; for such food, &c., is pure and acceptable. (7)

A monk or a nun on a begging-tour should not accept flattened grains, grains containing much chaff, &c. (see II, 1, 1, § 5), which a layman, for the sake of the mendicant, has ground[1], grinds, or will grind, has winnowed, winnows, or will winnow on a rock or a piece of clay containing life, &c. (see II, 1, 5, § 2, all down to) cobwebs; for such large, parched grains, &c., are impure and unacceptable. (8)

A monk or a nun on a begging-tour should not accept fossil salt or sea salt which a householder, for the sake of the mendicant, has ground or pounded, grinds or pounds, will grind or pound on a rock or a piece of clay containing life, &c.; for such-like fossil salt or sea salt is impure and unacceptable. (9)

A monk or a nun on a begging-tour should not

[1] The subject asamgae, the uncontrolled one, i. e. layman, stands in the singular, but the verb in the plural. The same irregularity occurs in the next paragraph. The commentator accounts for it simply by saying: ekavakanâdhikâre pi khândasatvât tadvyatyayena bahuvakanam drashtavyam, pûrvatra vâ gâtâv ekavakanam.

accept food, &c., which is prepared over the fire; for such food is impure and unacceptable. The Kevalin says: This is the reason: A layman will kill the fire-bodies, by wetting or moistening, wiping or rubbing, throwing up or turning down the food, &c., for the sake of the mendicant. Hence it has been declared to the mendicants: This is the statement, this is the reason, this is the order, that they should not accept food, &c., which has been prepared over the fire, &c.

This certainly is the whole duty, &c.

Thus I say. (10)

Seventh Lesson.

A monk or a nun on a begging-tour should not accept food, &c., which has been placed on a post or pillar or beam or scaffold or loft[1] or platform or roof or some such-like elevated place; for such food fetched from above is impure and unacceptable. The Kevalin says: This is the reason: The layman might fetch and erect a stool or a bench or a ladder or a handmill, get upon it, and getting upon it fall or tumble down. Thus he might hurt his foot or arm or breast or belly or head or some other part of his body; or he might kill or frighten or bruise or smash or crush or afflict or pain or dislocate all sorts

[1] Mâla. The word is not explained in the *T*îkâ and Dîpikâ; the Guzerati translation says that the word is lokapratîta, commonly understood. It is probably the Marâthî mâ*l* or mâ*l*â; the former word denotes a loft, floored with bamboos; the second, the room formed by overlaying with slight sticks the cross-beams of a house, a loft, an erection or stand in a cornfield, scaffolding (of a building). Molesworth, Marâthî and English Dictionary, s. v.

of living beings. Therefore he should not accept such-like food, &c., fetched from above. (1)

A monk or a nun on a begging-tour should not accept food, &c., which a layman, for the sake of the mendicant, has taken from a granary or vault by contorting himself up and down and horizontally; thinking that such-like food is brought from underground[1]. (2)

A monk or a nun on a begging-tour should not accept food, &c., which is kept in earthenware. The Kevalin says: This is the reason: The layman might, for the sake of the mendicant, break the earthen vessel containing the food, &c., and thereby injure the earth-body; in the same way he might injure the fire-body, the wind-body, plants and animals; by putting it again (in earthenware), he commits the pa*kkh*âkamma sin. Hence it has been said to the mendicant, &c., that he should not accept food, &c., which is put in earthenware. (3)

A monk or a nun on a begging-tour should not accept food, &c., placed on the earth-body, the wind-body, the fire-body, for such food is impure and unacceptable. The Kevalin says: This is the reason: A layman might, for the sake of the mendicant, stir or brighten the fire, and taking the food, &c., down from it, might give it to the mendicant. Hence it has been said, &c., that he should accept no such food. (4)

When a monk or a nun on a begging-tour sees that a layman might, for the sake of the mendicant,

[1] The original has bho mâloha*dam* ti na*kk*â. Bho mâloha*d*a is explained adhomâlâh*ri*tam. Mâloha*d*a, which I translate 'fetched from above,' is the technical term for things affected by the dosha under question.

cool too hot food, &c., by blowing or fanning with a winnowing basket or fan or a palm leaf or a branch or a part of a branch or a bird's tail or a peacock's tail or a cloth or a corner of a cloth or the hand or the mouth, they should, after consideration, say (to the householder or his wife): 'O long-lived one! (or, O sister!) do not blow or fan the hot food, &c., with a winnowing basket, &c.; but if you want to give it me, give it as it is.' After these words the other might give it after having blown or fanned it with a winnowing basket, &c.; such-like food they should not accept, because it is impure and unacceptable. (5)

A monk or a nun on a begging-tour should not accept food, &c., which is placed on vegetable or animal matter[1]; for such food is impure and unacceptable. (6)

A monk or a nun on a begging-tour should not accept water which has been used for watering flour or sesamum or rice, or any other such-like water which has been recently used for washing, which has not acquired a new taste, nor altered its taste or nature, nor has been strained; for such-like water is impure and unacceptable. But if it has long ago been used for washing, has acquired a new taste, has altered its taste or nature, and has been strained, it may be accepted, for it is pure and acceptable. (7)

When a monk or a nun on a begging-tour finds water used for washing sesamum, chaff or barley, or rainwater[2] or sour gruel or pure water, they should, after consideration, say (to the householder or his wife): 'O long-lived one! (or, O sister!) will you give

[1] Va*n*assaikâyapati*tth*iya and tasakâyapati*tth*iya.
[2] Âyâma, â*k*âmlam ava*s*yânam.

me some of this water?' Then the other may answer him: 'O long-lived *S*rama*n*a! take it yourself by drawing it with, or pouring it in, your bowl!' Such-like water, whether taken by himself or given by the other, he may accept. (8)

A monk or a nun on a begging-tour should not accept such water as has been taken from the bare ground, &c. (see II, 1, 5, § 2, all down to) cobwebs, or water which the layman fetches in a wet or moist or dirty vessel, mixing it with cold water.

This certainly is the whole duty, &c.

Thus I say. (9)

Eighth Lesson.

A monk or a nun on a begging-tour should not accept juice of mangos, inspissated juice of mangos, juice of wood-apples, citrons, grapes, wild dates, pomegranates, cocoa-nuts, bamboos, jujubes, myrobalans, tamarinds, or any such-like liquor containing particles of the shell or skin or seeds, which liquor the layman, for the sake of the mendicant, pressed, strained, or filtered through a basket[1], cloth, or a cow's tail; for such liquor is impure and unacceptable. (1)

When a monk or a nun on a begging-tour smells, in travellers' houses or garden houses or householders' houses or ma*th*s, the scent of food or drink or sweet scents, they should not smell them, being indifferent against smell, and not eager or desirous or greedy or covetous of the pleasant smell. (2)

---

[1] *Kh*avva, Sanskrit *kh*abdaka (sic). The Hindî has *kh*avdâ, basket.

A monk or a nun on a begging-tour should not accept raw things which are not yet modified by instruments [1], as bulbous roots, growing in water or dry ground, mustard stalks; for they are impure and unacceptable. The same holds good with regard to long pepper, ground long pepper, common pepper, ground common pepper, ginger or ground ginger. (3)

A monk or a nun on a begging-tour should not accept such raw fruits which are not yet modified by instruments, as those of Mango, Amrâtaka, *Ghigghîrâ* [2], Surabhi [3], Sallakî [4]; for they, &c. (4)

The same holds good with regard to raw shoots which, &c., as those of Asvattha, Nyagrodha, Pilamkhu [5], Nîyûra [6], Sallakî. (5)

The same holds good with regard to raw berries which, &c., as those of Kapittha [7], pomegranate, or Pippala. (6)

A monk or a nun on a begging-tour should not accept raw, powdered fruits which are not well ground and still contain small seeds, as those of Umbara, Pilamkhu, Nyagrodha, and Asvattha; for &c. (7)

A monk or a nun on a begging-tour should not accept unripe wild rice [8], dregs, honey, liquor, ghee, or sediments of liquor, if these things be old or if living beings are engendered or grow or thrive in

---

[1] I. e. when they have undergone no operation which takes the life out of them.

[2] Name of a shrub.

[3] Explained by satagru.

[4] Boswellia Thurifera.

[5] Explained by pipparî.

[6] Cedrela Toona.

[7] The wood-apple tree, Feronia Elephantum.

[8] Âmadâga, explained in the commentary âmapannam, unripe or half ripe, aranikatandulîyakâdi.

them, or are not taken out, or killed or destroyed in them. (8)

A monk or a nun on a begging-tour should not accept any such-like raw plants[1] as Ikshumeru, Aṅkakarelu, Kaseru, Samghâtika, Pûtiâlu. (9)

A monk or a nun on a begging-tour should not accept any such-like (vegetables) as Nymphaea or stalk of Nymphaea or the bulb of Nelumbium or the upper part or the filament of Lotus or any part of the plant. (10)

A monk or a nun on a begging-tour should not accept such-like raw substances as seeds or sprouts, growing on the top or the root or the stem or the knots (of a plant), likewise the pulp or blossoms of the plantain, cocoa-nut, wild date, and palmyra trees. (11)

A monk or a nun on a begging-tour should not accept any such-like raw unmodified substances as sugar-cane, which is full of holes, or withering or peeling off or corroded by wolves; or the points of reeds or the pulp of plantains. (12)

The same holds good with regard to garlic or its leaves or stalk or bulb or integument. (13) Likewise with regard to cooked fruits of Atthiya[2], Tinduka[3], Vilva[4], Srîparnî[5]. (14)

A monk or a nun on a begging-tour should not accept such raw, unmodified substances as corn, clumps of corn, cakes of corn, sesamum, ground sesamum, or cakes of sesamum.

This is the whole duty, &c.

Thus I say. (15)

---

[1] Of these plants only Kaseru, a kind of grass, and Samghâtika Trapa Bispinosa are specialised in our dictionaries.

[2] A certain tree.

[3] Diospyros Glutinosa.

[4] Aegle Marmelos.

[5] Pistia Stratiotes.

Ninth Lesson.

In the east or west or south or north, there are some faithful householders, &c., (all down to) servants who will speak thus: 'It is not meet that these illustrious, pious, virtuous, eloquent, restrained, controlled, chaste ascetics, who have ceased from sensual intercourse, should eat or drink food, &c., which is âdhâkarmika[1]; let us give to the ascetics all food, &c., that is ready for our use, and let us, afterwards, prepare food for our own use.' Having heard such talk, the mendicant should not accept such-like food, &c., for it is impure and unacceptable. (1)

A monk or a nun on a begging-tour or in their residence or on a pilgrimage from village to village, who know that in a village or scot-free town, &c., dwell a mendicant's nearer or remoter relations—viz. a householder or his wife, &c.—should not enter or leave such houses for the sake of food or drink. The Kevalin says: This is the reason: Seeing him, the other might, for his sake, procure or prepare food, &c. Hence it has been said to the mendicant, &c., that he should not enter or leave such houses for the sake of food or drink.

Knowing this, he should go apart and stay where no people pass or see him. In due time he may enter other houses, and having begged for alms which are acceptable and given out of respect for

[1] For the meaning of this frequently used term, see note 5 on p. 81, and note 1 on p. 94.

his cloth, he may eat his dinner. If the other has, on the mendicant's timely entrance, procured or prepared food, &c., which is âdhâkarmika, he might silently examine it, and think: 'Why should I abstain from what has been brought.' As this would be sinful, he should not do so. But after consideration he should say: 'O long-lived one! (or, O sister!) as it is not meet that I should eat or drink food, &c., which is âdhâkarmika, do not procure or prepare it.' If after these words the other brings and gives him âdhâkarmika food which he has prepared, he should not accept such-like food, &c., for it is impure and unacceptable. (2)

When a monk or a nun on a begging-tour sees that meat or fish is being roasted, or oil cakes, for the sake of a guest, are being prepared, they should not, quickly approaching, address the householder; likewise if the food is prepared for the sake of a sick person. (3)

A monk or a nun on a begging-tour might, of the received quantity of food, eat only the sweet-smelling parts and reject the bad-smelling ones. As this would be sinful, they should not do so; but they should consume everything, whether it be sweet smelling or bad smelling, and reject nothing. (4)

A monk or a nun on a begging-tour might, of the received quantity of drink, imbibe only the well-flavoured part, and reject the astringent part. As this would be sinful, they should not do so; but they should consume everything, whether it be well flavoured or astringent, and reject nothing. (5)

A monk or a nun, having received a more than sufficient quantity of food, might reject (the superfluous part) without having considered or consulted fellow-ascetics living in the neighbourhood, who follow the same rules of conduct, are agreeable and not to be shunned; as this would be sinful, they should not do so. Knowing this, they should go there and after consideration say: 'O long-lived *S*rama*n*as! this food, &c., is too much for me, eat it or drink it!' After these words the other might say: 'O long-lived *S*rama*n*a! we shall eat or drink as much of this food or drink as we require; or, we require the whole, we shall eat or drink the whole.' (6)

A monk or a nun on a begging-tour should not accept food, &c., which for the sake of another has been put before the door, if the householder has not permitted him to do so, or he gives it him; for such food, &c. But on the contrary he may accept it.

This is the whole duty, &c.

Thus I say. (7)

TENTH LESSON.

A single mendicant, having collected alms for many, might, without consulting his fellow-ascetics, give them to those whom he list; as this would be sinful, he should not do so. Taking the food, he should go there (where his teacher &c. is) and speak thus: 'O long-lived *S*rama*n*a! there are near or remote (spiritual) relations of mine: a teacher, a sub-teacher, a religious guide, a Sthavira, a head of a Ga*n*a, a Ga*n*adhara, a founder of a Ga*n*a; forsooth, I shall give it them.' The other may answer him: 'Well now, indeed, O long-lived one! give such a portion!' As much as the other commands, thus much he should give; if the other commands the whole, he should give the whole. (1)

A single mendicant, having collected agreeable food, might cover it with distasteful food, thinking: 'The teacher or sub-teacher, &c., seeing what I have received, might take it himself; indeed, I shall not give anything to anybody!' As this would be sinful, he should not do so.

Knowing this, he should go there (where the other mendicants are), should put the vessel in his out-stretched hand, show it (with the words): 'Ah, this! ah, this!' and hide nothing. (2)

A single mendicant, having received some food, might eat what is good, and bring what is discoloured and tasteless; as this would be sinful, he should not do so. (3)

A monk or a nun on a begging-tour should not accept any part of the sugar-cane[1], whether small or large, pea-pods, seed-pods, of which articles a small part only can be eaten, and the greater part must be rejected; for such things are impure and unacceptable. (4)

A monk or a nun on a begging-tour should not accept meat or fish containing many bones, so that only a part of it can be eaten and the greater part must be rejected; for such meat or fish, &c., is impure and unacceptable. (5)

A monk or a nun on a begging-tour may be invited to meat or fish containing many bones, (by the householder who addresses him thus): 'O long-lived *S*rama*n*a! will you accept meat with many bones?' Hearing such a communication, he should

[1] They are detailed in the original: a*m*taru*kkh*uya*m*, a piece between two knots; u*kkh*uga*md*iya*m*, a piece containing a knot; u*kkh*u*k*oyagam (?), u*kkh*umeraga*m*, top of a stalk; u*kkh*usâlaga*m*, long leaf; u*kkh*u*d*âlaga*m*, fragment of a leaf.

say, after consideration: 'O long-lived one! (or, O sister!) it is not meet for me to accept meat with many bones; if you want to give me a portion of whatever size, give it me; but not the bones!' If after these words the other (i.e. the householder) should fetch meat containing many bones, put it in a bowl and return with it, (the mendicant) should not accept such a bowl, whether out of the other's hand or a vessel[1]; for it is impure and unacceptable. But if he has inadvertently accepted it, he should not say: 'No, away, take it!' Knowing this, he should go apart, and in a garden or an upâsraya, where there are few eggs, &c., (all down to) cobwebs, eat the meat or fish, and taking the bones, he should resort to a secluded spot and leave them on a heap of ashes, &c. (see II, 1, 1, § 2). (6)

If a householder should fetch fossil salt or sea salt, put it in a bowl and return with it, a monk or a nun on a begging-tour should not accept it out of the other's hand or vessel; for, &c.

But if he has inadvertently accepted it, he should return with it to the householder, if he is not yet too far away, and say, after consideration[2]: 'Did you give me this with your full knowledge or without it?' He might answer: 'I did give it without my full knowledge; but indeed, O long-lived one! I now give it you; consume it or divide it (with others)!'

Then being permitted by, and having received it from, the householder, he should circumspectly eat it or drink it, and what he cannot eat or drink he

[1] Parahatthamsi vâ parapâyamsi vâ. This is a typical phrase, and seems rather out of place here.

[2] Âloeggâ, he should show, would perhaps be better.

should share with his fellow-ascetics in the neighbourhood, who follow the same rules of conduct, are agreeable, and not to be shunned; but if there are no fellow-ascetics, the same should be done as in case one has received too much food.

This is the whole duty, &c.

Thus I say. (7)

Eleventh Lesson.

Some mendicants say unto (others) who follow the same rules of conduct, or live in the same place, or wander from village to village, if they have received agreeable food and another mendicant falls sick[1]: 'Take it! give it him! if the sick mendicant will not eat it, thou mayst eat it.' But he (who is ordered to bring the food) thinking, 'I shall eat it myself,' covers it and shows it (saying): 'This is the lump of food, it is rough to the taste[2], it is pungent, it is bitter, it is astringent, it is sour, it is sweet; there is certainly nothing in it fit for a sick person.' As this would be sinful, he should not do so. But he should show him which parts are not fit for a sick person (saying): 'This particle is pungent, this one bitter, this one astringent, this one sour, this one sweet.' (1)

Some mendicants say unto (others) who follow the same rules of conduct, or live in the same place, or wander from village to village, if they have received agreeable food and another mendicant falls sick: 'Take it! give it him! if the mendicant will not eat it, bring it to us!' 'If nothing prevents me, I shall

[1] This is the way in which the commentator construes the sentence. There is some confusion in the text, which cannot easily be removed.

[2] Loe, Sanskrit rûksha?

bring it.' (Then he might act as stated in § 1, which would be sinful.) (2)

For the avoidance of these occasions to sin there are seven rules for begging food and as many for begging drink, to be known by the mendicants.

Now, this is the first rule for begging food. Neither hand nor vessel are wet[1]: with such a hand or vessel he may accept as pure, food, &c., for which he himself begs or which the other gives him. That is the first rule for begging food. (3)

Now follows the second rule for begging food. The hand and the vessel are wet. The rest as in the preceding rule. That is the second rule for begging food. (4)

Now follows the third rule for begging food. In the east, &c., there are several faithful householders, &c., (all down to) servants: they have put (food) in some of their various vessels, as a pan, a pot, a winnowing basket, a basket, a precious vessel. Now (the mendicant) should again know: is the hand not wet and the vessel wet; or the hand wet and the vessel not wet? If he collect alms with an alms-bowl or with his hand[2], he should say, after consideration: 'O long-lived one! (or, O sister!) with your not-wet hand, or with your wet vessel, put (alms) in this my bowl, or hand, and give it me!' Such-like food, for which he himself begs or which the other gives him, he may accept; for it is pure and acceptable. That is the third rule for begging food. (5)

Now follows the fourth rule for begging food. A

[1] Sa*m*sa*tth*a; it would perhaps be more correct to translate this word, soiled with the food in question.

[2] These are the pa*d*iggahadhârî and the pâ*n*ipa*d*iggahiya, lit. one who uses his hand instead of an alms-bowl.

monk or a nun may accept flattened grains, &c. (cf. II, 1, 1, § 5), for which they beg themselves or which the other gives them, if it be such as to require little cleaning or taking out (of chaff); for it is pure, &c. That is the fourth rule for begging food. (6)

Now follows the fifth rule for begging food. A monk or a nun may accept food which is offered on a plate or a copper cup or any vessel, if the moisture on the hands of the giver is almost dried up; for, &c. That is the fifth rule for begging food. (7)

Now follows the sixth rule for begging food. A monk or a nun may accept food which had been taken up from the ground, either taken up for one's own sake or accepted for the sake of somebody else, whether it be placed in a vessel or in the hand; for, &c. That is the sixth rule for begging food. (8)

Now follows the seventh rule for begging food. A monk or a nun may accept food of which only a part may be used, and which is not wanted by bipeds, quadrupeds, *S*rama*n*as, Brâhma*n*as, guests, paupers, and beggars, whether they beg for it themselves, or the householder gives it them. That is the seventh rule for begging food. (9)

These are the seven rules for begging food; now follow the seven rules for begging drink. They are, however, the same as those about food, only the fourth gives this precept: A monk or a nun may accept as drink water which has been used for watering flour or sesamum, &c. (II, 1, 7, § 7), if it be such as to require little cleaning and taking out (of impure) articles; for, &c. (10)

One who has adopted one of these seven rules for begging food or drink should not say: 'These reverend persons have chosen a wrong rule, I alone have rightly chosen.' (But he should say): 'These reverend persons, who follow these rules, and I who follow that rule, we all exert ourselves according to the commandment of the *G*ina, and we respect each other accordingly.'

This certainly is the whole duty, &c.

Thus I say. (11)

End of the First Lecture, called Begging of Food.

SECOND LECTURE,

CALLED

BEGGING FOR A COUCH[1].

FIRST LESSON.

If a monk or a nun want to ask for a lodging, and having entered a village or scot-free town, &c., conceive that lodging to contain eggs, living beings, &c., they should not use it for religious postures, night's-rest, or study[2]. (1)

But if the lodging contains only few eggs or few living beings, &c., they may, after having inspected and cleaned it, circumspectly use it for religious postures, &c. Now, if they conceive that the householder, for the sake of a Nirgrantha and on behalf of a fellow-ascetic (male or female, one or many), gives a lodging which he has bought or stolen or taken, though it was not to be taken nor given, but was taken by force, by acting sinfully towards all sorts of living beings, they should not use for religious postures, &c., such a lodging which has been appropriated by the giver himself, &c. (see II, 1, 1, § 11).

The same holds good if there be instead of a fellow-ascetic many *S*rama*n*as and Brâhma*n*as, guests, paupers, and beggars. But if the lodging has been

[1] Seggâ.

[2] Tahappagâre uvassae no *th*â*n*a*m* vâ segga*m* vâ nisîhiya*m* vâ *k*eteggâ. *Th*â*n*a = sthâna is explained kâyotsarga; seggâ = *s*ayyâ, sa*m*stâraka; nisîhiyâ = ni*s*ithikâ, svâdhyâya; *k*eteggâ = *k*intayet. The last word is elsewhere translated dadyât.

appropriated by another man than the giver, &c., they may, after having inspected and cleaned it, circumspectly use it for religious postures, &c. (2)

A monk or a nun, knowing that the layman has, for the sake of the mendicant, matted the lodging, whitewashed it, strewn it (with grass, &c.), smeared it (with cowdung), levelled, smoothed, or perfumed it (or the floor of it), should not use that lodging, which has been prepared by the giver himself, &c., for religious postures. But if it has been prepared by another person, &c., they may circumspectly use it for religious postures. (3)

A monk or a nun, knowing that a layman will, for the sake of a mendicant, make small doors large, &c. (all as in II, 1, 2, § 7, down to) spread his couch or place it outside, should not use such a lodging which has been appropriated by the giver himself, &c., for religious postures, &c. But if it has been appropriated by another person, &c., they may circumspectly use it for religious postures, &c. (4)

Again, a monk or a nun, knowing that the layman, for the sake of the mendicant, removes from one place to another, or places outside, bulbs or roots or leaves or flowers or fruits or seeds or grass-blades of water plants, should not use such a lodging, which is appropriated by the giver himself, for religious postures, &c. But if it has been prepared by another person, &c., they may circumspectly use it for religious postures, &c. (5)

A monk or a nun, knowing that the layman, for the sake of the mendicant, removes from one place to another, or places outside, a chair or a board or a ladder or a mortar, should not use such a lodging-place, &c. (all as at the end of the last paragraph). (6)

A monk or a nun should not use for religious postures, &c., a lodging-place above ground, as a pillar or a raised platform or a scaffold or a second story or a flat roof, likewise no underground place (except under urgent circumstances). If by chance they are thus lodged, they should there not wash or clean their hands or feet or eyes or teeth or mouth with hot or cold water; nor should they put forth there any other secretion, as excrements, urine, saliva, mucus, bilious humour, ichor, blood, or any other part of the bodily humours.

The Kevalin says: This is the reason: Making secretions he might stumble or fall; stumbling or falling he might hurt his hand, &c. (II, 1, 7, § 1), or any other limb of his body, or kill, &c., all sorts of living beings. Hence it has been said to the mendicant, &c., that he should use no above-ground lodging-place for religious postures, &c. (7)

A monk or a nun on a begging-tour should not use, for religious postures, a lodging-place used by the householder, in which there are women, children, cattle, food, and drink. This is the reason: A mendicant living together with a householder's family may have an attack of gout, dysentery, or vomiting; or some other pain, illness, or disease may befall him; the layman might, out of compassion, smear or anoint the mendicant's body with oil or ghee or butter or grease, rub or shampoo it with perfumes, drugs, lodhra, dye, powder, padmaka, then brush or rub it clean; clean, wash, or sprinkle it with hot or cold water, kindle or light a fire by rubbing wood on wood; and having done so, he might dry or warm (the mendicant's body).

Hence it has been said to the mendicant, &c.,

that he should not use for religious postures, &c., a lodging-place which is used by the householder. (8)

This is (another) reason: While a mendicant lives in a lodging used by the householder, the householder or his wife, &c., might bully, scold[1], attack or beat each other. Then the mendicant might direct his mind to approval or dislike: 'Let them bully each other!' or, 'Let them not bully each other!' &c. &c.

Hence it has been said to the mendicant, &c., that he should not use, for religious postures, &c., a lodging-place used by the householder. (9)

This is (another) reason: While the mendicant lives together with householders, the householder might, for his own sake, kindle or light or extinguish a fire-body. Then the mendicant might direct his mind to approval or dislike: 'Let them kindle or light or extinguish a fire-body;' or, 'Let them not do so.'

Hence it has been said to the mendicant, &c. (see above). (10)

This is (another) reason: While the mendicant lives together with householders, he might see the householder's earrings or girdle or jewels or pearls or gold and silver[2] or bracelets (those round the wrist and those round the upper arm) or necklaces (those consisting of three strings, or those reaching halfway down the body, or those consisting of eighty

---

[1] Vaha*m*ti. The Guzerati translation renders it nirbha*mkh*e, which is derived from Sanskrit nirbharts.

[2] Hira*nn*e suva*nn*e. The commentators explain these two words, which are synonyms in the later language, as 'raw and wrought gold, or coined gold.' I translate 'gold and silver,' because the distinction of the commentators seems rather farfetched, and because silver would be missed in enumerations like the present one.

strings or forty strings or one string or strings of pearls, golden beads or jewels) or a decked or ornamented girl or maiden. Thus the mendicant might direct his mind to approval or dislike: 'Let her be thus;' or, 'Let her not be thus.' So he might say, so he might think. Hence it has been said to the mendicant, &c. (see above). (11)

This is (another) reason: While a mendicant lives together with householders, the householder's wives, daughters, daughters-in-law, nurses, slave-girls or servant-girls might say: 'These reverend *S*rama*n*as, &c., have ceased from sexual intercourse; it behoves them not to indulge in sexual intercourse: whatever woman indulges with them in sexual intercourse, will have a strong, powerful, illustrious, glorious, victorious son of heavenly beauty.' Hearing and perceiving such talk, one of them might induce the mendicant ascetic to indulge in sexual intercourse.

Hence it has been said to the mendicant, &c., that he should not use for religious postures, &c., a lodging used by the householder.

This is the whole duty, &c.

Thus I say. (12)

Second Lesson.

Some householders are of clean habits and the mendicants, because they never bathe, are covered with uncleanliness; they smell after it, they smell badly, they are disagreeable, they are loathsome. Hence the householders, with regard to the mendicant, put off some work which otherwise they would have done before, and do some work which otherwise they would have put off.

Hence it has been said to the mendicant, &c.,

that he should not use, for religious postures, &c., a lodging used by the householder. (1)

This is the reason: While a mendicant lives together with householders, the householder might, for his own sake, have prepared something to eat. Then, afterwards, he might, for the sake of the mendicant, prepare or dress food, &c., and the mendicant might desire to eat or drink or swallow it.

Hence it has been said to the mendicant, &c. (see above). (2)

This is the reason: While the mendicant lives together with a householder, there may be ready wood cleft for the use of the householder. Then, afterwards, (the householder) might, for the sake of the mendicant, cleave or buy or steal wood, kindle or light, by rubbing wood on wood, the fire-body, and the mendicant might desire to dry or warm himself at, or enjoy, the fire.

Hence it has been said to the mendicant, &c. (see above). (3)

When in the night or twilight a mendicant, to ease nature, leaves the door open, a thief, watching for an occasion, might enter. It is not meet for the mendicant to say: This thief enters or does not enter, he hides himself or does not hide himself, he creeps in or does not creep in, he speaks or does not speak; he has taken it, another has taken it, it is taken from that man; this is the thief, this is the accomplice, this is the murderer, he has done so[1]. The householder will suspect the ascetic, the men-

[1] For if he gives warning of the thief, the warner or the thief might be slain; but if he gives no warning, no life will be lost, though the mendicant's integrity may be doubted.

dicant, who is not a thief, to be the thief. Hence it has been said to the mendicant, &c. (4)

A monk or a nun should not use, for religious postures, &c., sheds of grass or straw which contain eggs, living beings, &c. But they may do so if they contain few eggs, few living beings, &c. (5)

A mendicant should not stay in halting-places, garden houses, family houses, monasteries, where many fellow-ascetics are frequently arriving.

1. If the reverend persons continue to live in those places after staying there for a month[1] in the hot or cold seasons or for the rainy season (he should say): 'O long-lived one! you sin by overstaying the fixed time.' (6)

2. If the reverend persons repeatedly live in halting-places, &c., after staying there for the proper time, without passing two or three intermediate months somewhere else, (he should say): 'O long-lived one! you sin by repeating your retreat in the same place.' (7)

3. Here, in the east, west, north, or south, there are, forsooth, some faithful householders, householders' wives, &c., who are not well acquainted with the rules of monastic life (with regard to the fitness of lodging-places); nevertheless they believe in, perceive, are convinced of, (the merit of) giving lodging to mendicants. They (accordingly) give lodging-places for the sake of many *S*rama*n*as and Brâhma*n*as, guests, paupers, and beggars, in workshops, chapels, temples, assembly halls, wells, houses or halls for shopkeeping or for keeping or building carriages, distilleries, houses where Darbha-grass,

[1] Or any fixed period, which the mendicant has vowed not to exceed staying in one place.

bark, trees, wood or charcoal are being worked, houses on burial-places, rooms for retirement near the place of sacrifice[1], empty houses, hill-houses, caves, stone-houses, or palaces. He should say to those reverend persons who live in such-like places as workshops, &c., together with other guests: 'O long-lived one! you sin by living in a place frequented by other sectarians.' (8)

4. Here, in the east, &c. They accordingly give, &c. (all as in § 8 down to) palaces. If the mendicants come there while the other religious men do not come there, they sin by living in a place not frequented by other mendicants. (9)

5. In the east, west, north, or south there are faithful householders, viz. a householder or his wife, &c., who will speak thus: 'It is not meet that these illustrious, pious, virtuous, eloquent, controlled, chaste ascetics, who have ceased from sexual intercourse, should dwell in a lodging which is âdhâkarmika[2]: let us give to the mendicants the lodgings which are ready for our use, viz. workshops, &c., and let us, afterwards, prepare lodgings for our own use, viz. workshops, &c.' Hearing and perceiving such talk, if the reverend persons frequent such-like lodgings, viz. workshops, &c., and live in them which are ceded by other people (they should be warned): 'O long-lived one! that (lodging is infected by the sin called) varg*a*kriyâ.' (10)

6. Here, in the east, &c. (see § 8 all down to) they give lodging-places for the sake of many *S*ramanas and Brâhma*n*as, guests, paupers, and beggars, after having well counted them, in workshops, &c.

[1] *S*ântig*ri*ha.

[2] See note 5 on p. 81.

If the reverend persons frequent such-like lodgings, viz. workshops, &c., and live in them which are ceded by other people (they should be warned): 'O long-lived one! that (lodging is infected by the sin called) mahâvar*g*akriyâ.' (11)

7. Here, in the east, &c. They accordingly give, for the sake of many sorts of *S*rama*n*as[1], after having well counted them, lodging-places, viz. workshops, &c. If the reverend persons frequent such-like lodgings, viz. workshops, &c., and live in them which are ceded by other people (they should be warned): 'O long-lived one! that (lodging is infected by the sin called) sâvadyakriyâ.' (12)

8. Here, in the east, &c. They accordingly prepare, for the sake of one sort of *S*rama*n*as, lodgings, viz. workshops, &c., for which purpose great injury is done to the earth, water, fire, wind-bodies, plants, and animals, great injury, great cruelty, great and manifold sinful acts; by wasting cold water or strewing (the ground), smearing it with cowdung, shutting the doors and securing the bed, lighting a fire. If the reverend persons frequent such-like lodgings, viz. workshops, &c., and lead in such ceded lodgings an ambiguous[2] life (they should be warned): 'O long-lived one! that (lodging is infected by the sin called) mahâsâvadyakriyâ.' (13)

9. But if the lodgings, viz. workshops, &c., are

[1] There are five sorts of *S*rama*n*as enumerated in the following hemistich, which occurs not only in *S*îlâṅka's commentary, but also in that of the Sthânâṅga Sûtra, as Dr. Leumann informs me: Nigga*m*tha, Sakka, Tâvasa, Gerua, Â*g*îva pa*mk*ahâ sama*n*â. Nirgranthas, *S*âkyas, Tâpasas, Gairikas, Â*g*îvakas.

[2] Dupakkha*m* te kamma seva*m*ti, lit. use twofold work; the meaning is, according to the commentary, that they act like householders, though they make a show of monastic life.

prepared by the householders for their own sake under the same circumstances as detailed in the preceding paragraph, and the reverend persons frequent such-like lodgings, they lead, in those lodgings, an unambiguous life. 'O long-lived one! that (lodging is infected by the very small sin called) alpasâvadyakriyâ.'

This is the whole duty, &c.

Thus I say. (14)

THIRD LESSON.

'It[1] is difficult to obtain pure, acceptable alms; it is indeed not free from such preparations as strewing the ground (with Darbha-grass), smearing it (with cowdung), shutting the doors and securing the beds. And he (the mendicant) delights in pilgrimage, religious exercises, study, begging for a bed, a couch, or other alms.'

Some mendicants explain thus (the requisites of a lodging); they are called upright, searching after liberation, practising no deceit.

Some householders (who, having learned the requisites of a lodging-place, fit one out accordingly, try to deceive the mendicants, saying): 'This lodging, which we offer you, has been assigned to you, it has been originally prepared for our sake, or for the sake of some relations, it has been used, it has been relinquished.'

Explaining[2] thus, he truly explains. (The teacher says): Well, he is (an explainer of the truth). (1)

[1] The commentators say that this passage contains the mendicant's answer to an invitation to live in this or that village. By the second it is meant the lodging.

[2] The commentator supposes here the householder to further

If a mendicant, at night or at the twilight, leaves or enters a small lodging, one with a small door, a low or crammed lodging, (he should put forward) first his hand, then his foot, and thus circumspectly leave or enter it.

The Kevalin says: This is the reason: There might be a badly bound, badly placed, badly fastened, loose umbrella, pot, stick, staff, robe, hide, leather boots or piece of leather belonging to *S*rama*n*as or Brâhma*n*as; and the mendicant, when leaving or entering (the lodging) at night or twilight, might stumble or fall; stumbling or falling he might hurt his hand or foot, &c. (see IV, 1, 7, § 1), kill, &c., all sorts of living beings.

Hence it has been said to the mendicant, &c., that one (should put forward) first the hand, then the foot, and thus circumspectly leave or enter such a lodging. (2)

He (the mendicant) should, at halting-places, &c., ask for a lodging-place, after having inquired who is the landlord or who is the tenant. He should ask permission to use the lodging-place in this way: 'By your favour, O long-lived one! we shall dwell here for a while (for the time and in the place) which you will concede.' (If the landlord should object and say that he owns the lodging for a limited time only, or if he asks for the number of monks for which the lodging is required, he should answer)[1]: 'As long as this lodging belongs to you, (or) for the sake of as

inquire after the requisites of, and the objections to, the lodging-place. The mendicant should explain them.

[1] The passage in parentheses contains what the commentator supplies.

many fellow-ascetics (as shall stand in need of it), we shall occupy the lodging; afterwards we shall take to wandering.' (3)

A monk or a nun may know the name and gotra of him in whose lodging he lives; in that case they should not accept food, &c., in that house whether invited or not invited; for it is impure and unacceptable. (4)

A monk or a nun should not use for religious postures, &c., a lodging-place which is used by the householder, which contains fire or water; for it is not fit for a wise man to enter or leave it, &c. (cf. II, 1, 4, § 1). (5)

A monk or a nun should not use for religious postures, &c., a lodging for which they have to pass through the householder's abode, or to which there is no road; for it is not fit, &c. (see last paragraph). (6)

A monk or a nun should not use for religious postures, &c., a lodging where the householder or his wife, &c., might bully or scold, &c., each other (see II, 2, 1, § 9); for it is not fit, &c. (7)

A monk or a nun should not use for religious postures, &c., a lodging where the householder or his wife, &c., rub or anoint each other's body with oil or ghee or butter or grease; for it is not fit, &c. (8)

A monk or a nun should not use for religious postures, &c., a lodging where the householder or his wife, &c., rub or shampoo each other's body with perfumes, ground drugs, powder, lodhra, &c. (see II, 2, 1, § 8); for it is not fit, &c. (9)

A monk or a nun should not use for religious postures, &c., a lodging where the householder or his wife, &c., clean, wash, or sprinkle each other's body with cold or hot water; for it is not fit, &c. (10)

A monk or a nun should not use for religious postures, &c., a lodging where the householder or his wife, &c., go about naked or hide themselves, or talk about sexual pleasures, or discuss a secret plan; for it is not fit, &c. (11)

A monk or a nun should not use for religious postures, &c., a lodging which is a much-frequented playground[1]; for it is not fit, &c. (12)

1. If a monk or a nun wish to beg for a couch, they should not accept one which they recognise full of eggs, living beings, &c. (13)

2. If the couch is free from eggs, living beings, but is heavy, they should not accept such a couch. (14)

3. If the couch is free from eggs, living beings, light, but not movable, they should not accept such a couch. (15)

4. If the couch is free from eggs, living beings, &c., light, movable, but not well tied, they should not accept such a couch[2]. (16)

5. If the couch is free from eggs, living beings, light, movable, and well tied, they may accept such a couch. (17)

For the avoidance of these occasions to sin there are four rules, according to which the mendicant should beg for a couch.

---

[1] Âi*nn*asa*m*lekkha*m*. I am not certain whether I have found the correct meaning.

[2] In the first case, there would be sa*m*yamavirâdhanâ, or obstruction to control; in the second, âtmavirâdhanâ, injury to him who lifts the couch; in the third, tatparityâga; in the fourth, bandhanâdipalimantha, friction of the ropes. The word which I have translated movable is pa*d*ihâriya pratihâruka. The translation is conjectural.

Now this is the first rule for begging for a couch.

If a monk or a nun beg for a couch, specifying (its quality), viz. one of Ikka*t*a-reed, a hard one, one of *G*antuka-grass, of Para-grass[1], of peacock feathers, of hay, of Ku*s*a-grass, of brush-hair, of Pa*kk*aka, of Pippala, of straw, they should, after consideration, say: 'O long-lived one! (or, O sister!) please give me this here!' If the householder prepares one of the above-specified couches, or if the mendicant asks himself, and the householder gives it, then he may accept it as pure and acceptable.

This is the first rule. (18)

Now follows the second rule.

If a monk or a nun beg for a couch (of the above-detailed description) after having well inspected it, they should, after consideration, say: 'O long-lived one! &c.' (all as in the first rule).

This is the second rule[2]. (19)

If a monk or a nun beg for a couch of the above-detailed description, viz. one of Ikka*t*a-grass, &c., from him in whose house he lives, they may use it if they get it; if not, they should remain in a squatting or sitting posture (for the whole night).

This is the third rule. (20)

Now follows the fourth rule.

If a monk or a nun beg for a couch such as it is spread, either on the ground or on a wooden plank, they may use it if they get it; if not, they

---

[1] The commentator says that from this grass artificial flowers are produced.

[2] According to the commentary the first and second rules may not be adopted by a ga*kkh*a-nirgata, or a monk who is attached to no order of monks.

should remain in a squatting or sitting posture (for the whole night).

This is the fourth rule. (21)

A monk who has adopted one of these four rules, should not say, &c. (all as in II, 1, 11, § 12, down to) we respect each other accordingly. (22)

If a monk or a nun wish to give back a couch, they should not do so, if the couch contains eggs, living beings, &c. But if it contains few living beings, &c., they may restrainedly do so, after having well inspected, swept, and dried it[1]. (23)

A monk or a nun on a begging-tour or in a residence or on a pilgrimage from village to village should first inspect the place for easing nature. The Kevalin says: This is the reason: If a monk or a nun, in the night or the twilight, ease nature in a place which they have not previously inspected, they might stumble or fall, stumbling or falling they might hurt the hand or foot, &c., kill, &c., all sorts of living beings. (24)

A monk or a nun might wish to inspect the ground for their couch away from[2] that occupied by a teacher or sub-teacher, &c. (see II, 1, 10, § 1), or by a young one or an old one or a novice or a sick man or a guest, either at the end or in the middle, either on even or uneven ground, or at a place where there is a draught or where there is no draught. They should then well inspect and sweep

[1] One past preterite participle vi*n*i*th*u*n*iya is left out in the translation, as I do not know its meaning.

[2] Nannattha with instr., here explained muktvâ. Though I suspect the correctness of this translation, I have nothing better to offer.

(the floor), and circumspectly spread a perfectly pure bed or couch. (25)

Having spread a perfectly pure bed or couch, a monk or a nun might wish to ascend it. When doing so, they should first wipe their body from head to heels; then they may circumspectly ascend the perfectly pure bed or couch, and circumspectly sleep in it. (26)

A monk or a nun sleeping in a perfectly pure bed or couch (should have placed it at such a distance from the next one's) that they do not touch their neighbour's hand, foot, or body with their own hand, foot, or body; and not touching it, should circumspectly sleep in their perfectly pure bed or couch. (27)

Before inhaling or breathing forth, or coughing or sneezing or yawning or vomiting or eructating, a monk or a nun should cover their face or the place where it lies; then they may circumspectly inhale or breathe forth, &c. (28)

Whether his lodging[1] be even or uneven; full of, or free from, draughts; full of, or free from, dust; full of, or free from, flies and gnats; full of, or free from, dangers and troubles—in any such-like lodging one should contentedly stay, nor take offence at anything.

This is the whole duty, &c.

Thus I say. (29)

End of the Second Lecture, called Begging for a Couch.

---

[1] *Seggâ*, here explained by vasati.

THIRD LECTURE,

CALLED

WALKING[1].

FIRST LESSON.

When the rainy season has come and it is raining, many living beings are originated and many seeds just spring up, the roads between (different places) contain many living beings, seeds, &c. (see II, 1, 1, § 2), the footpaths are not used, the roads are not recognisable. Knowing this (state of things) one should not wander from village to village, but remain during the rainy season in one place[2]. (1)

When a monk or a nun knows that in a village or scot-free town, &c. (see I, 7, 6, § 3), there is no large place for religious practices nor for study; that there cannot easily be obtained a stool, bench, bed, or couch, nor pure, acceptable alms; that there have come or will come many *S*rama*n*as and Brâhma*n*as, guests, paupers, and beggars; that the means of existence are extremely small; that it is not fit for a wise man to enter or leave it, &c. (see II, 1, 4, § 1); in such a village, scot-free town, &c., they should not remain during the cold season. (2)

When a monk or a nun knows that in a village or scot-free town, &c., there is a large place for religious practices or for study; that there can easily

[1] Iriyâ.

[2] I. e. keep the pa*gg*usan.

be obtained a stool, bench, bed, or couch, or pure, acceptable alms; that there have not come nor will come *S*rama*n*as and Brâhma*n*as, guests, paupers, and beggars; that the means of existence are not small, &c., they may remain in such a village, &c., during the rainy season. (3)

Now they should know this: After the four months of the rainy season are over, and five or ten days of the winter have passed, they should not wander from village to village, if the road contains many living beings, &c., and if many *S*rama*n*as and Brâhma*n*as, &c., do not yet travel[1]. (4)

But if after the same time the road contains few living beings, and many *S*rama*n*as and Brâhma*n*as, &c., travel, they may circumspectly wander from village to village. (5)

A monk or a nun wandering from village to village should look forward for four cubits, and seeing animals they should move on by walking on his toes or heels or the sides of his feet. If there be some bypath, they should choose it, and not go straight on; then they may circumspectly wander from village to village. (6)

A monk or a nun wandering from village to village, on whose way there are living beings, seeds, grass, water, or mud, should not go straight if there be an unobstructed byway; then they may circumspectly wander from village to village. (7)

A monk or a nun on the pilgrimage, whose road (lies through) places belonging to borderers, robbers, Mle*kkh*as, non-Aryan people[2], half-civilised people,

[1] He should in that case stay in the same place for the whole month Mârga*s*îrsha, where he was during the rainy season.

[2] According to the commentary mle*kkh*a (milakkhu) means

unconverted people, people who rise or eat at an improper time, should, if there be some other place for walking about or friendly districts, not choose the former road for their voyage. (8)

The Kevalin says: This is the reason: The ignorant populace might bully, beat, &c., the mendicant, in the opinion that he is a thief or a spy, or that he comes from yonder (hostile village); or they might take away, cut off, steal or rob his robe, alms-bowl, mantle, or broom. Hence it has been said to the mendicant, &c., that one whose road (lies through) places belonging, &c. (all as in the last paragraph); then he may circumspectly wander from village to village. (9)

A monk or a nun on the pilgrimage, whose road (lies through) a country where there is no king or many kings or an unanointed king or two governments or no government or a weak government, should, if there be some other place for walking about or friendly districts, not choose the former road for their voyage. The Kevalin says: This is the reason: The ignorant populace might bully or beat, &c., the mendicant, &c. (all as in § 9). (10)

A monk or a nun on the pilgrimage, whose road lies through a forest[1] which they are not certain of crossing in one or two or three or four or five days, should, if there be some other place for walking about or friendly districts, not choose the former road for their voyage. (11)

The Kevalin says: This is the reason: During

---

the Varvara, *S*arvara, Pulindra, &c.; the non-Aryans are those who live not in the 36½ countries.

[1] Viha*m*, forest, as explained in the third lesson. But the commentator here explains it, a journey of some days.

the rain (he might injure) living beings, mildew, seeds, grass, water, mud. Hence it has been said to the mendicant that one whose road lies through such a forest, &c. (all as in the last paragraph); then he may circumspectly wander from village to village. (12)

A monk or a nun on the pilgrimage, on whose way there is some watercourse which must be crossed by a boat, should not ascend such a boat which plies up or down or across (the river), neither for one yogana's or half a yogana's distance, neither for a shorter nor a longer voyage, if they know that the householder[1] will buy or purloin the boat, or doing the work necessary to put the boat in order, pull it ashore out of the water, or push it from the shore into the water, or bale it, if it is filled (with water), or cause a sinking boat to float. (13)

A monk or a nun, knowing that a boat will cross the river, should, after having received the owner's permission, step apart, examine their outfit, put aside their provender, wipe their body from head to heels, reject the householder's food, and putting one foot in the water and the other in the air[2], they should circumspectly enter the boat. (14)

A monk or a nun in entering the boat should not choose for that purpose the stern or the prow or the middle of the boat; nor should they look at it holding up their arms, pointing at it with their finger, bowing up and down. (15)

If, on board, the boatman should say to the monk, 'O long-lived *S*rama*n*a! pull the boat forward or back-

[1] By householder is here intended the host of the mendicant.

[2] Thale=sthale. The commentator explains it by âkâ*s*e.

ward, or push it, or draw it with the rope towards you, or, let us do it together,' he should not comply with his request, but look on silently. (16)

If, on board, the other should say to him, 'O long-lived *S*rama*n*a! you cannot pull the boat forward or backward, or push it, or draw it with a rope towards you; give us the rope, we will ourselves pull the boat forward or backward, &c.,' he should not comply with his request, but look on silently. (17)

If, on board, the other should say to him, 'O long-lived *S*rama*n*a! if you can, pull the boat by the oar, the rudder, the pole, and other nautical instruments[1],' he should not comply with his request, but look on silently. (18)

If, on board, the other should say to him, 'O long-lived *S*rama*n*a! please, lade out the water with your hand, or pitcher[2], or vessel, or alms-bowl, or bucket,' he should not comply with his request, but look on silently. (19)

If, on board, the other should say to him, 'O long-lived *S*rama*n*a! please, stop the boat's leak with your hand, foot, arm, thigh, belly, head, body, the bucket, or a cloth, or with mud, Ku*s*a-grass, or lotus leaves,' he should not comply with his request, but look on silently. (20)

If a monk or a nun see that water enters through a leak in the boat, and the boat becomes dirty all over, they should not approach the boatman and say: 'O long-lived householder! water enters through a leak into the boat, and it becomes dirty all over.'

---

[1] Rudder is a guess for pî*dh*a, nautical instruments for valaya and avallaya.

[2] Pâe*n*a = pâtre*n*a. The Guzerati commentator takes it for pâdena, foot.

One should not think so or speak so; but undisturbed, the mind not directed outwardly, one should collect one's self for contemplation; then one may circumspectly complete one's journey by the boat on the water.

This is the whole duty, &c.

Thus I say. (21)

SECOND LESSON.

If, on board, the boatman should say to the mendicant, 'O long-lived *S*rama*n*a! please, take this umbrella, pot, &c. (see II, 2, 3, § 2), hold these various dangerous instruments[1], let this boy or girl drink,' he should not comply with his request, but look on silently. (1)

If, on board, the boatman should say to another of the crew, 'O long-lived one! this *S*rama*n*a is only a heavy load for the boat, take hold of him with your arms and throw him into the water!' hearing and perceiving such talk, he should, if he wears clothes, quickly take them off or fasten them or put them in a bundle on his head. (2)

Now he may think: These ruffians, accustomed to violent acts, might take hold of me and throw me from the boat into the water. He should first say to them: 'O long-lived householders! don't take hold of me with your arms and throw me into the water! I myself shall leap from the boat into the water!' If after these words the other, by force and violence, takes hold of him with his arms and throws him into the water, he should be neither glad nor sorry, neither in high nor low spirits, nor should he offer

[1] Satthag*â*ya = *s*astrag*â*ta. About *s*astra, see I, 1, 2.

violent resistance to those ruffians; but undisturbed, his mind not directed to outward things, &c. (see II, 3, 1, § 21), he may circumspectly swim in the water. (3)

A monk or a nun, swimming in the water, should not touch (another person's or their own?) hand, foot, or body with their own hand, foot, or body; but without touching it they should circumspectly swim in the water. (4)

A monk or a nun, swimming in the water, should not dive up or down, lest water should enter into their ears, eyes, nose, or mouth; but they should circumspectly swim in the water. (5)

If a monk or a nun, swimming in the water, should be overcome by weakness, they should throw off their implements (clothes, &c.), either all or a part of them, and not be attached to them. Now they should know this: If they are able to get out of the water and reach the bank, they should circumspectly remain on the bank with a wet or moist body. (6)

A monk or a nun should not wipe or rub or brush or stroke[1] or dry or warm or heat (in the sun) their body. But when they perceive that the water on their body has dried up, and the moisture is gone, they may wipe or rub, &c., their body in that state; then they may circumspectly wander from village to village. (7)

A monk or a nun on the pilgrimage should not wander from village to village, conversing with householders; they may circumspectly wander from village to village. (8)

If a monk or a nun on the pilgrimage come

---

[1] The original has six words for different kinds of rubbing, which it would be impossible to render adequately in any other language.

across a shallow water[1], they should first wipe their body from head to heels, then, putting one foot in the water and the other in the air, they should wade through the shallow water in a straight line[2]. (9)

If a monk or a nun on the pilgrimage come across a shallow water, they should wade through it in a straight line, without being touched by or touching (another person's or their own ?) hand, foot, or body with their own hand, foot, or body. (10)

A monk or a nun, wading through shallow water in a straight line, should not plunge in deeper water for the sake of pleasure or the heat; but they should circumspectly wade through the shallow water in a straight line. Now they should know this: If one is able to get out of the water and reach the bank, one should circumspectly remain on the bank with a wet or moist body. (11)

A monk or a nun should not wipe or rub, &c. (all as in § 7). (12)

A monk or a nun on the pilgrimage, with their feet soiled with mud, should not, in order that the grass might take off the mud from the feet, walk out of the way and destroy the grass by cutting, trampling, and tearing it. As this would be sinful, they should not do so. But they should first inspect a path containing little grass; then they may circumspectly wander from village to village. (13)

If a monk or a nun on the pilgrimage come upon walls or ditches or ramparts or gates or bolts

---

[1] *Gam*ghâsa*m*târime udae, literally, a water which is to be crossed by wading through it up to the knees; or perhaps water to be crossed on foot.

[2] Ahâriya*m*=yathâ *rig*u bhavati. It might also mean, in the right way. Another explanation is yathâtâryam.

or holes to fit them, or moats or caves, they should, in case there be a byway, choose it, and not go on straight. (14)

The Kevalin says: This is the reason: Walking there, the mendicant might stumble or fall down; when he stumbles or falls down, he might get hold of trees, shrubs, plants, creepers, grass, copsewood, or sprouts to extricate himself. He should ask travellers who meet him, to lend a hand; then he may circumspectly lean upon it and extricate himself; so he may circumspectly wander from village to village. (15)

If a monk or a nun perceive in their way (transports of) corn, waggons, cars, a friendly or hostile army[1], some encamped troops, they should, in case there be a byway, circumspectly choose it, and not walk on straight. One trooper might say to another: 'O long-lived one! this *S*rama*n*a is a spy upon the army; take hold of him with your arms, and drag him hither!' The other might take hold of the mendicant with his arms and drag him on. He should neither be glad nor sorry for it, &c. (see § 3); then he may circumspectly wander from village to village. (16)

If on his road travellers meet him and say, 'O long-lived *S*rama*n*a! how large is this village or scot-free town, &c.? how many horses, elephants, beggars, men dwell in it? is there much food, water, population, corn? is there little food, water, population, corn?' he should not answer such questions if asked, nor ask them himself.

This is the whole duty, &c.

Thus I say. (17)

---

[1] Sva*k*akrâ*n*i vâ para*k*akrâ*n*i vâ. My translation is merely a guess.

THIRD LESSON.

A monk or a nun on the pilgrimage, in whose way there are walls or ditches or ramparts or gates, &c. (see II, 3, 2, § 14), hill houses, palaces, underground houses, houses in trees, mountain caves, a sacred tree or pillar, workshops, &c. (see II, 2, 2, § 8), should not look at them holding up their arms, pointing at them with their fingers, bowing up and down. Then they may circumspectly wander from village to village. (1)

A monk or a nun on the pilgrimage, on whose way there are marshes, pasture-grounds, moats, fortified places, thickets, strongholds in thickets, woods, mountains, strongholds on mountains, caves[1], tanks, lakes, rivers, ponds, lotus ponds, long winding ponds, water-sheets, rows of water-sheets, should not look at them holding up their arms, &c. (see § 1). (2)

The Kevalin says: This is the reason: The deer, cattle, birds, snakes, animals living in water, on land, in the air might be disturbed or frightened, and strive to get to a fold or (other place of) refuge, (thinking): 'The *S*rama*n*a will harm me!'

Hence it has been said to the mendicant, &c., that he should not look at the objects (mentioned in § 2) holding up his arms, &c.[2] (3)

---

[1] The word aga*d*a has been left out in the translation.

[2] The passage closes: 'then he may circumspectly wander from village to village together with the master and teacher (âyariovag*gh*âya).' But as the master and teacher have not been mentioned before, and will be mentioned in the next Sûtra, it is almost certain that the words in question have been brought over from the next Sûtra, or that they ought to be supplied to all Sûtras from the beginning of the third lesson.

A monk or a nun, wandering from village to village together with the master or teacher, should not touch the master's or teacher's hand with their own, &c.; but without touching or being touched they should circumspectly wander from village to village together with the master or teacher. (4)

A monk or a nun, wandering from village to village together with the master or teacher, might be met on the road by travellers and asked: 'O long-lived *S*rama*n*a! who are you? whence do you come, and where do you go?' The master or teacher may answer and explain; but whilst the master or teacher answers and explains, one should not mix in their conversation. Thus they may wander from village to village with a superior priest[1]. (5)

A monk or a nun, wandering from village to village with a superior priest, should not touch the superior's hand with their own, &c. (see § 4). (6).

A monk or a nun, wandering from village to village with superior priests, might be met on the road by travellers, and be asked: 'O long-lived *S*rama*n*a! who are you?' He who has the highest rank of them all, should answer and explain; but whilst the superior answers and explains, one should not mix in their conversation, &c. (see § 5). (7)

A monk or a nun, wandering from village to village, might be met on the road by travellers, and be asked: 'O long-lived *S*rama*n*a! did you see somebody on the road? viz. a man, cow, buffalo, cattle, bird, snake, or aquatic animal—tell us, show

[1] Ahârâti*n*iyâe, Com. yathâratnâdhikam. Râti*n*iya is opposed to seha (disciple); it is elsewhere explained by *g*yesh*th*a; see Kalpa Sûtra, Sâm. 59. I am not sure if the phrase ought not to be translated, with due respect for his superior.

us!' The mendicant should not tell it, nor show it, he should not comply with their request, but look on silently, or, though knowing it, he should say that he did not know. Then he may circumspectly wander from village to village. (8)

He should act in the same manner, if asked about bulbs of water-plants, roots, bark, leaves, flowers, fruits, seeds, water in the neighbourhood, or a kindled fire; (9)

Likewise, if asked about (transports of) corn, waggons, cars, &c. (see II, 3, 2, § 16). (10)

Likewise, if asked: 'O long-lived *S*rama*n*a! how large is this village or scot-free town, &c.?' (11)

Likewise, if asked: 'O long-lived *S*rama*n*a! How far is it to that village or scot-free town, &c.?' (12)

If a monk or a nun, wandering from village to village, sees a vicious cow coming towards them, &c. (see II, 1, 5, § 3), they should not, from fear of them, leave the road, or go into another road, nor enter a thicket, wood, or stronghold, nor climb a tree, nor take a plunge in a large and extended water-sheet, nor desire a fold or any other place of refuge, or an army or a caravan; but undisturbed, the mind not directed to outward things, they should collect themselves for contemplation; thus they may circumspectly wander from village to village. (13)

If the road of a monk or a nun on the pilgrimage lies through a forest, in which, as they know, there stroll bands of many thieves desirous of their property, they should not, for fear of them, leave the road, &c. (all as in § 13). (14)

If these thieves say, 'O long-lived *S*rama*n*a! bring us your clothes, &c., give them, put them down!' the mendicant should not give or put them down.

Nor should he reclaim (his things) by imploring (the thieves), or by folding his hands, or by moving their compassion, but by religious exhortation or by remaining silent. (15)

If the thieves, resolving to do it themselves, bully him, &c., tear off his clothes, &c., he should not lodge an information in the village or at the king's palace; nor should he go to a layman, and say, 'O long-lived householder! these thieves, resolving to do (the robbing) themselves, have bullied me, &c., they have torn off my clothes,' &c. He should neither think so, nor speak so; but undisturbed, &c. (see § 13).

This is the whole duty, &c.

Thus I say. (16)

End of the Third Lecture, called Walking.

FOURTH LECTURE,

CALLED

MODES OF SPEECH[1].

First Lesson.

A monk or a nun, hearing and perceiving these uses of speech, should know that the following ones are not to be employed and have not hitherto been employed (by persons of exemplary conduct); those who speak in wrath or in pride, for deception or for gain, who speak, knowingly or unknowingly, hard words. They should avoid all this, which is blamable. Employing their judgment, they should know something for certain and something for uncertain[2]: (1) (N. N.) having received food or not having received food, having eaten it or not having eaten it, has come or has not come, comes or does not come, will come or will not come. (2)

Well considering (what one is to say), speaking with precision, one should employ language in moderation and restraint: the singular, dual, plural; feminine, masculine, neuter gender; praise, blame,

[1] Bhâsagâya.

[2] The commentator understands this passage and the following paragraph in a different way: a man of ripe judgment should utter no such positive assertions, e. g. it is certain (that it will rain), or it is not certain, &c. He seems to have been of opinion that the prohibition in the last sentence, savvam eta*m* sâva*gg*am va*gg*e*gg*â, extends also to the following sentence. But this is not probable, as eta*m* generally refers to what precedes, and ima*m* to what follows.

praise mixed with blame, blame mixed with praise; past, present, or future (tenses), the first and second, or third (person)[1]. If one thinks it necessary to speak in the singular, he should speak in the singular; if he thinks it necessary to speak in the plural, he should speak in the plural, &c. Considering well: this is a woman, this is a man, this is a eunuch, this is to be called thus, this is to be called otherwise, speaking with precision, he should employ language in moderation and restraint. (3)

For the avoidance of these occasions to sin, a mendicant should know that there are four kinds of speech: the first is truth; the second is untruth; the third is truth mixed with untruth; what is neither truth, nor untruth, nor truth mixed with untruth, that is the fourth kind of speech: neither truth nor untruth[2]. Thus I say.

All past, present, and future Arhats have taught and declared, teach and declare, will teach and declare these four kinds of speech; and they have explained all those things which are devoid of intellect, which possess colour, smell, taste, touch, which are subject to decay and increase, which possess various qualities. (4)

A monk (or a nun should know that) before (the utterance) speech is speech in (antecedent) non-existence[3]; that while uttered, it is (real) speech;

---

[1] Pa*kk*akkhavaya*n*am, parokkhavaya*n*am.

[2] The first, second, and third cases refer to assertions, the fourth (asatyam*ri*shâ) to injunctions.

[3] Literally, non-speech. The commentary has the terms used in the translation, which are taken from the Vai*s*eshika philosophy. But it is well known that many *G*ainas have adopted and written on the Vai*s*eshika philosophy, and that the *G*ainas themselves maintain

that the moment after it has been uttered, the spoken speech is speech in (subsequent) non-existence. (5)

A monk or a nun, well considering, should not use speech whether truth or untruth, or truth mixed with untruth, if it be sinful, blamable, rough, stinging, coarse, hard, leading to sins, to discord and factions, to grief and outrage, to destruction of living beings. (6)

A monk or a nun, considering well, should use true and accurate speech, or speech which is neither truth nor untruth (i.e. injunctions); for such speech is not sinful, blamable, rough, stinging, &c. (7)

A monk or a nun, if addressing a man who, if addressed, does not answer, should not say: 'You loon! you lout[1]! you *S*ûdra! you low-born wretch! you slave! you dog! you thief! you robber! you cheat! you liar! &c.; you are such and such! your parents[2] are such and such!' Considering well, they should not use such sinful, blamable, &c., speech. (8)

But in that case they should say: 'N. N.! O long-lived one! O long-lived ones! O layman! O pupil! O faithful one! O lover of faith!' Considering well, they should use such sinless, blameless, &c., speech. (9)

A monk or a nun, if addressing a woman who, if addressed, does not answer, should not say: 'You hussy! you wench! &c.' (repeat the above list of

that one of their own creed, *Kh*uluya-Rohagutta, is the author of the Vai*s*eshika Dar*s*anam; see Kalpa Sûtra, p. 119.

[1] The original has hole, gole, which are said by the commentator to have been used, in another country, as abusive words. My conjectural translation is based on the meaning of the Sanskrit words ho*d*â, golâ.

[2] It is well known that the Hindus include the parents of the abused party in their maledictions.

abusive words adapted to females). Considering well, they should not use such sinful, blamable, &c., speech. (10)

A monk or a nun, if addressing a woman who, if addressed, does not answer, should say: 'O long-lived one! O sister! madam! my lady! O lay-sister! O pupil! O faithful one! O lover of faith!' Considering well, they should use such sinless, blameless, &c., speech. (11)

A monk or a nun should not say: 'The god[1] of the sky! the god of the thunderstorm! the god of lightning! the god who begins to rain! the god who ceases to rain! may rain fall or may it not fall! may the crops grow or may they not grow! may the night wane or may it not wane! may the sun rise or may it not rise! may the king conquer or may he not conquer!' They should not use such speech. (12)

But knowing the nature of things, he should say: 'The air; the follower of Guhya; a cloud has gathered or come down; the cloud has rained.'

This is the whole duty, &c.

Thus I say. (13)

Second Lesson.

A monk or a nun, seeing any sort (of diseases), should not talk of them in this way: 'He has got boils, or leprosy, &c. (see I, 6, 1, § 3); his hand is cut, or his foot, nose, ear, lip is cut.' For as all such people, spoken to in such language, become

[1] This prohibition to use the word god in such phrases as the god (deva) rains, is a curious instance of the rationalism of the early *G*ainas. As they were allowed to speak nothing but the truth, they were enjoined not to say, 'the god rains,' but 'the air (a*m*talikkha*m*) rains.'

angry, hence, considering well, they should not speak to them in such language. (1)

A monk or a nun, seeing any sort (of good qualities), should speak thus: 'He is strong, powerful, vigorous, famous, well-formed, well-proportioned, handsome.' For as all such people, spoken to in such language, do not become angry, they should, considering well, speak to them in such language. (2)

A monk or a nun, seeing any sort of such things as walls or ditches, &c. (see II, 3, 2, § 14), should not speak of them in this way: 'This is well-executed, finely executed, beautiful, excellent, (so done) or to be done;' they should not use such sinful, &c., language. (3)

A monk or a nun, seeing walls, &c., should speak about them in this way: 'This has been executed with great effort, with sin, with much labour; it is very magnificent, it is very beautiful, it is very fine, it is very handsome;' considering well, they should use such sinless, &c., language. (4)

A monk or a nun, seeing food, &c., prepared, should not speak about it in this way: 'This is well executed, finely executed, beautiful, excellent, (so done) or to be done;' considering well, they should not use such sinful, &c., language. (5)

A monk or a nun, seeing food, &c., prepared, should speak about it in this way: 'This has been executed with great effort, with sin, with much labour; it is very good, it is excellent, it is well seasoned, it is most delicious, it is most agreeable;' considering well, they should use such sinless, &c.. language. (6)

A monk or a nun, seeing a man, a cow, a buffalo, deer, cattle, a bird, a snake, an aquatic animal of increased bulk, should not speak about them in this way: 'He (or it) is fat, round, fit to be killed or cooked;' considering well, they should not use such sinful, &c., language. (7)

A monk or a nun, seeing a man, a cow, &c., of increased bulk, should speak about them in this way: 'He is of increased bulk, his body is well grown, well compacted, his flesh and blood are abundant, his limbs are fully developed;' considering well, they should use such sinless, &c., language. (8)

A monk or a nun, seeing any sort of cows (or oxen), should not speak about them in this way: 'These cows should be milked or tamed or covered, should draw a waggon or car;' considering well, they should not use such sinful, &c., language. (9)

A monk or a nun, seeing any sort of cows (or oxen), should speak about them in this way: 'It is a young cow, a milch cow, she gives much milk, it is a short or a large one, a beast of burden;' considering well, they should use such sinless, &c., language. (10)

A monk or a nun, seeing big trees in parks, on hills, or in woods, should speak about them in this way: 'These (trees) are fit for palaces, gates, houses, benches, bolts, boats, buckets, stools, trays, ploughs, mattocks (?), machines, poles, the nave of a wheel (?), ga*nd*î[1], seats, beds, cars, sheds;' considering well, they should not use such sinful, &c., language. (11)

A monk or a nun, seeing big trees in parks, on hills, or in woods, should speak about them in this way: 'These trees are noble, high and round, big;

---

[1] The Guzerati commentator explains ga*nd*î by a kind of utensil. The Sanskrit commentaries give no explanation.

they have many branches, extended branches, they are very magnificent,' &c. (see § 4); considering well, they should use such sinless, &c., language. (12)

A monk or a nun, seeing many wild fruits, should not speak about them in this way: 'They are ripe, they should be cooked or eaten, they are just in season, or soft, or they have just split;' considering well, they should not use such sinful, &c., language. (13)

A monk or a nun, seeing many wild fruits, should speak about them in this way: 'They are very plentiful, they contain many seeds, they are fully grown, they have developed their proper shape;' considering well, they should use such sinless, &c., language. (14)

A monk or a nun, seeing many vegetables, should not speak about them in this way: 'They are ripe, they are dark coloured, shining, fit to be fried or roasted or eaten;' considering well, they should not use such sinful, &c., language. (15)

A monk or a nun, seeing many vegetables, should speak about them in this way: 'They are grown up, they are fully grown, they are strong, they are excellent, they are run to seed, they have spread their seed, they are full of sap;' considering well, they should use such sinless, &c., language. (16)

A monk or a nun, hearing any sort of sounds, should not speak about them in this way: 'This is a good sound, this is a bad sound;' considering well, they should not use such sinless, &c., language; but they should call them good, if they are good; bad, if they are bad; considering well, they should use such sinless, &c., language. (17)

In the same manner they should speak about the

(five) colours, as black, &c.; the (two) smells, as pleasant or unpleasant; the (five) tastes, as sharp &c.; the (five) kinds of touch, as hard, &c. (18)

A monk or a nun, putting aside wrath, pride, deceit, and greed, considering well, speaking with precision, what one has heard, not too quick, with discrimination, should employ language in moderation and restraint.

This is the whole duty, &c.

Thus I say. (19)

End of the Fourth Lecture, called Modes of Speech.

FIFTH LECTURE,

CALLED

BEGGING OF CLOTHES[1].

First Lesson.

A monk or a nun wanting to get clothes, may beg for cloth made of wool, silk, hemp, palm-leaves, cotton, or Arkatûla, or such-like clothes. If he be a youthful, young, strong, healthy, well-set monk, he may wear one robe, not two; if a nun, she should possess four raiments, one two cubits broad, two three cubits broad, one four cubits broad[2]. If one does not receive such pieces of cloth, one should afterwards sew together one with the other. (1)

A monk or a nun should not resolve to go further than half a yogana to get clothes. As regards the acceptance of clothes, those precepts which have been given in the (First Lesson of the First Lecture, called) Begging of Food[3], concerning one fellow-ascetic, should be repeated here; also concerning many fellow-ascetics, one female fellow-ascetic, many female fellow-ascetics, many *S*rama*n*as and Brâhma*n*as; also about (clothes) appropriated by another person[4]. (2)

A monk or a nun should not accept clothes which the layman, for the mendicant's sake, has bought,

[1] Vatthesa*n*â.

[2] The first to wear in the cloister, the second and third for out-of-door, the fourth for assemblies.

[3] See II, 1, 1, § 11.

[4] See II, 1, 1, § 13.

washed, dyed, brushed, rubbed, cleaned, perfumed, if these clothes be appropriated by the giver himself. But if they be appropriated by another person, they may accept them; for they are pure and acceptable. (3)

A monk or a nun should not accept any very expensive clothes of the following description: clothes made of fur, fine ones, beautiful ones; clothes made of goats' hair, of blue cotton, of common cotton, of Bengal cotton, of Pa*tt*a, of Malaya fibres, of bark fibres, of muslin, of silk; (clothes provincially called) Desaraga, Amila, Ga*gg*ala, Phâliya, Kâyaha; blankets or mantles. (4)

A monk or a nun should not accept any of the following plaids of fur and other materials: plaids made of Udra, Pe*s*a fur[1], embroidered with Pe*s*a fur, made of the fur of black or blue or yellow deer, golden plaids, plaids glittering like gold, interwoven with gold, set with gold, embroidered with gold, plaids made of tigers' fur, highly ornamented plaids, plaids covered with ornaments. (5)

For the avoidance of these occasions to sin there are four rules for begging clothes to be known by the mendicants.

Now, this is the first rule:

A monk or a nun may beg for clothes specifying (their quality), viz. wool, silk, hemp, palm-leaves, cotton, Arkatûla. If they beg for them, or the householder gives them, they may accept them; for they are pure and acceptable.

This is the first rule. (6)

Now follows the second rule:

---

[1] According to the commentary udra and pe*s*a are animals in Sindh.

A monk or a nun may ask for clothes which they have well inspected, from the householder or his wife, &c. After consideration, they should say: 'O long-lived one! (or, O sister!) please give me one of these clothes!' If they beg for them, or the householder gives them, they may accept them; for they are pure and acceptable.

This is the second rule. (7)

Now follows the third rule:

A monk or a nun may beg for an under or upper garment. If they beg for it, &c. (see § 7).

This is the third rule. (8)

Now follows the fourth rule:

A monk or a nun may beg for a left-off robe, which no other *S*rama*n*a or Brâhma*n*a, guest, pauper or beggar wants. If they beg, &c. (see § 7).

This is the fourth rule.

A monk or a nun who have adopted one of these four rules should not say, &c. (all as in II, 1, 11, § 12, down to) we respect each other accordingly. (9)

A householder may perhaps say to a mendicant begging in the prescribed way: 'O long-lived *S*rama*n*a! return after a month, ten nights, five nights, to-morrow, to-morrow night; then we shall give you some clothes.' Hearing and perceiving such talk, he should, after consideration, say: 'O long-lived one! (or, O sister!) it is not meet for me to accept such a promise. If you want to give me (something), give it me now!'

After these words the householder may answer: 'O long-lived *S*rama*n*a! follow me! then we shall give you some clothes.' The mendicant should give the same answer as above.

After his words the householder may say (to one

of his people): 'O long-lived one! (or, O sister!) fetch that robe! we shall give it the *S*rama*n*a, and afterwards prepare one for our own use, killing all sorts of living beings.'

Hearing and perceiving such talk, he should not accept such clothes; for they are impure and unacceptable. (10)

The householder[1] may say (to one of his people): 'O long-lived one! (or, O sister!) fetch that robe, wipe or rub it with perfume, &c. (see II, 2, 1, § 8); we shall give it to the *S*rama*n*a.'

Hearing and perceiving such talk, the mendicant should, after consideration, say: 'O long-lived one! (or, O sister!) do not wipe or rub it with perfume, &c. If you want to give it me, give it, such as it is!'

After these words the householder might nevertheless offer the clothes after having wiped or rubbed them, &c.; but the mendicant should not accept them, for they are impure and unacceptable. (11)

The householder may say (to another of his people): 'O long-lived one! (or, O sister!) bring that robe, clean or wash it with cold or hot water!'

The mendicant should return the same answer as above (in § 11) and not accept such clothes. (12)

The householder may say (to another of his

[1] Here and in the following paragraph the original adds nettâ, which may be = nîtvâ, bringing (the clothes); but the following words seem to militate against this rendering. For the householder's order to fetch (âhara) the clothes would be superfluous, if he had already brought (nettâ) them. Unless âhara has here some other meaning than the common one, perhaps 'take it,' nettâ cannot be translated 'having brought them.'

people): 'O long-lived one! (or, O sister!) bring that cloth, empty it of the bulbs, &c. (see II, 2, 1, § 5); we shall give it to the *S*rama*n*a.' Hearing and perceiving such talk, the mendicant should say, after consideration: 'O long-lived one! (or, O sister!) do not empty that cloth of the bulbs, &c.; it is not meet for me to accept such clothes.' After these words the householder might nevertheless take away the bulbs, &c., and offer him the cloth; but he should not accept it; for it is impure and unacceptable. (13)

If a householder brings a robe and gives it to the mendicant, he should, after consideration, say: 'O long-lived one! (or, O sister!) I shall, in your presence, closely inspect the inside of the robe.'

The Kevalin says: This is the reason: There might be hidden in the robe an earring or girdle or gold and silver, &c. (see II, 2, 1, § 11), or living beings or seeds or grass. Hence it has been said to the mendicant, &c. that he should closely inspect the inside of the robe. (14)

A monk or a nun should not accept clothes which are full of eggs or living beings, &c.; for they are impure, &c. A monk or a nun should not accept clothes which are free from eggs or living beings, &c., but which are not fit nor strong nor lasting nor to be worn[1]—which though pleasant are not fit (for a mendicant); for they are impure and unacceptable. (15)

[1] If they contain stains of mustard or A*ñg*ana, &c. The commentator quotes two *s*lokas which, as I understand them, assign to the different parts of the cloth different significations as omina. They run thus: *K*attâri deviyâ bhâgâ do ya bhâgâ ya mâ*n*usâ ı asurâ*n*a ya do bhâgâ ma*ggh*e vatthassa rakkhaso ıı devesu uttamo lobho mâ*n*usesu ya ma*ggh*imo ı asuresu ya gala*nnam* mara*nam* *g*â*n*a rakkhase ıı

A monk or a nun may accept clothes which are fit, strong, lasting, to be worn, pleasant and fit for a mendicant; for they are pure and acceptable. (16)

A monk or a nun should not wash his clothes, rub or wipe them with ground drugs, &c., because they are not new.

A monk or a nun should not clean or wash his clothes in plentiful water, because they are not new. (17)

A monk or a nun should not make his clothes undergo the processes (prohibited in § 17), because they have a bad smell. (18)

A monk or a nun wanting to air or dry (in the sun) their clothes, should not do so on the bare ground or wet earth or rock or piece of clay containing life, &c. (see II, 1, 5, § 2). (19)[1]

A monk or a nun wanting to air or dry (in the sun) their clothes, should not hang them for that purpose on a post of a house, on the upper timber of a door-frame, on a mortar, on a bathing-tub, or on any such-like above-ground place, which is not well fixed or set, but shaky and movable. (20)

A monk or a nun wanting to air or dry (in the sun) their clothes, should not lay them for that purpose on a dyke, wall, rock, stone, or any such-like above-ground place, &c. (21)

A monk or a nun wanting to air or dry (in the sun) their clothes, should not do it on a pillar, a raised platform, a scaffold, a second story, a flat roof, or any such-like above-ground place, &c. (22)

[1] If the garment falls on the ground, it would come in contact with dust, &c., then it would contain living beings and be no more pure.

Knowing this, he should resort to a secluded spot, and circumspectly air or dry his clothes there on a heap of ashes or bones, &c. (see II, 1, 1, § 1), which he has repeatedly inspected and cleaned.

This is the whole duty, &c.

Thus I say. (23)

SECOND LESSON.

A monk or a nun should beg for acceptable clothes, and wear them in that state in which they get them; they should not wash or dye them, nor should they wear washed or dyed clothes, nor (should they) hide (their clothes) when passing through other villages, being careless of dress. This is the whole duty for a mendicant who wears clothes[1].

A monk or a nun wanting, for the sake of alms, to enter the abode of a householder, should do so outfitted with all their clothes; in the same manner they should go to the out-of-door place for religious practices or study, or should wander from village to village.

Now they should know this: A monk or a nun dressed in all their clothes should not enter or leave, for the sake of alms, the abode of a householder, &c. &c., on perceiving that a strong and widely spread rain pours down, &c. (see II, 1, 3, § 9). (1)

If a single mendicant borrows for a short time a robe[2] (from another mendicant) and returns after staying abroad for one, two, three, four, or five days,

[1] See I, 7, 4, § 1.

[2] Padihâriyam, which is translated prâtihâruka. There are various readings as parihâriya, pâdihâriya; but the meaning of the word remains uncertain, and my translation is but conjectural.

he (the owner) should not take such a robe for himself, nor should he give it to somebody else, nor should he give it on promise (for another robe after a few days), nor should he exchange that robe for another one. He should not go to another mendicant and say: 'O long-lived *S*rama*n*a! do you want to wear or use this robe?' He (the owner of the robe) should not rend the still strong robe, and cast it away; but give it him (who had borrowed it) in its worn state; he should not use it himself. (2)

The same rule holds good when many mendicants borrow for a short time clothes, and return after staying abroad for one, &c., days. All should be put in the plural. (3)

'Well, I shall borrow a robe and return after staying abroad for one, two, three, four, or five days; perhaps it will thus become my own.' As this would be sinful, he should not do so. (4)

A monk or a nun should not make coloured clothes colourless, or colour colourless clothes; nor should they give them to somebody else thinking that they will get other clothes; nor should they give it on promise (for other clothes); nor should they exchange them for other clothes; nor should they go to somebody else and say: 'O long-lived *S*rama*n*a! do you want to wear or use these clothes?' They should not rend the still strong clothes, and cast them away, that another mendicant might think them bad ones. (5)

If he sees in his way thieves, he should not from fear of them, and to save his clothes, leave the road or go into another road, &c. (see II, 3, 3, § 13), but undisturbed, his mind not directed to outward things, he should collect himself for contemplation; then he may circumspectly wander from village to village. (6)

If the road of a monk or a nun on the pilgrimage lies through a forest in which, as they know, there stroll bands of many thieves desirous of their clothes, they should not from fear of them, and to save their clothes, leave the road or go into another road, &c. (all as in § 6). (7)

If these thieves say: 'O long-lived *S*rama*n*a! bring us your robe, give it, deliver it!' he should not give or deliver it. He should act in such cases (as prescribed in II, 3, 3, §§ 15 and 16).

This is the whole duty, &c.

Thus I say. (8)

End of the Fifth Lecture, called Begging of Clothes.

SIXTH LECTURE,

CALLED

BEGGING FOR A BOWL[1].

FIRST LESSON.

A monk or a nun wanting to get a bowl, may beg for one made of bottle-gourd or wood or clay, or such-like bowls. If he be a youthful, young, &c. (see II, 5, 1, § 1) monk, he may carry with him one bowl, not two[2].

A monk or a nun should not resolve to go farther than half a Yo*g*ana to get a bowl.

As regards the acceptance of a bowl, those four precepts which have been given in (the First Lesson of the First Lecture, called)[3] Begging of Food, concerning one fellow-ascetic, &c., should be repeated here, the fifth is that concerning many *S*rama*n*as and Brâhma*n*as.

A monk or a nun should not accept a bowl which the layman has, for the mendicant's sake, bought, &c. (see the Lecture called Begging of Clothes[4]). (1)

A monk or a nun should not accept any very expensive bowls of the following description: bowls made of iron, tin, lead, silver, gold, brass, a mixture of

---

[1] Pâesa*n*â.

[2] This applies, according to the commentator, to *G*inakalpikas, &c. Ordinary monks may have a drinking vessel besides the alms-bowl.

[3] See II, 1, 1, § 11.

[4] II, 5, 1, § 3.

gold, silver, and copper, pearl, glass, mother of pearl, horn, ivory, cloth, stone, or leather; for such very expensive bowls are impure and unacceptable. (2)

A monk or a nun should not accept bowls which contain a band of the same precious materials specialised in § 2; for &c. (3)

For the avoidance of these occasions to sin there are four rules for begging a bowl to be known by the mendicants.

Now this is the first rule:

A monk or a nun may beg for a bowl specifying its quality, viz. bottle-gourd or wood or clay. If they beg for such a bowl, or the householder gives it, they may accept it, for it is pure and acceptable.

This is the first rule. (4)

Now follows the second rule:

A monk or a nun may ask for a bowl, which they have well inspected, from the householder or his wife, &c. After consideration, they should say: 'O long-lived one! (or, O sister!) please give me one of these bowls, viz. one made of bottle-gourds or wood or clay.' If they beg for such a bowl, or the householder gives it, they may accept it; for &c.

This is the second rule. (5)

Now follows the third rule:

A monk or a nun may beg for a bowl which has been used by the former owner or by many people. If they beg for it, &c. (see § 5).

This is the third rule. (6)

Now follows the fourth rule:

A monk or a nun may beg for a left-off bowl which no other *S*rama*n*a or Brâhma*n*a, guest, pauper, or beggar wants. If they beg for it, &c. (see § 5).

This is the fourth rule.

A monk or a nun having adopted one of these four rules should not say, &c. (see II, 1, 11, § 12, all down to) we respect each other accordingly. (7)

A householder may perhaps say to a mendicant begging in the prescribed way: 'O long-lived *S*ramana! return after a month,' &c. (all as in the Lecture called Begging of Clothes[1]). (8)

The householder may say (to one of his people): 'O long-lived one! (or, O sister!) fetch that bowl, rub it with oil, ghee, fresh butter or marrow, we shall give it,' &c. (see II, 5, 1, § 11); or 'wash, wipe, or rub it with perfumes,' &c.; or 'wash it with cold or hot water;' or 'empty it of the bulbs,' &c. (see II, 5, 1, §§ 11 and 12). (9)

The householder may say (to the mendicant): 'O long-lived *S*ramana! stay a while till they have cooked or prepared our food, &c., then we shall give you, O long-lived one! your alms-bowl filled with food or drink; it is not good, not meet that a mendicant should get an empty alms-bowl.' After consideration, the mendicant should answer: 'O long-lived one! (or, O sister!) it is indeed not meet for me to eat or drink food &c. which is âdhâkarmika; do not cook or prepare it; if you want to give me anything, give it as it is.' After these words the householder might offer him the alms-bowl filled with food or drink which had been cooked or prepared: he should not accept such an alms-bowl, for it is impure and unacceptable. (10)

Perhaps the householder will bring and give the mendicant an alms-bowl; the mendicant should then, after consideration, say: 'O long-lived one! (or, O

[1] II, 5, 1, § 10.

sister!) I shall in your presence closely inspect the interior of the bowl.'

The Kevalin says: This is the reason: In the alms-bowl there might be living beings or seeds or grass. Hence it has been said to the mendicant, &c., that he should closely inspect the interior of the alms-bowl. (11)

All that has been said in the Lecture called Begging of Clothes (II, 5, 1, § 15 down to the end) is mutatis mutandis to be repeated here. (In § 15, add before perfumes) with oil, ghee, butter or marrow.

This is the whole duty, &c.

Thus I say. (12)

SECOND LESSON.

A monk or a nun, entering the abode of a householder for the sake of alms, should after examining their alms-bowl, taking out any living beings, and wiping off the dust, circumspectly enter or leave the householder's abode.

The Kevalin says: This is the reason: Living beings, seeds or dust might fall into his bowl. Hence it has been said to the mendicant, &c., that he should after examining his alms-bowl, taking out any living beings, circumspectly enter or leave the householder's abode. (1)

On such an occasion the householder might perhaps, going in the house, fill the alms-bowl with cold water and, returning, offer it him; (the mendicant) should not accept such an alms-bowl[1] either in

[1] Though the alms-bowl is expressly mentioned, it must stand here for water, as the commentators interpret the passage.

the householder's hand or his vessel; for it is impure and unacceptable. (2)

Perhaps he has, inadvertently, accepted it; then he should empty it again in (the householder's) water-pot; or (on his objecting to it) he should put down the bowl and the water somewhere, or empty it in some wet place. (3)

A monk or a nun should not wipe or rub a wet or moist alms-bowl. But when they perceive that on their alms-bowl the water has dried up and the moisture is gone, then they may circumspectly wipe or rub it. (4)

A monk or a nun wanting to enter the abode of a householder, should enter or leave it, for the sake of alms, with their bowl; also on going to the out-of-door place for religious practices or study; or on wandering from village to village.

If a strong and widely spread rain pours down, they should take the same care of their alms-bowl as is prescribed for clothes (in the preceding Lecture, Lesson 2, § 1).

This is the whole duty, &c.

Thus I say. (5)

End of the Sixth Lecture, called Begging for a Bowl.

SEVENTH LECTURE.

CALLED

REGULATION OF POSSESSION[1].

FIRST LESSON.

'I shall become a *S*rama*n*a who owns no house, no property, no sons, no cattle, who eats what others give him; I shall commit no sinful action; Master, I renounce to accept anything that has not been given.' Having taken such vows, (a mendicant) should not, on entering a village or scot-free town, &c., take himself, or induce others to take, or allow others to take, what has not been given. A mendicant should not take or appropriate any property, viz. an umbrella[2] or vessel or stick, &c. (see II, 2, 3, § 2), of those monks together with whom he stays, without getting their permission, and without having inspected and wiped (the object in question); but having got their permission, and having inspected and wiped (the object in question), he may take or appropriate it[3]. (1)

He may beg for a domicile in a traveller's hall, &c.

---

[1] Oggahapa*d*imâ.

[2] The commentator (*S*îlâṅka) states that the monks in Kuṅka*n*ade*s*a, &c., are allowed to carry umbrellas, because of the heavy rains in that country.

[3] Ogi*n*he*gg*â vâ paggi*n*he*gg*â vâ. The commentators explain these words 'to take for once' (sak*ri*t) and 'to take repeatedly (aneka*s*as). Later on the Guzerati commentator explains oggi*n*he*gg*â by mâge, 'he should ask.'

(see II, 1, 8, § 2), having reflected (on its fitness for a stay); he should ask permission to take possession of it from him who is the landlord or the steward of that place: 'Indeed, O long-lived one! for the time, and in the space which you concede us, we shall dwell here. We shall take possession of the place for as long a time as the place belongs to you; and of as much of it as belongs to you; for as many fellow-ascetics (as shall stand in need of it); afterwards we shall take to wandering[1].' (2)

Having got possession of some place, a mendicant should invite to that food, &c., which he himself has collected, any fellow-ascetics arriving there who follow the same rules and are zealous brethren; but he should not invite them to anything of which he has taken possession for the sake of somebody else. (3)

Having got possession of some place (in a traveller's hall, &c.), a mendicant should offer a footstool or bench or bed or couch, which he himself has begged, to any fellow-ascetics arriving there who follow other rules than he, yet are zealous brethren; but he should not offer them anything of which he has taken possession for the sake of somebody else. (4)

Having got possession of some place in a traveller's hall, &c., a mendicant might ask from a householder or his sons the loan of a needle or a Pippalaka[2] or an ear-picker or a nail-parer, he should not give or lend it to somebody else; but

[1] Compare the corresponding precept in II, 2, 3, § 3.

[2] The Guzerati commentator only says that pippalaka is some utensil. The older commentators do not explain this passage.

having done that for which he wanted one of the above articles, he should go with that article there (where the householder, &c., is), and stretching out his hands or laying the article on the ground, he should, after consideration, say: 'Here it is! here it is!' But he should not with his own hand put it in the hand of the householder. (5)

A monk or a nun should not take possession of anything[1] on the bare ground, on wet ground, where there are eggs, &c.; nor on pillars or such an above-ground place (II, 2, 1, § 7); nor on a wall, &c.; nor on the trunk of a tree, &c.; nor where the householder or fire or water, or women or children or cattle are, and where it is not fit for a wise man to enter or to leave, &c., nor to meditate on the law; nor where they have to pass through the householder's abode or to which there is no road, and where it is not fit, &c.; nor where the householder or his wife, &c., bully or scold each other, &c. (see II, 2, 1, § 9, and 3, § 7); nor where they rub or anoint each other's body with oil or ghee or butter or grease; nor where they take a bath, &c.; nor where they go about naked, &c. (all as in II, 2, 3, §§ 7-12).

This is the whole duty, &c.

Thus I say. (6-12)

SECOND LESSON.

He may beg for a domicile in a traveller's hall, &c. (see II, 1, 8, § 2), having reflected (on its fitness); he should ask permission to take possession

[1] Oggaha.

of it from the landlord or the steward of that place: 'Indeed, O long-lived one! for the time and in the space you concede us, we shall dwell here[1],' &c. (see 1, § 2). Now what further after the place is taken possession of? He should not remove from without to within, or vice versa, any umbrella or stick, &c. (see II, 2, 3, § 2) belonging to *S*rama*n*as or Brâhma*n*as (previously settled there); nor should he wake up a sleeping person, nor offend or molest the (inmates). (1)

A monk or a nun might wish to go to a mango park; they should then ask the landlord's or steward's permission (in the manner described above). Now what further after the place is taken possession of? Then they might desire to eat a mango. If the monk or the nun perceive that the mango is covered with eggs, living beings, &c. (see II, 1, 1, § 2), they should not take it; for it is impure, &c. (2)

If the monk or the nun perceive that the mango is free from eggs, living beings, &c., but not nibbled at by animals, nor injured, they should not take it; for it is impure, &c. But if they perceive that the mango is free from eggs, living beings, &c., and is nibbled at by animals and injured, then they may take it; for it is pure, &c.[2] (3)

The monk might wish to eat or suck one half of a mango or a mango's peel or rind or sap or smaller particles. If the monk or the nun perceive that the above-enumerated things are covered with eggs, or living beings, they should not take them; for they are impure, &c. But they may take them, if they are

---

[1] § 2 of the preceding Lesson is repeated word for word.
[2] See II, 1, 1, §§ 3, 4.

free from eggs, &c., and nibbled at by animals or injured[1]. (4)

A monk or a nun might wish to go to a sugar-cane plantation. They should ask permission in the manner described above. The monk or the nun might wish to chew or suck sugar-cane. In that case the same rules as for eating mango apply also; likewise if they wish to chew or to suck the sugar-cane's pulp, fibres, sap, or smaller particles. (5)

A monk or a nun might wish to go to a garlic field. They should ask permission in the manner described above. The monk or the nun might wish to chew or suck garlic. In that case the same rules as for eating mangoes apply also; likewise if they wish to chew or suck the bulb or peel or stalk or seed of garlic[2]. (6)

A monk or a nun, having got possession of a place in a traveller's hall, &c., should avoid all occasions to sin (proceeding from any preparations made by) the householders or their sons, and should occupy that place according to the following rules. (7)

Now this is the first rule:

He may beg for a domicile in a traveller's hall, &c., having reflected (on its fitness for a stay), &c. (§ 2 of the preceding Lesson is to be repeated here). This is the first rule. (8)

Now follows the second rule:

A monk resolves: 'I shall ask for possession of a dwelling-place, &c., for the sake of other mendicants,

[1] In the text § 3 is repeated with the necessary alterations.

[2] *S*îlâṅka, in his commentary, remarks that the meaning of the Sûtras about eating mangoes, sugar-cane, and garlic should be learned from the Sixteenth Lesson of the Nishîtha Sûtra.

and having taken possession of it for their sake, I shall use it.'

This is the second rule. (9)

Now follows the third rule:

A monk resolves: 'I shall ask for possession of a dwelling-place, &c., for the sake of other mendicants, and having taken possession of it for their sake, I shall not use it.'

This is the third rule. (10)

Now follows the fourth rule:

A monk resolves: 'I shall not ask for possession of a dwelling-place, &c., for the sake of other mendicants; but if the dwelling-place, &c., has already been ceded to them, I shall use it.'

This is the fourth rule. (11)

Now follows the fifth rule:

A monk resolves: 'I shall ask for possession of a dwelling-place for my own sake, not for two, three, four, or five persons.'

This is the fifth rule. (12)

Now follows the sixth rule:

If a monk or a nun, occupying a dwelling-place in which there is Ikka*d*a reed, &c. (see II, 2, 3, § 18) get this thing, then they may use it; otherwise they should remain in a squatting or sitting posture.

This is the sixth rule. (13).

Now follows the seventh rule:

A monk or a nun may beg for a dwelling-place paved with clay or wood. If they get it, then they may use it; otherwise they should remain in a squatting or sitting posture.

This is the seventh rule.

One who has adopted one of these seven rules, should not say, &c. (all as in II, 1, 11, § 12). (14)

I have heard the following explanation by the venerable (Mahâvîra): The Sthaviras, the venerable ones, have declared that dominion[1] is fivefold:

The lord of the gods' dominion;
The king's dominion;
The houseowner's[2] dominion;
The householder's[3] dominion;
The religious man's[4] dominion.
This is the whole duty, &c.
Thus I say. (15)

End of the Seventh Lecture, called Regulation of Possession.

---

[1] Oggaha, avagraha.

[2] Gâhâvaî, *gri*hapati. In another part of the commentary it is explained grâmamahattarâdi, his dominion is grâmapâ*t*akâdikam.

[3] Sâgâriya, sâgârika. It is explained *s*ayyatara, host. His dominion is shampasâlâdi.

[4] Sâhammiya, sâdharmika. His dominion is vasatyâdi, his domicile which extends for a Yogana and a quarter. When he takes possession (parigraha) of it, he must ask permission of the possessors.

SECOND PART.

THE SEVEN LECTURES[1].

Eighth Lecture[2].

When a monk or a nun wishes to perform religious postures[3], they should enter a village or a scot-free town, &c.; having entered it, they should not accept a place, even if it is offered, which is infected by eggs or living beings, &c.; for such a place is impure and unacceptable. In this way all that has been said about couches (in the Second Lecture) should be repeated here as far as 'water-plants' (II, 2, 1, § 5). (1)

Avoiding these occasions to sin, a mendicant may choose one of these four rules for the performance of religious postures.

This is the first rule:

I shall choose something inanimate[4], and lean against it; changing the position of the body, and moving about a little, I shall stand there.

This is the first rule. (2)

Now follows the second rule:

I shall choose something inanimate, and lean

[1] Sattikao.

[2] *Thâna*sattikkaya*m*, sthânasaptaikakam.

[3] *Thâna*m *th*âittae.

[4] As a wall, &c.

against it; changing the position of the body, but not moving about a little, I shall stand there.

This is the second rule. (3)

Now follows the third rule:

I shall choose something inanimate, and lean against it; not changing the position of the body, nor moving about a little, I shall stand there.

This is the third rule. (4)

Now follows the fourth rule:

I shall choose something inanimate, but I shall not lean against it; not changing the position of the body, nor moving about a little, I shall stand there. Abandoning the care of the body, abandoning the care of the hair of the head, beard, and the other parts of the body, of the nails, perfectly motionless, I shall stand there.

This is the fourth rule. (5)

One who has adopted one of these four rules, &c. (see II, 1, 11, § 12).

This is the whole duty, &c.

Thus I say.

NINTH LECTURE[1].

When a monk or a nun wishes to go to a pure place for study, they[2] should not accept one which is infected by eggs or living beings, &c.; for it is impure and unacceptable. But if that place for study to which they wish to go, is free from eggs or living beings, &c., they may accept it; for it is pure and acceptable.

[1] Nisîhiyasattikkaya*m*; nishîthikâ = svâdhyâyabhûmi*h*.

[2] The original has the first person *k*etissâmi.

In this way all that has been said in the corresponding passage about couches[1] should be repeated here as far as 'water-plants.' (1)

If parties of two, three, four, or five (mendicants) resolve to go to the place for study, they should not embrace or hug, bite with their teeth or scratch with their nails each other's body.

This is the whole duty, &c.

Thus I say. (2)

TENTH LECTURE[2].

A monk or a nun being pressed by nature should, in case they have not their own broom, beg for that of a fellow-ascetic. A monk or a nun, seeing that the ground is infected by eggs or living beings, &c., should not ease nature on such an unfit ground. But if the ground is free from eggs or living beings, &c., then they may ease nature on such a ground. (1)

A monk or a nun, knowing that the householder with regard to such a place for the sake of one or many, male or female fellow-ascetics, for the sake of many *S*rama*n*as or Brâhma*n*as whom he has well counted, kills living beings and commits various sins, should not ease nature on such a place or any other of the same sort, whether that place be appropriated by another person or not[3], &c. (see II, 1, 1, § 13). (2 and 3).

[1] Se*gg*â-game*n*a.

[2] U*kk*ârapâsava*n*asattikkao, discharging of feces and urine.

[3] Purisa*m*taraka*d*a, here translated svîk*ri*ta. The text proceeds *g*âva bahiyâ nîha*d*am vâ, which I do not know how to apply to the object in question. As § 3 differs from § 2 only in giving

Now he should know this: If that place has not been appropriated by another person, &c., he may ease nature on such a place (after having well inspected and cleaned it). (4)

A monk or a nun should not ease nature on a ground which for their sake has been prepared or caused to be prepared (by the householder), or has been occupied by main force, or strewn with grass, or levelled, or smeared (with cowdung), or smoothed, or perfumed. (5)

A monk or a nun should not ease nature on a ground where the householders or their sons remove from outside to inside, or vice versa, bulbs, roots, &c. (see II, 2, 1, § 5). (6)

A monk or a nun should not ease nature on a pillar or bench or scaffold or loft or tower or roof. (7)

A monk or a nun should not ease nature on the bare ground or on wet ground or on dusty ground or on a rock or clay containing life, or on timber inhabited by worms or on anything containing life, as eggs, living beings, &c. (8)

A monk or a nun should not ease nature in a place where the householders or their sons have, do, or will put[1] by bulbs, roots, &c. (9)

A monk or a nun should not ease nature in a place where the householders or their sons have sown, sow, or will sow rice, beans, sesamum, pulse, or barley. (10)

A monk or a nun should not ease nature in a place where there are heaps of refuse, furrows, mud,

the negative attributes (apurisa*m*taraka*d*a*m*), I have contracted both paragraphs in the translation.

[1] Parisâ*d*e*m*su vâ, explained parikshepa*n*âdikâ*h* kriyâ*h* kuryu*h*.

stakes, sprigs, holes, caves, walls, even or uneven places[1]. (11)

A monk or a nun should not ease nature in fire-places, layers (or nests) of buffaloes, cattle, cocks, monkeys, quails, ducks[2], partridges, doves, or franco-line partridges. (12)

A monk or a nun should not ease nature in a place where suicide is committed, or where (those who desire to end their life) expose their body to vultures, or precipitate themselves from rocks or trees[3], or eat poison, or enter fire. (13)

A monk or a nun should not ease nature in gardens, parks, woods, forests, temples, or wells. (14)

A monk or a nun should not ease nature in towers, pathways, doors, or town gates. (15)

A monk or a nun should not ease nature where three or four roads meet, nor in courtyards or squares. (16)

A monk or a nun should not ease nature where charcoal or potash is produced, or the dead are burnt, or on the sarcophagues or shrines of the dead. (17)

A monk or a nun should not ease nature at sacred places near rivers, marshes or ponds, or in a conduit. (18)

A monk or a nun should not ease nature in fresh clay pits, fresh pasture grounds for cattle, in meadows or quarries. (19)

A monk or a nun should not ease nature in a field of shrubs, vegetables, or roots. (20)

---

[1] The translation of some of the words in the text is merely conjectural.

[2] Va*ll*aya. I think this is the modern ba*ll*ak, duck.

[3] The commentator says: where they fall like a tree, having starved themselves to death, or where they fall from trees.

A monk or a nun should not ease nature in woods of A*s*aṇa[1], *S*ana[2], Dhâtakî[3], Ketaki[4], Mango, A*s*oka, Punnâga, or other such-like places which contain leaves, flowers, fruits, seeds, or sprouts. (21)

A monk or a nun should take their own chamber-pot or that of somebody else, and going apart with it, they should ease nature in a secluded place where no people pass or see them, and which is free from eggs or living beings, &c.; then taking (the chamber-pot), they should go to a secluded spot, and leave the excrements there on a heap of ashes, &c. (see II, 1, 1, § 2).

This is the whole duty, &c.

Thus I say. (22)

ELEVENTH LECTURE[5].

A monk or a nun should not resolve to go where they will hear sounds of a M*ri*daṅga, Nandîm*ri*daṅga, or *Gh*allarî[6], or any such-like various sounds of drums. (1)

If a monk or a nun hear any sounds, viz. of the Vî*n*â, Vipa*mk*î, Vadvîsaka, Tu*n*aka, Pa*n*aka, Tumbavî*n*ikâ, or Dha*m*ku*n*a, they should not resolve to go where they will hear any such-like various sounds of stringed instruments. (2)

The same precepts apply to sounds of kettle-drums, viz. of the Tâla, Lattiyâ, Gohiyâ[7], or Kirikiriyâ; (3)

---

[1] Terminalia Tomentosa.
[2] Crotolaria Juncea.
[3] Grislea Tomentosa.
[4] Pandanus Odoratissimus.
[5] Saddasattikkayam. Lecture on Sounds.
[6] These are different kinds of drums.
[7] Lattiyâ and gohiyâ would be in Sanskrit lattikâ and godhikâ; both words are names of lizards.

Also to sounds of wind instruments, viz. the conch, flute, Kharamukhî, or Piripiriyâ. (4)

A[1] monk or a nun should not, for the sake of hearing sounds, go to walls or ditches, &c. (see II, 3, 3, §§ 1 and 2); (5)

Nor to marshes, pasture grounds, thickets, woods, strongholds in woods, mountains, strongholds in mountains; (6)

Nor to villages, towns, markets, or a capital, hermitages, cities, halting-places for caravans; (7)

Nor to gardens, parks, woods, forests, temples, assembly halls, wells; (8)

Nor to towers, pathways, doors, or town gates; (9)

Nor where three or four roads meet, nor to courtyards or squares; (10)

Nor to stables (or nests) of buffaloes, cattle, horses, elephants, &c. (see 10, § 12); (11)

Nor to places where buffaloes, bulls, horses, &c., fight; (12)

Nor to places where herds of cattle, horses, or elephants are kept; (13)

Nor to places where story-tellers or acrobaṭs perform, or where continuously story-telling, dramatical plays, singing, music, performance on the Vînâ, beating of time, playing on the Tûrya, clever playing on the Pa*t*aha is going on; (14)

Nor to places where quarrels, affrays, riots, conflicts between two kingdoms, anarchical or revolutionary disturbances occur; (15)

[1] The beginning, 'If a monk or a nun hear particular sounds somewhere, viz.,' and the end, 'they should not resolve to go to suchlike or other places for the sake of hearing sounds,' are in the text repeated in all, §§ 5-16. In the translation the text has been somewhat abridged.

Nor to places where a young well-attended girl, well-attired and well-ornamented, is paraded, or where somebody is led to death. (16)

A monk or a nun should not, for the sake of hearing sounds, go to places where there are many great temptations[1], viz. where many cars, chariots, Mle*kkh*as, or foreigners meet. (17)

A monk or a nun should not, for the sake of hearing sounds, go to great festivals where women or men, old, young, or middle-aged ones are well-dressed and ornamented, sing, make music, dance, laugh, play, sport, or give, distribute, portion or parcel out plenty of food, drink, dainties, and spices. (18)

A monk or a nun should not like or love, desire for, or be enraptured with, sounds of this or the other world, heard or unheard ones, seen or unseen ones.

This is the whole duty, &c.

Thus I say. (19)

TWELFTH LECTURE.

If a monk or a nun see various colours (or forms), viz. in wreaths, dressed images, dolls, clothes[2], wood-work, plastering, paintings, jewelry, ivory-work, strings, leaf-cutting, they should not for the sake of pleasing the eye resolve to go where they will see various colours (or forms). All that has been said

---

[1] Mahâsava, mahâsrava. The word has probably here the original meaning, conflux; or mahâsava is a mistake for mahosava, which would be identical with mahussava, great festivals, in the next paragraph.

[2] I have translated the last four words, ga*m*thimâ*n*i, ve*dh*imâ*n*i, pûrimâ*n*i, sa*m*ghâtimâ*n*i, according to the commentary. Later on I shall translate them garlands, ribbons, scarfs, and sashes.

in the last chapter with regard to sounds should be repeated here with regard to colours (or forms); only the passages on music are to be omitted. (1.)

THIRTEENTH LECTURE.

One should neither be pleased with nor prohibit the action of another which relates to one's self, and produces karman.

One should neither be pleased with nor prohibit it [1];

If another (i. e. a householder) wipes [or rubs] the mendicant's feet; (1)

If he kneads or strokes them; (2)

If he touches or paints them; (3)

If he smears or anoints them with oil, ghee, or marrow; (4)

If he rubs or shampoos them with Lodhra, ground drugs, powder, or dye; (5)

If he sprinkles or washes them with hot or cold water; (6)

If he rubs or anoints them with any sort of ointment; (7)

If he perfumes or fumigates them with any sort of incense; (8)

If he extracts or removes a splinter or thorn from them; (9)

If he extracts or removes pus or blood from them. (10)

If he wipes or rubs the mendicant's body, &c.[2] (see §§ 2–8 down to) if he perfumes or fumigates it with any sort of incense. (11)

If he wipes or rubs a wound in (the mendicant's)

---

[1] In the text these words are repeated after each Sûtra in §§ 1–10.

[2] The text gives the whole in extenso.

body (&c.[1], down to) if he sprinkles or washes it with hot or cold water; (12)

If he cuts or incises it with any sharp instrument; if after having done so, he extracts or removes pus or blood from it. (13)

If he wipes or rubs a boil, abscess, ulcer, or fistula (&c.[1], down to) if he cuts or incises it with any sharp instrument; if after having done so, he extracts or removes pus or blood from it; (14)

If he removes, or wipes off, the sweat and uncleanliness on his body; (15)

If he removes, or wipes off, the dirt of his eyes, ears, teeth, or nails. (16)

If he cuts or dresses the long hair of his head or his brows or his armpits; (17)

If he removes, or wipes off, the nit or lice from his head. (18)

One should neither be pleased with nor prohibit it, if the other, sitting in the Aṅka or Paryaṅka posture, wipes or rubs (the mendicant's) feet; in this way the §§ 1–18 should be repeated here. (19)

One should neither be pleased with nor prohibit it, if the other, sitting in the Aṅka or Paryaṅka posture, fastens or ties a necklace of many or less strings, a necklace hanging down over the breast, a collar, a diadem, a garland, a golden string; (20)

If the other, leading him to, or treating him in, a garden or a park, wipes or rubs (the mendicant's) feet, &c. (all as above); similarly with actions done reciprocally. (21)

One should neither be pleased with nor prohibit it, if the other tries to cure him by pure charms;

---

[1] The text gives the whole in extenso as in § 11.

If the other tries to cure him by impure charms;

If he tries to cure him, digging up and cutting, for the sake of a sick monk, living bulbs, roots, rind, or sprouts. (22)

For sensation is the result of former actions; all sorts of living beings experience sensation.

This is the whole duty, &c.

Thus I say. (23)

Fourteenth Lecture.

One should not be pleased with nor prohibit a reciprocal action, which relates to one's self, and produces karman.

A mendicant should not be pleased with nor prohibit it, if (he and the other) wipe or rub each other's feet, &c.

In this way the whole Thirteenth Lecture should be repeated here.

This is the whole duty, &c.

Thus I say. (1)

End of the Second Part, called the Seven Lectures.

THIRD PART.

FIFTEENTH LECTURE,

CALLED

THE CLAUSES[1].

In that period, in that age lived the Venerable Ascetic Mahâvîra, the five (most important moments of whose life happened) when the moon was in conjunction with the asterism Uttaraphalgunî[2]; to wit: In Uttaraphalgunî he descended (from heaven), and having descended (thence), he entered the womb (of Devânandâ); in Uttaraphalgunî he was removed from the womb (of Devânandâ) to the womb (of Trisalâ); in Uttaraphalgunî he was born; in Uttaraphalgunî tearing out his hair, he left the house, and entered the state of houselessness; in Uttaraphalgunî he obtained the highest knowledge and intuition, called Kevala, which is infinite, supreme, unobstructed, unimpeded, complete, and perfect. But in Svâti the Venerable One obtained final liberation[3]. (1)

When in this Avasarpinî era, the Sushama-sushamâ period, the Sushamâ period, the Sushamaduhshamâ period, and much time of the Duhshamasushamâ period had elapsed, seventy-five years nine and a half

[1] Bhâvanâ. The bhâvanâs are subdivisions of the five great vows.

[2] Hatthottarâ in the original.

[3] Kalpa Sûtra, § 1.

months of it being left; in the fourth month of summer, in the eighth fortnight, in the light fortnight of Âshâdha, on its sixth day, while the moon was in conjunction with Uttaraphalgunî, the Venerable Ascetic Mahâvîra descended from the great Vimâna[1], the all-victorious and all-prosperous Pushpottara, which is like the lotus amongst the best (and highest flowers), and like the Svastika and Vardhamânaka amongst the celestial regions, where he had lived for twenty Sâgaropamas till the termination of his allotted length of life, (divine) nature and existence (among gods). Here, forsooth, in the continent of *G*ambudvîpa, in Bharatavarsha, in the southern part of it, in the southern brahmanical part of the place Ku*nd*apura, he took the form of an embryo in the womb of Devânandâ, of the *G*âlandharâya*n*a gotra, wife of the Brâhma*n*a *Ri*shabhadatta, of the gotra of Ko*d*âla, taking the form of a lion[2]. (2) The knowledge of the Venerable Ascetic Mahâvîra (with reference to this transaction) was threefold: he knew that he was to descend; he knew that he had descended; he knew not when he was descending. For that time has been declared to be infinitesimally small. (3)

Then in the third month of the rainy season, the fifth fortnight, the dark (fortnight) of Â*s*vina, on its thirteenth day, while the moon was in conjunction with Uttaraphalgunî, after the lapse of eighty-two days, on the eighty-third day current, the compassionate god (Indra), reflecting on what was the established custom (with regard to the birth of Tîrthakaras), removed the embryo from the southern

[1] Vimânas are palaces of the gods. [2] Cf. Kalpa Sûtra, § 2.

brahmanical part of the place Ku*nd*apura to the northern Kshatriya part of the same place, rejecting the unclean matter, and retaining the clean matter, lodged the fetus in the womb of Tri*s*alâ of the Vâsish*th*a gotra, wife of the Kshatriya Siddhârtha, of the Kâ*s*yapa gotra, of the clan of the *G*ñât*ri*s, and lodged the fetus of the Kshatriyâ*n*î Tri*s*alâ in the womb of Devânandâ of the *G*âlandharâya*n*a gotra, wife of the Brâhma*n*a *Ri*shabhadatta, of the gotra of Ko*d*âla, in the southern brahmanical part of the place Ku*nd*apurî. (4) The knowledge of the Venerable Ascetic Mahâvîra (with regard to this transaction) was threefold: he knew that he was to be removed; he knew that he was removed; he also knew when he was being removed. (5)

In that period, in that age, once upon a time, after the lapse of nine complete months and seven and a half days, in the first month of summer, in the second fortnight, the dark (fortnight) of *K*aitra, on its thirteenth day, while the moon was in conjunction with Uttaraphalgunî, the Kshatriyâ*n*î Tri*s*alâ, perfectly healthy herself, gave birth to a perfectly healthy (boy), the Venerable Ascetic Mahâvîra. (6)

In that night in which the Kshatriyâ*n*î Tri*s*alâ, perfectly healthy herself, gave birth to a perfectly healthy (boy), the Venerable Ascetic Mahâvîra, there was one great divine, godly lustre (originated) by descending and ascending gods and goddesses (of the four orders of) Bhavanapatis, Vyantaras, *G*yotishkas, and Vimânavâsins; and in the conflux of gods the bustle of gods amounted to confusion[1]. (7)

In that night, &c., the gods and goddesses rained

[1] Cf. Kalpa Sûtra, § 97.

down one great shower of nectar, sandal powder, flowers, gold, and pearls[1]. (8)

In that night the gods and goddesses (of the above-mentioned four orders) performed the customary ceremonies of auspiciousness and honour, and his anointment as a Tîrthakara. (9)

Upwards from the time when the Venerable Mahâvîra was placed in the womb of the Kshatriyâ*n*î Tri*s*alâ, that family's (treasure) of gold, silver, riches, corn, jewels, pearls, shells, precious stones, and corals increased[2]. (10) When the parents of the Venerable Ascetic Mahâvîra had become aware of this, after the lapse of the tenth day, and the performance of the purification, they prepared much food, drink, sweetmeats, and spices; and having invited a host of friends, near and remote relatives, they distributed, portioned out, bestowed (the above-mentioned materials) to *S*rama*n*as, Brâhma*n*as, paupers, beggars[3], eunuchs, &c., and distributed gifts to those who wanted to make presents; then they gave a dinner to the host of friends, near and remote relatives, and after dinner they announced the name (of the child) to their guests: (11) 'Since the prince was placed in the womb of the Kshatriyâ*n*î Tri*s*alâ, this family's (treasure) of gold, silver, riches, corn, jewels, pearls, shells, precious stones, and corals increased; therefore the prince shall be called Vardhamâna (i.e. the Increasing).' (12)

The Venerable Ascetic Mahâvîra was attended by five nurses: a wet-nurse, a nurse to clean him,

[1] Cf. Kalpa Sûtra, § 98.

[2] Cf. Kalpa Sûtra, § 90.

[3] The next word, bhivvu*m*daga, has been left out in the translation.

one to dress him, one to play with him, one to carry him; being transferred from the lap of one nurse to that of another, he grew up on that beautiful ground, paved with mosaic of precious stones, like a *K*ampaka[1] tree growing in the glen of a mountain. (13)

Then the Venerable Ascetic Mahâvîra, after his intellect had developed and the childhood had passed away, lived in the enjoyment of the allowed, noble, fivefold joys and pleasures: (consisting in) sound, touch, taste, colour, and smell[2]. (14)

The Venerable Ascetic Mahâvîra belonged to the Kâ*s*yapa gotra. His three names have thus been recorded by tradition: by his parents he was called Vardhamâna, because he is devoid of love and hate; (he is called) *S*rama*n*a (i.e. Ascetic), because he sustains dreadful dangers and fears, the noble nakedness, and the miseries of the world; the name Venerable Ascetic Mahâvîra has been given to him by the gods[3].

The Venerable Ascetic Mahâvîra's father belonged to the Kâ*s*yapa gotra; he had three names: Siddhârtha, *S*reyâ*m*sa, and *G*asa*m*sa[4]. His mother belonged to the Vâsish*th*a gotra, and had three names: Tri*s*alâ, Videhadattâ, and Priyakâri*n*î. His paternal uncle Supâr*s*va belonged to the Kâ*s*yapa gotra. His eldest brother, Nandivardhana, and his eldest sister, Sudar*s*anâ, belonged both to the Kâ*s*yapa gotra. His wife Ya*s*odâ belonged to the Kau*nd*inya gotra. His daughter, who belonged to the Kâ*s*yapa gotra, had two names: A*n*og*g*â and

[1] Michelia Champaka.

[2] Cf. Kalpa Sûtra, § 10.

[3] Cf. Kalpa Sûtra, § 108.

[4] The spaced words are Prâkrit, the Sanskrit form of which cannot be made out with certainty.

Priyadarsanâ. His granddaughter, who belonged to the Kausika gotra, had two names: Seshavatî and Yasovatî[1]. (15)

The Venerable Ascetic Mahâvîra's parents were worshippers of Pârsva and followers of the Sramanas. During many years they were followers of the Sramanas, and for the sake of protecting the six classes of lives they observed, blamed, repented, confessed, and did penance according to their sins. On a bed of Kusa-grass they rejected all food, and their bodies dried up by the last mortification of the flesh, which is to end in death. Thus they died in the proper month, and, leaving their bodies, were born as gods in Adbhuta Kalpa. Thence descending after the termination of their allotted length of life, they will, in Mahâvideha, with their departing breath, reach absolute perfection, wisdom, liberation, final Nirvâna, and the end of all misery. (16)

In that period, in that age the Venerable Ascetic Mahâvîra, a *Gñâtri* Kshatriya, *Gñâtri*putra, a Videha, son of Videhadattâ, a native of Videha, a prince of Videha, lived thirty years amongst the householders under the name of 'Videha[2].'

After his parents had gone to the worlds of the gods and he had fulfilled his promise, he gave up his gold and silver, his troops and chariots, and distributed, portioned out, and gave away his valuable treasures (consisting of) riches, corn, gold, pearls, &c., and distributed among those who wanted to make presents to others. Thus he gave away during a whole year. In the first month of winter, in the first fortnight, in the dark (fortnight) of Mârgasiras,

---

[1] Cf. Kalpa Sûtra, § 109.

[2] Cf. Kalpa Sûtra, § 110.

on its tenth day, while the moon was in conjunction with Uttaraphalgunî, he made up his mind to retire from the world. (17)

A year before the best of *G*inas will retire from the world, they continue to give away their property, from the rising of the sun. i.

One krore and eight lacks of gold is his gift at the rising of the sun, as if it were his morning meal. ii.

Three hundred and eighty-eight krores and eighty lacks were given in one year. iii.

The Ku*nd*aladharas of Vai*s*rama*n*a, the Laukântika and Maharddhika gods in the fifteen Karmabhûmis[1] wake the Tîrthakara. iv.

In Brahma Kalpa and in the line of K*ri*sh*n*as, the Laukântika Vimânas are eightfold and infinite in number. v.

These orders of gods wake the best of *G*inas, the Venerable Vîra: 'Arhat! propagate the religion which is a blessing to all creatures in the world!' vi.

When the gods and goddesses (of the four orders of) Bhavanapatis, Vyantaras, *G*yotishkas, and Vimânavâsins had become aware of the Venerable Ascetic Mahâvîra's intention to retire from the world, they assumed their proper form, dress, and ensigns, ascended with their proper pomp and splendour, together with their whole retinue, their own vehicles and chariots, and rejecting all gross matter, retained only the subtile matter. Then they rose and with that excellent, quick, swift, rapid, divine motion of the gods they came down again crossing numberless continents and oceans till they arrived in *G*ambû-

[1] Those parts of the world which are inhabited by men who practise religious duties, are called Karmabhûmi. In *G*ambûdvîpa they are Bharata, Airâvata, and Videha.

dvîpa at the northern Kshatriya part of the place Ku*nd*apura; in the north-eastern quarter of it they suddenly halted. (18)

*S*akra, the leader and king of the gods, quietly and slowly stopped his vehicle and chariot, quietly and slowly descended from it and went apart. There he underwent a great transformation, and produced by magic a great, beautiful, lovely, fine-shaped divine pavilion[1], which was ornamented with many designs in precious stones, gold, and pearls. In the middle part of that divine pavilion he produced one great throne of the same description, with a footstool. (19)

Then he went where the Venerable Ascetic Mahâvîra was, and thrice circumambulating him from left to right, he praised and worshipped him. Leading him to the divine pavilion, he softly placed him with the face towards the east on the throne, anointed him with hundredfold and thousandfold refined oil, with perfumes and decoctions, bathed him with pure water, and rubbed him with beautifying cool sandal[2], laid on a piece of cloth worth a lack. He clad him in a pair of robes so light that the smallest breath would carry them away; they were manufactured in a famous city, praised by clever artists, soft as the fume of horses, interwoven with gold by skilful masters, and ornamented with designs of flamingos. Then (the god) decked him with necklaces of many and fewer strings, with one hanging down over his breast and one consisting of one row of pearls, with a garland, a golden string, a turban, a diadem, wreaths of precious stones, and decorated him with

[1] Deva*kkham*daya in the original. My translation is but a guess.
[2] Go*s*îrsha and red sandal.

garlands, ribbons, scarves, and sashes like the Kalpavriksha. (20)

The god then, for a second time, underwent a great transformation, and produced by magic the great palankin, called Kandraprabhâ[1], which a thousand men carry. (This palankin) was adorned with pictures of wolves, bulls, horses, men, dolphins, birds, monkeys, elephants, antelopes, sarabhas[2], yacks, tigers, lions, creeping plants, and a train of couples of Vidyâdharas; it had a halo of thousands of rays; it was decorated with thousands of brilliant glittering rupees; its lustre was mild and bright; the eyes could not bear its light; it shone with heaps and masses of pearls; it was hung with strings and ribbons, and with golden excellent necklaces, extremely beautiful; it was embellished with designs of lotuses and many other plants; its cupola was adorned with many precious stones of five colours, with bells and flags; it was conspicuous, lovely, beautiful, splendid, magnificent. (21)

This palankin was brought for the best of Ginas, who is free from old age and death; it was hung with wreaths and garlands of divine flowers, grown in water or on dry ground. vii.

In the middle of the palankin (was) a costly throne covered with a divine cloth, precious stones and silver, with a footstool, for the best of Ginas. viii.

He wore on his head a chaplet and a diadem, his body was shining, and he was adorned with many ornaments; he had put on a robe of muslin worth a lack. ix.

---

[1] I. e. shining like the moon.

[2] A fabulous animal with eight legs.

After a fast of three days, with a glorious resolution he ascended the supreme palankin, purifying all by his light. x.

He sat on his throne, and *S*akra and Î*s*âna, on both sides, fanned him with chowries, the handles of which were inlaid with jewels and precious stones. xi.

In front it was uplifted by men, covered with joyful horripilation; behind the gods carried it: the Suras and Asuras, the Garu*d*as and the chiefs of Nâgas. xii.

The Suras carried it on the eastern side, and the Asuras on the southern one; on the western side the Garu*d*as carried it, and the Nâgas on the northern side. xiii.

As a grove in blossom, or a lotus-covered lake in autumn looks beautiful with a mass of flowers, so did (then) the firmament with hosts of gods. xiv.

As a grove of Siddhârtha[1], of Kar*n*ikâra[2] or of *K*ampaka[3] looks beautiful with a mass of flowers, so did (then) the firmament with hosts of gods. xv.

In the skies and on earth the sound of musical instruments produced by hundreds of thousands of excellent drums, kettle-drums, cymbals, and conches was extremely pleasant. xvi.

Then the gods ordered many hundreds of actors to perform a very rich concert of four kinds of instruments: stringed instruments and drums, cymbals and wind-instruments. xvii.

At that period, in that age, in the first month of winter, in the first fortnight, the dark (fortnight) of Mârga*s*iras, on its tenth day, called Suvrata[4], in

---

[1] White mustard. [2] Cassia Fistula.

[3] Michelia Champaka.

[4] Correct suvvate*n*am in the printed text.

the Muhûrta called Vigaya, while the moon was in conjunction with the asterism Uttaraphalgunî, when the shadow had turned towards the east, and the first Paurushî[1] was over, after fasting three days without taking water, having put on one garment, the Venerable Ascetic Mahâvîra, in his palankin *K*andraprabhâ, which only a thousand men can carry, with a train of gods, men, and Asuras left the northern Kshatriya part of the place Ku*nd*apura by the high way for the park *G*ñâtri Sha*nd*a. There, just at the beginning of night, he caused the palankin *K*andraprabhâ to stop quietly on a slightly raised untouched ground, quietly descended from it, sat quietly down on a throne with the face towards the east, and took off all his ornaments and finery. (22)

The god Vai*s*rama*n*a, prostrating himself[2], caught up the finery and ornaments of the Venerable Ascetic Mahâvîra in a cloth of flamingo-pattern. Mahâvîra then plucked out with his right and left (hands) on the right and left (sides of his head) his hair in five handfuls. But *S*akra, the leader and king of the gods, falling down before the feet of the Venerable Ascetic Mahâvîra, caught up the hair in a cup of diamond, and requesting his permission, brought them to the Milk Ocean. After the Venerable Ascetic Mahâvîra had plucked out his hair in five handfuls (as described above), he paid obeisance to all liberated spirits, and vowing to do no sinful act, he adopted the holy conduct. At that moment the

[1] Wake, Yâma, or time of three hours.

[2] *Gam*tuvâyapa*d*ie, according to the Guzerati Bâlbodh this means making obeisance to the Lord of the world by touching his feet. Another MS. has: Then *S*akra the chief and king of the gods.

whole assembly of men and gods stood motionless, like the figures on a picture.

At the command of *S*akra, the clamour of men and gods, and the sound of musical instruments suddenly ceased, when Mahâvîra chose the holy conduct. xviii.

Day and night following that conduct which is a blessing to all animated and living beings, the zealous gods listen to him with joyful horripilation. xix.

When the Venerable Ascetic Mahâvîra had adopted the holy conduct which produced that state of soul in which the reward of former actions is temporarily counteracted, he reached the knowledge called Mana*h*paryâya[1], by which he knew the thoughts of all sentient beings, with five organs, which are not defective, and possess a developed intellect, (living) in the two and a half continents and the two oceans. Then he formed the following resolution: I shall for twelve years neglect my body and abandon the care of it; I shall with equanimity bear, undergo, and suffer all calamities arising from divine powers, men or animals[2]. (23)

The Venerable Ascetic Mahâvîra having formed this resolution, and neglecting his body, arrived in the village Kummâra when only one Muhûrta of the day remained. Neglecting his body, the Venerable Ascetic Mahâvîra meditated on his Self, in blameless lodgings, in blameless wandering, in restraint, kindness, avoidance of sinful influence (sa*m*vara), chaste life, in patience, freedom from passion, contentment; control, circumspectness, practising religious postures and acts; walking the path of

[1] Or Mana*h*paryaya.

[2] Cf. Kalpa Sûtra, § 117.

Nirvâna and liberation, which is the fruit of good conduct. Living thus he with equanimity bore, endured, sustained, and suffered all calamities arising from divine powers, men, and animals, with undisturbed and unafflicted mind, careful of body, speech, and mind. (24)

The Venerable Ascetic Mahâvîra passed twelve years in this way of life; during the thirteenth year in the second month of summer, in the fourth fortnight, the light (fortnight) of Vaisâkha, on its tenth day, called Suvrata, in the Muhûrta called Vigaya, while the moon was in conjunction with the asterism Uttaraphalgunî, when the shadow had turned towards the east, and the first wake was over, outside of the town *Gri*mbhikagrâma[1], on the northern bank of the river *Rig*upâlikâ[2], in the field of the householder Sâmâga, in a north-eastern direction from an old temple[3], not far from a Sâl tree, in a squatting position with joined heels exposing himself to the heat of the sun, with the knees high and the head low, in deep meditation, in the midst of abstract meditation, he reached Nirvâna[4], the complete and full, the unobstructed, unimpeded, infinite and supreme, best knowledge and intuition, called Kevala. (25) When the Venerable One had become an Arhat and *G*ina, he was a Kevalin, omniscient and comprehending all objects, he knew all conditions of the world, of gods, men, and demons; whence

[1] *G*ambhiyagâma in Prâkrit.

[2] U*gg*upâliyâ in Prâkrit.

[3] Or, a temple called Vigayâvartta.

[4] Nivvâ*n*e or nevvâ*n*e; it may also be an adjective, belonging to nirvâ*n*a. This is of course not the final nirvâ*n*a, which is reached at the dissolution of the body, but that state which the orthodox philosophers call *g*îvanmukti.

they come, where they go, whether they are born as men or animals (*k*yavana), or become gods or hell-beings (upapâda); their food, drink, doings, desires, open and secret deeds, their conversation and gossip, and the thoughts of their minds; he saw and knew all conditions in the whole world of all living beings. (26)

On the day when the Venerable Ascetic Mahâvîra reached the Kevala, the gods (of the four orders of) Bhavanapatis, Vyantaras, *G*yotishkas, and Vimânavâsins descended from, and ascended to heaven, &c. (as on the moment of his birth, see above, § 7). (27)

Then when the Venerable Ascetic Mahâvîra had reached the highest knowledge and intuition, he reflected on himself and the world: first he taught the law to the gods, afterwards to men. (28)

The Venerable Ascetic Mahâvîra endowed with the highest knowledge and intuition taught the five great vows, with their clauses, the six classes of lives to the *S*rama*n*as and Nirgranthas, to Gautama, &c.

The six classes of lives are earth-body, &c. (down to) animals. (29)

---

i. The first great vow, Sir, runs thus:

I renounce all killing of living beings, whether subtile or gross, whether movable or immovable. Nor shall I myself kill living beings (nor cause others to do it, nor consent to it). As long as I live, I confess and blame, repent and exempt myself of these sins, in the thrice threefold way[1], in mind, speech, and body.

---

[1] I.e. acting, commanding, consenting, either in the past or the present or the future.

There are five clauses.

The first clause runs thus:

A Nirgrantha is careful in his walk, not careless[1]. The Kevalin assigns as the reason, that a Nirgrantha, careless in his walk, might (with his feet) hurt or displace or injure or kill living beings. Hence a Nirgrantha is careful in his walk, not careless in his walk.

This is the first clause. (1)

Now follows the second clause:

A Nirgrantha searches into his mind (i.e. thoughts and intentions). If his mind is sinful, blamable, intent on works, acting on impulses[2], produces cutting and splitting (or division and dissension), quarrels, faults, and pains, injures living beings, or kills creatures, he should not employ such a mind in action; but if, on the contrary, it is not sinful, &c., then he may put it in action.

This is the second clause. (2)

Now follows the third clause:

A Nirgrantha searches into his speech; if his speech is sinful, blamable, &c. (all down to) kills creatures, he should not utter that speech. But if, on the contrary, it is not sinful, &c., then he may utter it.

This is the third clause. (3)

Now follows the fourth clause:

A Nirgrantha is careful in laying down his utensils of begging, he is not careless in it. The Kevalin says: A Nirgrantha who is careless in laying down his utensils of begging, might hurt or displace or

[1] This could also be translated: he who is careful in his walk is a Nirgrantha, not he who is careless.

[2] A*n*hayakare explained by karmâsravakâri.

injure or kill all sorts of living beings. Hence a Nirgrantha is careful in laying down his utensils of begging, he is not careless in it.

This is the fourth clause. (4)

Now follows the fifth clause:

A Nirgrantha eats and drinks after inspecting his food and drink; he does not eat and drink without inspecting his food and drink. The Kevalin says: If a Nirgrantha would eat and drink without inspecting his food and drink, he might hurt and displace or injure or kill all sorts of living beings. Hence a Nirgrantha eats and drinks after inspecting his food and drink, not without doing so.

This is the fifth clause. (5)

In this way the great vow is correctly practised, followed, executed, explained, established, effected according to the precept.

This is, Sir, the first great vow: Abstinence from killing any living beings. i.

---

ii. The second great vow runs thus:

I renounce all vices of lying speech (arising) from anger or greed or fear or mirth. I shall neither myself speak lies, nor cause others to speak lies, nor consent to the speaking of lies by others. I confess and blame, repent and exempt myself of these sins in the thrice threefold way, in mind, speech, and body.

There are five clauses.

The first clause runs thus:

A Nirgrantha speaks after deliberation, not without deliberation. The Kevalin says: Without deliberation a Nirgrantha might utter a falsehood in his speech. A Nirgrantha speaks after deliberation, not without deliberation.

This is the first clause. (1)

Now follows the second clause:

A Nirgrantha comprehends (and renounces) anger, he is not angry. The Kevalin says: A Nirgrantha who is moved by anger, and is angry, might utter a falsehood in his speech. A Nirgrantha, &c.

This is the second clause. (2)

Now follows the third clause:

A Nirgrantha comprehends (and renounces) greed, he is not greedy. The Kevalin says: A Nirgrantha who is moved by greed, and is greedy, might utter a falsehood in his speech. A Nirgrantha, &c.

This is the third clause. (3)

Now follows the fourth clause:

A Nirgrantha comprehends (and renounces) fear, he is not afraid. The Kevalin says: A Nirgrantha who is moved by fear, and is afraid, might utter a falsehood in his speech. A Nirgrantha, &c.

This is the fourth clause. (4)

Now follows the fifth clause:

A Nirgrantha comprehends (and renounces) mirth, he is not mirthful. The Kevalin says: A Nirgrantha who is moved by mirth, and is mirthful, might utter a falsehood in his speech. A Nirgrantha, &c.

This is the fifth clause. (5)

In this way the great vow is correctly practised, followed, &c.

This is, Sir, the second great vow. ii.

---

iii. The third great vow runs thus:

I renounce all taking of anything not given, either in a village or a town or a wood, either of little or much, of small or great, of living or lifeless things. I shall neither take myself what is not given, nor cause others to take it, nor consent to their taking it. As long as I live, I confess and blame, &c. (all down to) body.

There are five clauses.

The first clause runs thus:

A Nirgrantha begs after deliberation, for a limited ground, not without deliberation. The Kevalin says: If a Nirgrantha begs without deliberation for a limited ground, he might take what is not given. A Nirgrantha, &c.

This is the first clause. (1)

Now follows the second clause:

A Nirgrantha consumes his food and drink with permission (of his superior), not without his permission. The Kevalin says: If a Nirgrantha consumes his food and drink without the superior's permission, he might eat what is not given. A Nirgrantha, &c.

This is the second clause. (2)

Now follows the third clause:

A Nirgrantha who has taken possession of some ground, should always take possession of a limited part of it and for a fixed time. The Kevalin says: If a Nirgrantha who has taken possession of some ground, should take possession of an unlimited part of it and for an unfixed time, he might take what is not given. A Nirgrantha, &c.

This is the third clause. (3)

Now follows the fourth clause:

A Nirgrantha who has taken possession of some ground, should constantly have his grant renewed. The Kevalin says: If a Nirgrantha has not constantly his grant renewed, he might take possession of what is not given. A Nirgrantha, &c.

This is the fourth clause. (4)

Now follows the fifth clause:

A Nirgrantha begs for a limited ground for his co-religionists after deliberation, not without deliberation. The Kevalin says: If a Nirgrantha should beg without deliberation, he might take possession of what is not given. A Nirgrantha, &c.

This is the fifth clause. (5)

In this way the great vow, &c.

This is, Sir, the third great vow. iii.

---

iv. The fourth great vow runs thus:

I renounce all sexual pleasures, either with gods or men or animals. I shall not give way to sensuality, &c. (all as in the foregoing paragraph down to) exempt myself.

There are five clauses.

The first clause runs thus:

A Nirgrantha does not continually discuss topics relating to women. The Kevalin says: If a Nirgrantha discusses such topics, he might fall from the law declared by the Kevalin, because of the destruction or disturbance of his peace. A Nirgrantha, &c.

This is the first clause. (1)

Now follows the second clause:

A Nirgrantha does not regard and contemplate the lovely forms of women. The Kevalin says: If a Nirgrantha regards and contemplates the lovely forms of women, he might, &c. A Nirgrantha, &c.

This is the second clause. (2)

Now follows the third clause:

A Nirgrantha does not recall to his mind the pleasures and amusements he formerly had with women. The Kevalin says: If a Nirgrantha recalls to his mind the pleasures and amusements he formerly had with women, he might, &c. A Nirgrantha, &c.

This is the third clause. (3)

Now follows the fourth clause:

A Nirgrantha does not eat and drink too much, nor does he drink liquors or eat highly-seasoned dishes. The Kevalin says: If a Nirgrantha did eat and drink too much, or did drink liquors and eat highly-seasoned dishes, he might, &c. A Nirgrantha, &c.

This is the fourth clause. (4)

Now follows the fifth clause:

A Nirgrantha does not occupy a bed or couch affected[1] by women, animals, or eunuchs. The Kevalin says: If a Nirgrantha did occupy a bed or couch affected by women, animals, or eunuchs, he might, &c. A Nirgrantha, &c.

This is the fifth clause. (5)

In this way the great vow, &c.

This is, Sir, the fourth great vow. iv.

---

v. The fifth great vow runs thus:

I renounce all attachments[2], whether little or much, small or great, living or lifeless; neither shall I myself form such attachments, nor cause others to do so, nor consent to their doing so, &c. (all down to) exempt myself.

There are five clauses.

The first clause runs thus:

If a creature with ears hears agreeable and disagreeable sounds, it should not be attached to, nor delighted with, nor desiring of, nor infatuated by,

---

[1] This may mean belonging to, or close by.

[2] This means the pleasure in external objects.

nor covetous of, nor disturbed by the agreeable or disagreeable sounds. The Kevalin says: If a Nirgrantha is thus affected by the pleasant or unpleasant sounds, he might fall, &c. (see above, IV, 1).

If it is impossible not to hear sounds, which reach the ear, the mendicant should avoid love or hate, originated by them.

A creature with ears hears agreeable and disagreeable sounds.

This is the first clause. (1)

Now follows the second clause:

If a creature with eyes sees agreeable and disagreeable forms (or colours), it should not be attached, &c., to them.

The Kevalin says, &c. (the rest as in the last clause. Substitute only see and forms for hear and sounds).

This is the second clause. (2)

Now follows the third clause:

If a creature with an organ of smell smells agreeable or disagreeable smells, it should not be attached to them. (The rest as above. Substitute smell and nose.)

This is the third clause. (3)

Now follows the fourth clause:

If a creature with a tongue tastes agreeable or disagreeable tastes, it should not be attached, &c., to them. (The rest as above. Substitute taste and tongue.)

This is the fourth clause. (4)

Now follows the fifth clause:

If a creature with an organ of feeling feels agreeable or disagreeable touches, it should not be attached to them. (The rest as above. Substitute feel and touch.)

This is the fifth clause. (5)

In this way the great vow, &c. (see above). v.

He who is well provided with these great vows and their twenty-five clauses is really Houseless, if he, according to the sacred lore, the precepts, and the way correctly practises, follows, executes, explains, establishes, and, according to the precept, effects them.

End of the Fifteenth Lecture, called the Clauses.

FOURTH PART.

SIXTEENTH LECTURE,

CALLED

THE LIBERATION.

The creatures attain only a temporary residence (in one of the four states of being); hearing this supreme truth (i.e. the doctrine of the Tîrthakara's) one should meditate upon it. The wise man should free himself from the family bonds; fearless should he give up acts and attachments. (1)

A mendicant, living thus[1], self-controlled towards the eternal (world of living beings), the matchless sage, who collects his alms, is insulted with words by the people assailing him, like an elephant in battle with arrows. (2)

Despised by such-like people, the wise man, with undisturbed mind, sustains their words and blows, as a rock is not shaken by the wind. (3)

Disregarding (all calamities) he lives together with clever (monks, insensible) to pain and pleasure, not hurting the movable and immovable (beings), not killing, bearing all: so is described the great sage, a good *S*rama*n*a. (4)

As the lustre of a burning flame increases, so increase the austerity, wisdom, and glory of a steadfast sage who, with vanquished desires, meditates

[1] Tahâgaya, i.e. tathâgata.

on the supreme place of virtue[1], though suffering pain[2]. (5)

The great vows which are called the place of peace, the great teachers, and the producers of disinterestedness have, in all quarters of the earth, been proclaimed by the infinite *G*ina, the knowing one[3], as light, illumining the three worlds, (repels) darkness. (6)

The unbound one, living amongst the bound (i.e. householders), should lead the life of a mendicant; unattached to women, he should speak with reverence. Not desiring this or the next world, the learned one is not measured by the qualities of love. (7)

The dirt (of sins) formerly committed by a thus liberated mendicant who walks in wisdom (and restraint), who is constant, and bears pain, vanishes as the dirt covering silver (is removed) by fire. (8)

He lives, forsooth, in accordance with wisdom (and restraint), and walks free from desire, and with conquered sensuality. As a snake casts off its old skin, so is the Brâhma*n*a freed from the bed of pain. (9)

As they call the great ocean a boundless flood of water, difficult to traverse with the arms (alone), so should the learned one know (and renounce) it (the sa*m*sâra): that sage is called 'Maker of the end.' (10)

Here amongst men bondage and deliverance have

---

[1] Dhammapada*m*.

[2] Vidû*n*ate, which I take to be the genitive of the present participle corresponding to vidunvata*h*. The commentators divide the word into vidû *n*ate = vidvân nata*h*, which gives no sense.

[3] Nâti*n*â in the original. I would prefer to translate it *gñatri*, the name of the clan to which Nâtaputta belonged.

been declared; he who, according to that doctrine (of the church), knows bondage and deliverance: that sage is called 'Maker of the end.' (11)

He for whom there is no bondage whatever in this world, and besides in the two (other continents, or heaven and hell), is indeed a (monk needing) no support and no standing place; he has quitted the path of births. (12)

End of the Sixteenth Lecture, called the Liberation.

End of the Second Book.

End of the Â*k*ârâṅga Sûtra.

THE KALPA SÛTRA

OF

BHADRABÂHU.

KALPA SÛTRA.

LIVES OF THE *G*INAS.

LIFE OF MAHÂVÎRA.

Obeisance to the Arhats!
Obeisance to the Liberated Ones!
Obeisance to the Religious Guides!
Obeisance to the Religious Instructors!
Obeisance to all Saints in the World!

This fivefold obeisance, destroying all sins, is of all benedictions the principal benediction.

1 In that period, in that age lived the Venerable Ascetic Mahâvîra, the five (most important moments of whose life happened) when the moon was in conjunction with the asterism Uttaraphalgunî; to wit, in Uttaraphalgunî he descended (from heaven), and having descended (thence), he entered the womb (of Devânandâ); in Uttaraphalgunî he was removed from the womb (of Devânandâ) to the womb (of Trisalâ); in Uttaraphalgunî he was born; in Uttaraphalgunî, tearing out his hair, he left the house and entered the state of houselessness; in Uttaraphalgunî he obtained the highest knowledge and intuition, called Kevala, which is infinite, supreme, unobstructed,

unimpeded, complete, and perfect. But in Svâti the Venerable One obtained final liberation. (1)[1]

End of the First Lecture[2].

In that period, in that age the Venerable Ascetic Mahâvîra, having on the sixth day of the fourth month of summer, in the eighth fortnight, the light (fortnight) of Âshâ*dh*a, descended from the great Vimâna, the all-victorious and all-prosperous Pushpottara, which is like the lotus amongst the best things, where he had lived for twenty Sâgaropamas till the termination of his allotted length of life, of his (divine nature, and of his existence (among gods); here in the continent of *G*ambûdvîpa, in Bharatavarsha,—when of this Avasarpi*n*î era the Sushamasushamâ, the Sushamâ, and Sushamadu*h*shamâ periods, and the greater part of the Du*h*shamasushamâ period (containing a Ko*d*âko*d*i[3] of Sâgaropamas, less forty-two thousand years) had elapsed, and only seventy-two years, eight and a half months were left, after twenty-one Tîrthakaras of the race of Ikshvâku and of the Kâ*s*yapa gotra, and two of the race of Hari and of the Gautama gotra, on the whole twenty-three Tîrthakaras had appeared,—the Venerable Ascetic Mahâvîra, the last of the Tîrthakaras, took the form of an embryo in the womb of Devânandâ, of the *G*âlandharâya*n*a gotra, the wife of the Brâhma*n*a *Ri*shabhadatta, of the gotra of Ko*d*âla, in the

---

[1] Cf. Â*k*âráṅga Sûtra II, 15, § 1.

[2] Vâ*k*anâ. These vâ*k*anâs are the parts into which the Kalpa Sûtra is generally divided by some commentators. I have adopted the distribution of Samayasundara.

[3] A ko*t*i of ko*t*is or 100,000,000,000,000.

brahmanical part of the town Ku*nd*agrâma in the middle of the night, when the moon was in conjunction with the asterism Uttaraphalgunî, after his allotted length of life, of his (divine) nature, and of his existence (amongst gods) had come to their termination. (2)[1]

The knowledge of the Venerable Ascetic Mahâvîra (about this) was threefold; he knew that he was to descend, he knew that he had descended, he knew not when he was descending[2].

In that night in which the Venerable Ascetic Mahâvîra took the form of an embryo in the womb of the Brâhma*n*î Devânandâ of the *G*âlandharâya*n*a gotra, the Brâhma*n*î Devânandâ was on her couch, taking fits of sleep, in a state between sleeping and waking, and having seen the following fourteen illustrious, beautiful, lucky, blest, auspicious, fortunate great dreams, she woke up. (3) To wit:

An elephant, a bull, a lion, the anointing (of the goddess *S*rî), a garland, the moon, the sun, a flag, a vase, a lotus lake, the ocean, a celestial abode, a heap of jewels, and a flame. (4)

When the Brâhma*n*î Devânandâ, having seen these dreams, woke up, she—glad, pleased, and joyful in her mind, delighted, extremely enraptured, with a heart widening under the influence of happiness, with the hair of her body all erect in their pores like the flowers of the Kadamba touched by rain-drops—firmly fixed the dreams (in her mind), and rose from her couch. Neither hasty nor trembling, with a quick and even[3] gait, like that of the

[1] Cf. Â*k*ârâṅga Sûtra II, 15, § 2.
[2] Cf. Â*k*ârâṅga Sûtra II, 15, § 3.
[3] Add in the text asa*m*bha*m*tâe after avila*m*biyâe.

royal swan, she went to the Brâhma*n*a *Ri*shabha-datta, and gave him the greeting of victory. Then she comfortably sat down in an excellent chair of state; calm and composed, joining the palms of her hands so as to bring the ten nails together, she laid the folded hands on her head, and spoke thus: (5)

'O beloved of the gods, I was just now on my couch taking fits of sleep, in a state between sleeping and waking, when I saw the following fourteen illustrious, &c., great dreams; to wit, an elephant, &c. (6)

'O beloved of the gods, what, to be sure, will be the happy result portended by these fourteen illustrious, &c., great dreams?' (7)

When the Brâhma*n*a *Ri*shabhadatta had heard and perceived this news from the Brâhma*n*î Devânandâ, he, glad, pleased, and joyful (see § 5, down to) rain-drops, firmly fixed the dreams (in his mind), and entered upon considering them. He grasped the meaning of those dreams with his own innate intellect and intuition, which were preceded by reflection, and thus spoke to the Brâhma*n*î Devânandâ: (8)

'O beloved of the gods, you have seen illustrious dreams; O beloved of the gods, you have seen beautiful, lucky, blest, auspicious, fortunate dreams, which will bring health, joy, long life, bliss, and fortune! We shall have success, O beloved of the gods, we shall have pleasure; we shall have happiness, O beloved of the gods, we shall have a son! Indeed, O beloved of the gods, after the lapse of nine complete months and seven and a half days you will give birth to a lovely and handsome boy with tender hands and feet, with a body containing the entire and complete five organs of sense, with the lucky signs, marks, and good qualities; a boy on whose body all limbs will be well formed, and of full volume, weight, and length, of a lovely figure like that of the moon! (9) And this boy, after having passed his childhood[1], and, with just ripened intellect, having reached the state of youth, will repeat, fully understand, and well retain (in his mind) the four Vedas: the *Ri*g-veda, Ya*g*ur-veda, Sâma-veda, Atharva-veda—to which the Itihâsa[2] is added as a fifth, and the Nigghan*t*u[3] as a sixth (Veda)—together with their Aṅgas and Upâṅgas, and the Rahasya[4]; he will know the six Aṅgas, he will be versed in the philosophy of the sixty categories[5], and well grounded in arithmetic, in phonetics, ceremonial, grammar, metre, etymology, and astronomy[6], and in many other brahmanical [and monastic] sciences besides. (10) Therefore, O beloved of the gods, you have seen illustrious dreams, &c. (see § 9).'

In this way he repeatedly expressed his extreme satisfaction. (11)

When the Brâhma*n*î Devânandâ had heard and perceived this news from the Brâhma*n*a *Ri*shabhadatta, she—glad, pleased, and joyful, &c. (see § 5)—

---

[1] That is, having reached his eighth year.

[2] Purâ*n*a.

[3] Dictionary.

[4] According to the commentators, works which treat of the aidamparya of the Vedas.

[5] The Sâṅkhya philosophy of Kapila, according to the commentary; but see Max Müller, What can India teach us? p. 362.

[6] These are the six Aṅgas which in the same order occur in the well-known versus memorialis. Indeed, that verse is nearly identical with the passage in our text.

joining the palms of her hands, &c. (see § 5, down to) and spoke thus: (12)

'That is so, O beloved of the gods; that is exactly so, O beloved of the gods; that is true, O beloved of the gods; that is beyond doubt, O beloved of the gods; that is what I desire, O beloved of the gods; that is what I accept, O beloved of the gods; that is what I desire and accept, O beloved of the gods; that matter is really such as you have pronounced it.'

Thus saying, she accepted the true meaning of the dreams, and enjoyed together with *Ri*shabhadatta the noble permitted pleasures of human nature. (13)

In that period, in that age, *S*akra,—the chief and king of the gods, the wielder of the thunderbolt, the destroyer of towns, the performer of a hundred sacrifices, the thousand-eyed one, Maghavan, the punisher of the Daitya Pâka, the lord of the southern half of the earth[1], the lord of the thirty-two thousand celestial abodes, the bestrider of the elephant Airavata, the chief of the Suras, who wears spotless clothes and robes[2], and puts on garlands and the diadem, whose cheeks were stroked by fine, bright, and trembling earrings of fresh gold [the most prosperous, the most brilliant, the most mighty, the most glorious, the most powerful, and the most happy one], with a splendid body, ornamented with a long down-reaching garland,—this *S*akra was in the Saudharma Kalpa, in the celestial abode Saudharma Avata*m*saka, in the council-hall Sudharman, on his throne *S*akra; he who exercises and maintains the supreme command, government,

[1] I. e. of that part of it which lies to the south of mount Meru.

[2] According to the commentators, wearing clothes resembling the dustless sky.

management, guidance, direction, and sovereign power and generalship over the thirty-two thousand gods of the celestial abodes, the eighty-four thousand gods of a rank equal with that of himself, the thirty-two chief gods, the four guardians of the world, the eight principal queens with their trains, the three courts, the seven armies, and the seven commanders of these armies. He was then enjoying the permitted pleasures of divine nature under the great din of uninterrupted story-telling, dramatical plays, singing, and music, as beating of time, performance on the V*î*n*â*, the Tûrya, the great drum, and the Pa*t*upa*t*aha. (14)

And he viewed this whole continent *G*ambûdvîpa with his extensive (knowledge called) Avadhi. There he saw in the continent *G*ambûdvîpa, in Bhâratavarsha, in the southern half of Bharata, in the brahmanical part of the town Ku*nd*agrâma, the Venerable Ascetic Mahâvîra taking the form of an embryo in the womb of the Brâhma*n*î Devânandâ of the *G*âlandharâya*n*a gotra, wife of the Brâhma*n*a *Ri*shabhadatta of the gotra of Ko*d*âla; and—glad, pleased, and joyful in his mind, delighted, extremely enraptured, with a heart widening under the influence of happiness, with the hair of his body bristling and erect in their pores like the fragrant flowers of Nîpa when touched by rain-drops, with his eyes and mouth open like full-blown lotuses, with his excellent, various[1], trembling bracelets, with diadem and earrings, his breast lighted up by necklaces, wearing long and swinging ornaments with a pearl pendant—the chief of the gods rose

[1] Ka*d*aga, tu*d*iya, keûra. Ka*t*aka is the well-known ka*n*ka*n*a, tru*t*ika is explained by bâhurakshikâ, keyûra by a*n*gada. The last two are bracelets worn on the upper arm.

with confusion, hasty and trembling from his throne, descended from the footstool, took off his shoes which were by a clever artist set with Vaidûrya and excellent Rish*t*a and A*ñg*ana[1], and ornamented with glittering jewels and precious stones, threw his seamless robe over his left shoulder, and, arranging the fingers of his hands in the shape of a bud, he advanced seven or eight steps towards the Tîrthakara. Bending his left knee and reposing on the right one, he three times placed his head on the ground and lifted it a little; then he raised his bracelet-encumbered arms, and joining the palms of his hands so as to bring the ten nails together, laid the hands on his head and spoke thus: (15)

'Reverence to the Arhats and Bhagavats; to the Âdikaras, the Tîrthakaras, the perfectly-enlightened ones; to the highest of men, the lions among men, the flowers among mankind[2], the Gandhahastins among men; to the highest in the world, the guides of the world, the benefactors of the world, the lights of the world, the enlighteners of the world; to the givers of safety, to the givers of sight, to the givers of the road, to the givers of shelter, to the givers of life, to the givers of knowledge[3]; to the givers of the law, the preachers of the law, the lords of the law, the leaders of the law, the universal emperors of the best law; to the light, the help, the shelter, the refuge, the resting-place, the possessors of unchecked know-

---

[1] Names of precious stones.

[2] The text has literally, the best lotus among men.

[3] These words are variously and always somewhat fancifully interpreted. One explanation is ascribed to the Aupanishadikas, whom I do not remember to have found noticed anywhere else in *G*aina books.

ledge and intuition who have got rid of unrighteousness; to the conquerors and the granters of conquest, the saved and the saviours, the enlightened and the enlighteners, the liberated and the liberators, to the all-knowing ones, the all-seeing ones, to those who have reached the happy, stable, unstained, infinite, unperishable, undecaying place, called the path of perfection, whence there is no return; reverence to the *G*inas who have conquered fear.

'Reverence to the Venerable Ascetic Mahâvîra, the Âdikara, the last of the Tîrthakaras who was predicted by the former Tîrthakaras, &c.[1] I here adore the Revered One yonder, may the Revered One yonder see me here!' With these words he adored, he worshipped the Venerable Ascetic Mahâvîra, and sat down on his excellent throne facing the east. Then the following internal, reflectional, desirable idea occurred to the mind of *S*akra, the chief of kings and gods: (16)

'It never has happened, nor does it happen, nor will it happen, that Arhats, *K*akravartins, Baladevas, or Vasudevas, in the past, present, or future, should be born in low families, mean families, degraded families, poor families, indigent families, beggars' families, or brahmanical families. (17) For indeed Arhats, *K*akravartins, Baladevas, and Vasudevas, in the past, present, and future, are born in high families, noble families, royal families, noblemen's families, in families belonging to the race of Ikshvâku, or of Hari, or in other suchlike families of pure descent on both sides. (18)

[1] According to the commentary all the epithets from 'the enlightened one' down to 'who has reached' are intended by this '&c.'

Now this is something which moves the wonder of the world: it happens in the lapse of numberless Avasarpi*n*îs and Utsarpi*n*îs, because the imperishable, indescribable, and undestroyable Karman relating to name and gotra must take effect, that Arhats, &c., in the past, present, and future, descend in (i.e. take the form of an embryo in the womb of a woman belonging to) low families, &c.; but they are never brought forth by birth from such a womb. (19) This Venerable Ascetic Mahâvîra, now, in the continent *G*ambûdvîpa, in Bharatavarsha, in the brahmanical part of the town Ku*nd*agrâma, has taken the form of an embryo in the womb of the Brâhma*n*î Devânandâ of the *G*âlandharâya*n*a gotra, wife of the Brâhma*n*a *Ri*shabhadatta of the gotra of Ko*d*âla. (20) Hence it is the established custom of all past, present, and future *S*akras, chiefs and kings of the gods, to cause the Arhats and Bhagavats to be removed from such-like low, mean, &c., families, to such-like high, noble, &c., families. (21) It is, therefore, better that I should cause the Venerable Ascetic Mahâvîra, the last of the Tîrthakaras who was predicted by the former Tîrthakaras, to be removed from the brahmanical part of the town Ku*nd*agrâma, from the womb of the Brâhma*n*î Devânandâ of the *G*âlandharâya*n*a gotra, wife of the Brâhma*n*a *Ri*shabhadatta of the gotra of Ko*d*âla, to the Kshatriya part of the town Ku*nd*agrâma, and to be placed as an embryo in the womb of the Kshatriyâ*n*î Tri*s*alâ of the Vâsish*th*a gotra, wife of the Kshatriya Siddhârtha of the Kâ*s*yapa gotra, belonging to the clan of the *Gñ*â*tri* Kshatriyas; and to cause the embryo of the Kshatriyâ*n*î Tri*s*alâ of the Vâsish*th*a gotra to be placed in the womb of the Brâhma*n*î Devânandâ of the *G*âlandharâya*n*a gotra.'

Thus he reflected and called Hari*n*egamesi[1], the divine commander of the foot troops; having called him, he spoke thus: (22)

'Well, now, beloved of the gods, it never has happened, &c. (§§ 17–20 are verbally repeated). (23–25)

'Therefore, go now and remove the Venerable Ascetic Mahâvîra from the brahmanical part, &c., and place the embryo of the Kshatriyâ*n*î Tri*s*alâ, &c. (see § 21). Having done this, return quickly to report on the execution of my orders.' (26)

When Hari*n*egamesi, the divine commander of the foot troops, was thus spoken to by *S*akra, the chief and king of the gods, he—glad, pleased, and joyful, &c. (see § 15)—laid his folded hands on his head and modestly accepted the words of command, saying, 'Just as your Majesty commands.' After this he left the presence of *S*akra, the chief and king of the gods, and descended towards the north-eastern quarter; then he transformed himself through his magical power of transformation, and stretched himself out for numerous Yo*g*anas like a staff, (during which he seized) jewels, Va*g*ra, Vai*d*ûrya, Lohitâksha, Masâragalla, Ha*m*sagarbha, Pulaka, Saugandhika, *G*yotisara, A*ñ*gana, A*ñ*ganapulaka, *G*âtarûpa, Subhaga, Spha*t*ika, and Rish*t*a; (of these precious materials) he rejected the gross particles, and retained the subtle particles. (27) Then

[1] This name is rendered Hari*n*aigamaishin in Sanskrit. He is represented in pictures as a man with the head of an antelope (hari*n*a). This is apparently the effect of a wrong etymology, interesting as the fact itself is.

for a second time he transformed himself through his magical power of transformation, and produced the definitive form (which gods adopt on entering the world of men); having done so, he passed with that excellent, hasty, trembling, active, impetuous, victorious, exalted, and quick divine motion of the gods right through numberless continents and oceans, and arrived in *G*ambûdvîpa, in Bharatavarsha, in the brahmanical part of the town Ku*nd*agrâma, at the house of the Brâhma*n*a *Ri*shabhadatta, where the Brâhma*n*î Devânandâ dwelt. Having arrived there, he made his bow in the sight of the Venerable Ascetic Mahâvîra, and cast the Brâhma*n*î Devânandâ, together with her retinue, into a deep sleep; then he took off all unclean particles, and brought forth the clean particles, and saying, 'May the Venerable One permit me,' he took the Venerable Ascetic Mahâvîra in the folded palms of his hands without hurting him. Thus he went to the Kshatriya part of the town Ku*nd*agrâma, to the house of the Kshatriya Siddhârtha, where the Kshatriyâ*n*î Tri*s*alâ dwelt; he cast her and her attendants into a deep sleep, took off all unclean particles, and brought forth the clean particles, and placed the embryo of the Venerable Ascetic Mahâvîra in the womb of the Kshatriyâ*n*î Tri*s*alâ, and the embryo of the Kshatriyâ*n*î Tri*s*alâ he placed in the womb of the Brâhma*n*î Devânandâ of the *G*âlandharâya*n*a gotra. Having done so, he returned in that direction in which he had come[1]. (28) With that excellent, &c. (see § 28), divine motion

[1] The contents of §§ 14-28 are contained in Â*k*ârâṅga Sûtra II, 15, § 4.

of the gods, he flew upwards right through numberless continents and oceans, taking thousands of Yoganas in each motion, and arrived in the Saudharma Kalpa, in the divine abode called Saudharma Avatamsaka, where Sakra, the chief and king of the gods, sat on the throne called Sakra, and reported to Sakra, the chief and king of the gods, on the execution of his orders.

In that period, in that age the knowledge of the Venerable Ascetic Mahâvîra was threefold; he knew that he was to be removed; he knew that he was removed; he knew not when he was being removed[1]. (29)

In that period, in that age, on the thirteenth day of the third month of the rainy season, in the fifth fortnight, the dark (fortnight) of Âsvina, after the lapse of eighty-two days, on the eighty-third day current (since his conception), the embryo of the Venerable Ascetic Mahâvîra was, on the command of Sakra, safely removed by Harinegamesi from the womb of the Brâhmanî Devânandâ to that of the Kshatriyânî Trisalâ[2], in the middle of the night, when the moon was in conjunction with the asterism Uttaraphalgunî. (30)

End of the Second Lecture.

In that night in which the embryo of the Venerable Ascetic Mahâvîra was removed from the womb of the Brâhmanî Devânandâ of the Gâlandharâyana gotra to that of the Kshatriyânî Trisalâ of the

---

[1] In some MSS. the last part of this paragraph is placed at the end of the next one.

[2] The text repeats the corresponding passage of § 21.

Vâsish*th*a gotra, the former was on her couch taking fits of sleep in a state between sleeping and waking; and seeing that these fourteen illustrious, beautiful, lucky, blest, auspicious, fortunate, great dreams were taken from her by the Kshatriyâ*n*î Tri*s*alâ, she awoke. (31)

In that night in which the embryo of the Venerable Ascetic Mahâvîra was removed from the womb of the Brâhma*n*î Devânandâ of the *G*âlandharâya*n*a gotra to that of the Kshatriyâ*n*î Tri*s*alâ of the Vâsish*th*a gotra, the latter was in her dwelling-place, of which the interior was ornamented with pictures, and the outside whitewashed, furbished and cleansed, the brilliant surface of the ceiling was painted, the darkness was dispelled by jewels and precious stones, the floor was perfectly level and adorned with auspicious figures; which, moreover, was furnished with offerings of heaps of delicious, fragrant, strewn flowers of all five colours, was highly delightful through curling, scented fumes of black aloe, the finest Kundurukka and Turushka[1], and burning frankincense; was exquisitely scented with fine perfumes, and turned as it were into a smelling-bottle; on a couch with a mattress of a man's length, with pillows at head and foot, raised on both sides and hollow in the middle, soft as if one walked on the sand of the banks of the Ganges, covered with the cloth of a robe of ornamented linen, containing a well-worked towel, and hung with red mosquito curtains, delightful, soft to the touch like fur, wadding, Pûra[2], butter, or cotton, with all the comforts of

[1] Different kinds of the resin of Boswellia.
[2] Name of a tree.

a bed, such as fragrant, excellent flowers and sandal-powder—(in such a room and on such a bed Trisalâ was) taking fits of sleep between sleeping and waking, and having seen the following fourteen, &c. (see § 3), dreams, viz. an elephant, &c. (see § 4), she awoke. (32)

1. Then Trisalâ saw in her first dream a fine, enormous elephant, possessing all lucky marks, with strong thighs and four mighty tusks; who was whiter than an empty great cloud, or a heap of pearls, or the ocean of milk, or the moon-beams, or spray of water, or the silver mountain (Vaitâ*dh*ya); whose temples were perfumed with fragrant musk-fluid, which attracted the bees; equalling in dimension the best elephant of the king of the gods (Airâvata); uttering a fine deep sound like the thunder of a big and large rain-cloud. (33)

2. Then she saw a tame, lucky bull, of a whiter hue than that of the mass of petals of the white lotus, illumining all around by the diffusion of a glory of light; (a bull) whose lovely, resplendent, beautiful hump was delightful through the collection of its charms, whose glossy skin (was covered with) thin, fine, soft hairs; whose body was firm, well made, muscular, compact, lovely, well proportioned, and beautiful; whose horns were large, round, excellently beautiful, greased at their tops, and pointed; whose teeth were all equal, shining, and pure. He foreboded innumerable good qualities. (34)

3. Then she saw a handsome, handsomely shaped, playful lion, jumping from the sky towards her face; a delightful and beautiful lion whiter than a heap of pearls, &c. (see § 33), who had strong and lovely fore-arms, and a mouth adorned with round, large,

and well-set teeth; whose lovely lips, splendent through their proportions, and soft like a noble lotus, looked as if they were artificially ornamented; whose palate[1] was soft and tender like the petals of the red lotus, and the top of whose tongue was protruding; whose eyes were like pure lightning, and revolved like red-hot excellent gold just poured out from the crucible; (a lion) with broad and large thighs, and with full and excellent shoulders, who was adorned with a mane of soft, white, thin, long hair of the finest quality; whose erect, well-shaped, and well-grown tail was flapping; the tops of whose nails were deeply set and sharp; whose beautiful tongue came out of his mouth like a shoot of beauty. (35)

4. Then she, with the face of the full moon, saw the goddess of famous beauty, *S*rî, on the top of Mount Himavat, reposing on a lotus in the lotus lake, anointed with the water from the strong and large trunks of the guardian elephants. She sat on a lofty throne. Her firmly placed feet resembled golden tortoises, and her dyed, fleshy, convex, thin, red, smooth nails were set in swelling muscles[2]. Her hands and feet were like the leaves of the lotus, and her fingers and toes soft and excellent; her round and well-formed legs were adorned with the Kuruvindâvarta[3], and her knees with dimples. Her fleshy thighs resembled the proboscis of an excellent elephant, and her lovely broad hips were encircled by a golden zone. Her large and beautiful belly was

---

[1] Another reading noticed in the commentary has tala, upper side of the tongue, instead of tâlu, palate.

[2] Literally, elevated and fat.

[3] An ornament according to the commentary.

adorned by a circular navel, and contained a lovely row of hairs (black as) collyrium, bees, or clouds, straight, even, continuous, thin, admirable, handsome, soft, and downy. Her waist, which contained the three folds, could be encompassed with one hand. On all parts of her body shone ornaments and trinkets, composed of many jewels and precious stones, yellow and red gold. The pure cup-like pair of her breasts sparkled, encircled by a garland of Kunda flowers, in which glittered a string of pearls. She wore strings of pearls made by diligent and clever artists, shining with wonderful strings, a necklace of jewels with a string of Dînârâs[1], and a trembling pair of earrings, touching her shoulders, diffused a brilliancy; but the united beauties and charms of these ornaments were only subservient to the loveliness of her face[2]. Her lovely eyes were large and pure like the water lily. She sprinkled about the sap from two lotus flowers which she held in her splendid hands, and gracefully fanned herself. Her glossy, black, thick, smooth hair hung down in a braid. (36)

5. Then she saw, coming down from the firmament, a garland charmingly interwoven with fresh Mandâra flowers. It spread the delicious smell of *K*ampaka[3], A*s*oka[4], Nâga[5] Punnâga[6], Priyangu[7],

[1] This word, corresponding to the Greek δηνάριον, proves the late composition of this part of the Kalpa Sûtra.

[2] I cannot accurately construe this passage; my translation is therefore rather free, but, I believe, comes near the meaning of the original.

[3] Michelia Champaka.

[4] Jonesia Asoka.

[5] Mesua Roxburghii.

[6] Rottlera Tinctoria.

[7] Panicum Italicum.

*S*irîsha[1], Mudgara[2], Mallikâ[3], *G*âti[4], Yûthika[5], Aṅkolla[6], Kora*nt*akapatra[7], Damanaka[8], Navamâlikâ[9], Bakula[10], Tilaka[11], Vâsantika[12], Nuphar, Nymphaea, Pâ*t*ala[13], Kunda[14], Atimukta[15], and Mango; and perfumed the ten divisions of the universe with its incomparably delightful fragrance. It was white through wreaths of fragrant flowers of all seasons, and brilliant through splendid, beautiful embellishments of many colours. Towards it came humming swarms of different kinds of bees[16], and filled with their sweet noise the whole neighbourhood. (37)

6. And the moon: white as cow-milk, foam, spray of water, or a silver cup, glorious, delighting heart and eyes, full, dispelling the compact darkness of the thickest wilderness, whose crescent shines at the end of the two halves of the month, opening the blossoms of the groups of Nymphaeas, adorning the night, resembling the surface of a well-polished mirror. She was of a white hue, like a flamingo, the stars' head-ornament, the quiver of Cupid's arrows, raising the waters of the ocean, burning as it were disconsolate

[1] Acacia Sirisa.
[2] A species of jasmine.
[3] Jasminum Zambac.
[4] Jasminum Grandiflorum.
[5] Jasminum Auriculatum.
[6] Alangium Hexapetalum.
[7] Not specialised in our dictionaries.
[8] Artemisia Indica.
[9] The many-flowered Nykanthes or Jasminum Zambac.
[10] Mimusops Elengi.
[11] Clerodendum Phlomoides or Symplocos Racemosa.
[12] Gaertnera Racemosa.
[13] Bignonia Suaveolens.
[14] Fragrant Oleander.
[15] Diospyros Glutinos or Dalbergia Ougeinense.
[16] Sha*t*pada, madhukarî, bhramara. The sha*t*pada are literally six-footed bees, as Stevenson correctly translated, but he strangely reckons them among the preternatural animals, like the four-tusked elephants, dear to the imagination of the *G*ains!

people when absent from their sweethearts, the large, glorious, wandering headmark of the celestial sphere—beloved in heart and soul by Rohinî[1]. Such was the glorious, beautiful, resplendent full moon which the queen saw. (38)

7. Then she saw the large sun, the dispeller of the mass of darkness, him of radiant form, red like the Asoka, the open Kimsuka, the bill of a parrot, or the Guñgârdha[2], the adorner of the lotus groups, the marker of the starry host, the lamp of the firmament, throttling as it were the mass of cold, the illustrious leader of the troop of planets, the destroyer of night, who only at his rising and setting may be well viewed, but (at all other times) is difficult to be regarded, who disperses evil-doers that stroll about at night, who stops the influence of cold, who always circles round Mount Meru, whose thousand rays obscure the lustre of other lights[3]. (39)

8. Then she saw an extremely beautiful and very large flag, a sight for all people, of a form attractive to the beholders. It was fastened to a golden staff with a tuft of many soft and waving peacock's feathers of blue, red, yellow, and white colours, and seemed as if it would pierce the brilliant, celestial sphere, with the brilliant lion on its top, who was white like crystal, pearlmother, Aṅka-stone, Kunda-flowers, spray of water, or a silver cup. (40)

---

[1] The commentators understand this passage (Rohinîmanahiyayavallabham) differently by explaining hiyaya by hitada, the lover of Rohinî who did her mind good.

[2] According to Stevenson: the red side of the retti seed.

[3] Or if we adopt a various reading, mentioned in the commentary, payadiya, we must translate: whose luminous glory was set forth by his thousand rays.

9. Then she saw a full vase of costly metal[1], splendent with fine gold, filled with pure water, excellent, of brilliant beauty, and shining with a bouquet of water lilies. It united many excellencies and all-auspicious marks, and stood on a lotus-(shaped foot), shining with excellent jewels[2]. It delighted the eyes, glittered and illumined all about; it was the abode of happy Fortune, free from all faults, fine, splendid, exquisitely beautiful, entwined with a wreath of fragrant flowers of all seasons. (41)

10. Then she saw a lake, called Lotus Lake, adorned with water lilies. Its yellow water was perfumed by lotuses opening in the rays of the morning sun; it abounded with swarms of aquatic animals, and fed fishes. It was large, and seemed to burn through the wide-spreading, glorious beauty of all kinds of lotuses[3]. Its shape and beauty were pleasing. The lotuses in it were licked by whole swarms of gay bees and mad drones. Pairs of swans, cranes, *K*akravâkas, ducks, Indian cranes, and many other lusty birds resorted to its waters, and on the leaves of its lotuses sparkled water-drops like pearls[4]. It was a sight, pleasing to the heart and the eye. (42)

11. Then she whose face was splendid like the

---

[1] The original has rayaya, silver, but as the commentary remarks, this would be in conflict with the epithet which we have put next, but which, in the original, is separated from it by many lines. Unless the author has blundered, which from his vague style seems far from impossible, the word must here have a more indefinite meaning than it usually has.

[2] This passage may also be translated: standing on a lotus filled with pollen, of excellent workmanship.

[3] Specialised in the text as kamala, kuvalaya, utpala, tâmarasa, and pu*nd*arîka.

[4] According to the commentary; the textus receptus is, many water-drops.

moon in autumn, saw the milk-ocean, equalling in beauty the breast of Lakshmî, which is white like the mass of moon-beams. Its waters increased in all four directions, and raged with ever-changing and moving, excessively high waves. It presented a splendid and pleasant spectacle as it rushed to and from the shore with its wind-raised, changeable, and moving billows, its tossing waves, and its rolling, splendid, transparent breakers. From it issued camphor-white foam under the lashing (tails) of great porpoises, fishes, whales, and other monsters of the deep[1]. Its agitated waters were in great uproar, occasioned by the vortex Gaṅgâvarta, which the vehemence and force of the great rivers produced; they rose, rushed onwards and backwards, and eddied. (43)

12. Then she saw a celestial abode excelling among the best of its kind, like the lotus (among flowers). It shone like the morning sun's disk, and was of a dazzling beauty. Its thousand and eight excellent columns (inlaid with) the best gold and heaps of jewels diffused a brilliant light like a heavenly lamp, and the pearls fastened to its curtains glittered. It was hung with brilliant divine garlands, and decorated with pictures of wolves, bulls, horses, men, dolphins, birds, snakes, Kinnaras, deer, *S*arabhas, Yaks, Sa*m*saktas[2], elephants, shrubs, and plants. There the Gandharvas performed their concerts, and the din of the drums of the gods,

[1] The original has timiṅgila-niruddha-tilitilika.

[2] Sa*m*sakta, which I do not find mentioned elsewhere, is explained, 'a kind of beast of prey;' I think that sa*m*sakta may be an adjective specifying the following word, and mean 'fighting' elephants.

imitating the sound of big and large rain-clouds, penetrated the whole inhabited world. It was highly delightful through curling, scented fumes of black aloe, the finest Kundurukka and Turushka, burning frankincense and other perfumes. It (shed) continuous light, was white, of excellent lustre, delighting the best of gods, and affording joy and pleasure. (44)

13. Then she saw an enormous heap of jewels containing Pulaka, Va*g*ra, Indranîla, Sasyaka, Karketana, Lohitâksha, Marakata, Prabâla, Saugandhika, Spha*t*ika, Ha*m*sagarbha, A*ñg*ana, and *K*andrakânta. Its base was on the level of the earth, and it illumined with its jewels even the sphere of the sky. It was high and resembled Mount Meru. (45)

14. And a fire. She saw a fire in vehement motion, fed with much-shining and honey-coloured ghee, smokeless, crackling, and extremely beautiful with its burning flames. The mass of its flames, which rose one above the other, seemed to interpenetrate each other, and the blaze of its flames appeared to bake the firmament in some places. (46)

After having seen these fine, beautiful, lovely, handsome dreams, the lotus-eyed queen awoke on her bed while the hair of her body bristled for joy.

Every mother of a Tîrthakara sees these fourteen dreams in that night in which the famous Arhat enters her womb. (46 b)

End of the Third Lecture.

When the Kshatriyâ*n*î Tri*s*alâ, having seen these fourteen illustrious, great dreams, awoke, she was glad, pleased, and joyful, &c. (see § 5, down to) rose from her couch, and descended from the footstool. Neither hasty nor trembling, with a quick and even gait like that of the royal swan, she went to the couch of the Kshatriya Siddhârtha. There she awakened the Kshatriya Siddhârtha, addressing him with kind, pleasing, amiable, tender, illustrious, beautiful, lucky, blest, auspicious, fortunate, heart-going, heart-easing, well-measured, sweet, and soft words. (47)

Then the Kshatriyânî Trisalâ, with the permission of king Siddhârtha, sat down on a chair of state inlaid with various jewels and precious stones in the form of arabesques; calm and composed, sitting on an excellent, comfortable chair, she addressed him with kind, pleasing, &c. (see last paragraph), words, and spoke thus: (48)

'O beloved of the gods, I was just now on my couch (as described in § 32), &c. (see § 5), and awoke after having seen the fourteen dreams; to wit, an elephant, &c. What, to be sure, O my lord, will be the happy result portended by these fourteen illustrious, great dreams?' (49)

When the Kshatriya Siddhârtha had heard and perceived this news from the Kshatriyânî Trisalâ, he glad, pleased, and joyful, &c. (see § 5, down to) firmly fixed the dreams in his mind, and entered upon considering them; he grasped the meaning of those dreams with his own innate intelligence and intuition which were preceded by reflection, and addressing the Kshatriyânî Trisalâ with kind, pleasing, &c., words, spoke thus: (50)

'O beloved of the gods, you have seen illustrious dreams, &c. (see § 9, down to) you will give birth to a lovely, handsome boy, who will be the ensign of our family, the lamp of our family, the crown[1] of our family, the frontal ornament

[1] Vadimsaya (avatamsaka) is here rendered by sekhara.

of our family, the maker of our family's glory, the sun of our family, the stay of our family, the maker of our family's joy and fame, the tree of our family, the exalter of our family; (a boy) with tender hands and feet, &c. (see § 9, down to the end). (51) And this boy, after having passed childhood, and, with just ripened intellect, having reached the state of youth, will become a brave, gallant, and valorous king, the lord of the realm, with a large and extensive army and train of waggons. (52) Therefore, O beloved of the gods, you have seen illustrious, &c. dreams, &c. (see § 9).'

In this way he repeatedly expressed his extreme satisfaction.

When the Kshatriyânî Trisalâ had heard and perceived this news from king Siddhârtha, she glad, pleased, and joyful, &c. (see § 12, down to) and spoke thus: (53)

'That is so, O beloved of the gods, &c. (see § 13, down to) as you have pronounced it.'

Thus saying she accepted the true meaning of the dreams, and with the permission of king Siddhârtha she rose from her chair of state, inlaid with various jewels and precious stones in the form of arabesques. She then returned to her own bed, neither hasty nor trembling, with a quick and even gait like that of the royal swan, and spoke thus: (54)

'These my excellent and pre-eminent dreams shall not be counteracted by other bad dreams.'

Accordingly she remained awake to save her dreams by means of (hearing) good, auspicious, pious, agreeable stories about gods and religious men. (55)

At the time of daybreak the Kshatriya Siddhârtha called his family servants and spoke thus: (56)

'Now, beloved of the gods, quickly make ready, or have made ready, the exterior hall of audience; see that it be sprinkled with scented water, cleaned, swept, and newly smeared, furnished with offerings of fragrant, excellent flowers of all five colours, made highly delightful through 'curling scented fumes, &c. (see § 32, down to) and turned, as it were, into a smelling box; also erect my throne, and having done this quickly return, and report on the execution of my orders.' (57)

When the family servants were thus spoken to by king Siddhârtha, they—glad, pleased, and joyful, &c. (see § 12, down to) on their heads, and modestly accepted the words of command, saying, 'Yes, master!' Then they left the presence of the Kshatriya Siddhârtha, and went to the exterior hall of audience, made it ready, and erected the throne (as described in the last paragraph). Having done this, they returned to the Kshatriya Siddhârtha; joining the palms of their hands so as to bring the ten nails together, laid the folded hands on their heads, and reported on the execution of their orders. (58)

Early at the wane of the night, when the bright morning disclosed the soft flowers of the full-blown lotuses and Nymphaeas, rose the sun: he was red like the A*s*oka, the open Ki*m*s*u*ka, the bill of a parrot or the Gu*ñg*ârdha; of an intense redness like that of the Bandhu*g*îvaka[1], the feet and eyes of the turtle dove, the scarlet eyes of the Indian cuckoo, a mass of China roses, or vermilion. He, the thousand-rayed maker of the day, shining in his radiance, awakened

[1] Pentapetes Phoenicea.

the groups of lotuses. When in due time the god of the day had risen and by the blows of his hands (or rays) the darkness was driven away, while the inhabited world was, as it were, dipped in saffron by the morning sun, the Kshatriya Siddhârtha rose from his bed, (59) descended from the footstool, went to the hall for gymnastic exercises, and entered it. There he applied himself to many wholesome exercises, jumped, wrestled, fenced, and fought till he got thoroughly tired: then he was anointed with hundredfold and thousandfold refined different kinds of oil, which nourished, beautified, invigorated, exhilarated, strengthened, and increased all senses and limbs. On an oiled hide he was shampooed by clever men with soft and tender palms of the hands and soles of the feet, who were well acquainted with the best qualities of the practices of anointing, kneading, and stretching; well trained, skilful, excellent, expert, intelligent, and never tiring. When by this fourfold agreeable treatment of the body the king's bones, flesh, skin, and hair had been benefited, and his fatigues banished, he left the hall for gymnastic exercises, (60) and entered the bathing-house. The pleasant bathing-room was very agreeable, and contained many windows[1], ornamented with pearls; its floor was decorated with mosaic of various jewels and precious stones. On the bathing-stool, inlaid with various jewels and precious stones in the form of arabesques, he comfortably sat down and bathed himself with water scented with flowers and perfumes, with tepid water and pure water, according to an excellent method of

[1] *Gâla*, windows formed by flat stones which are perforated so as to produce a network of more or less intricate design.

bathing, combined with healthy exercises. When this healthy excellent bathing under many hundred-fold pleasures was over, he dried his body with a long-haired, soft, scented, and coloured towel, put on a new and costly excellent robe, rubbed himself with fresh and fragrant Gosîrsha[1] and sandal, and ornamented himself with fine wreaths and sandal-ointment. He put on (ornaments) of jewels and pearls, hung round his neck fitting necklaces of eighteen, nine, and three strings of pearls, and one with a pearl pendant, and adorned himself with a zone. He put on a collar, rings, and charming ornaments of the hair, and encumbered his arms with excellent bracelets: he was of excessive beauty. His face was lighted up by earrings, and his head by a diadem; his breast was adorned and decked with necklaces, and his fingers were, as it were, gilded by his rings. His upper garment of fine cloth contained swinging pearl pendants. He put on, as an emblem of his undefeated knighthood, glittering, well-made, strong, excellent, beautiful armlets, made by clever artists of spotless and costly jewels, gold, and precious stones of many kinds. In short, the king was like the tree granting all desires, decorated and ornamented; an umbrella, hung with wreaths and garlands of Korin*t*a flowers, was held above him. He was fanned with white excellent chowries, while his appearance was greeted with auspicious shouts of victory. Surrounded by many chieftains, satraps, kings, princes, knights, sheriffs, heads of families, ministers, chief ministers, astrologers, counsellors, servants, dancing masters, citizens, traders, merchants, foremen of guilds, generals, leaders of cara-

[1] Gosîrsha is a superior kind of sandal.

vans, messengers, and frontier-guards, he—the lord and chief of men, a bull and a lion among men, shining with excellent lustre and glory, lovely to behold like the moon emerging from a great white cloud in the midst of the flock of the planets and of brilliant stars and asterisms—left the bathing-house, (61) entered the exterior hall of audience and sat down on his throne with the face towards the east. (62)

On the north-eastern side he ordered eight state chairs, covered with cloth and auspiciously decorated with white mustard, to be set down. Not too far from and not too near to himself, towards the interior of the palace, he had a curtain drawn. It was adorned with different jewels and precious stones, extremely worth seeing, very costly, and manufactured in a famous town; its soft cloth was all over covered with hundreds of patterns and decorated with pictures of wolves, bulls, horses, men, dolphins, birds, snakes, Kinnaras, deer, *S*arabhas, Yaks, Sa*m*saktas, elephants, shrubs, and plants. Behind it he ordered to be placed, for the Kshatriyâ*n*î Tri*s*alâ, an excellent chair of state, decorated with arabesques of different jewels and precious stones, outfitted with a coverlet and a soft pillow, covered with a white cloth, very soft and agreeable to the touch. Then he called the family servants and spoke thus: (63)

'Quickly, O beloved of the gods, call the interpreters of dreams who well know the science of prognostics with its eight branches, and are well versed in many sciences besides!'

When the family servants were thus spoken to by king Siddhârtha, they—glad, pleased, and joyful, &c.—laid the folded hands on their heads and modestly accepted the words of command, saying, 'Yes, master!' (64)

Then they left the presence of the Kshatriya Siddhârtha, went right through the town Ku*nd*apura to the houses of the interpreters of dreams, and called the interpreters of dreams. (65)

Then the interpreters of dreams, being called by the Kshatriya Siddhârtha's family servants, glad, pleased, and joyful, &c., bathed, made the offering (to the house-gods)[1], performed auspicious rites and expiatory[2] acts, put on excellent, lucky, pure court-dress, adorned their persons with small but costly ornaments, and put, for the sake of auspiciousness, white mustard and Dûrvâ grass on their heads. Thus they issued from their own houses and went right through the Kshatriya part of the town Ku*nd*a-pura to the front gate of king Siddhârtha's excellent palace, a jewel of its kind. (66)

There they assembled and went to the exterior hall of audience in the presence of the Kshatriya Siddhârtha. Joining the palms of their hands so as to bring the ten nails together, they laid the folded hands on their heads and gave him the greeting of victory. (67)

The king Siddhârtha saluted and honoured the interpreters of dreams, made them presents, and received them with respect. They sat down, one after the other, on the chairs of state which had been placed there before. (68) Then the Kshatriya Siddhârtha placed his wife Trisalâ behind the curtain, and taking flowers and fruits in his hands,

---

[1] Balikarman.

[2] Pâya*kkh*itta = prâya*s*kitta. The commentators explain it by pâda*kkh*upta, touching their feet in order to avoid the wicked eye.

addressed with utmost courtesy the interpreters of dreams: (69)

'O beloved of the gods, the Kshatriyâ*n*î Tri*s*alâ was just on her couch, &c. (see § 32, down to the end). (70 and 71) What to be sure, O beloved of the gods, will be the result portended by these fourteen illustrious great dreams?' (72)

When the interpreters of dreams had heard and perceived this news from the Kshatriya Siddhârtha, they—glad, pleased, and joyful, &c.—fixed the dreams in their minds, entered upon considering them, and conversed together. (73)

Having found, grasped, discussed, decided upon, and clearly understood the meaning of these dreams, they recited before king Siddhârtha the dream-books and spoke thus:

'O beloved of the gods, in our dream-books are enumerated forty-two (common) dreams and thirty great dreams. Now, O beloved of the gods, the mothers of universal monarchs or of Arhats wake up after seeing these fourteen great dreams out of the thirty great dreams, when the embryo of a universal monarch or an Arhat enters their womb; (74) viz. an elephant, a bull, &c. (75) The mothers of Vâsudevas wake up after seeing any seven great dreams out of these fourteen great dreams, when the embryo of a Vâsudeva enters their womb. (76) The mothers of Baladevas wake up after seeing any four great dreams out of these fourteen great dreams, when the embryo of a Baladeva enters their womb. (77) The mother of Mâ*nd*alikas wake up after seeing a single great dream out of these fourteen great dreams, when the embryo of a Mâ*nd*alika enters their womb. (78) Now, O beloved of the gods, the Kshatriyânî Trisalâ has seen these fourteen great dreams, &c. (see § 51, down to the end). (79) And this boy, &c. (see § 52, down to) the lord of a realm with a large and extensive army and train of waggons, a universal emperor or a Gina, the lord of the three worlds, the universal emperor of the law. (80). Therefore, O beloved of the gods, the Kshatriyânî Trisalâ has seen illustrious dreams,' &c. (see § 9). (81)

When king Siddhârtha had heard and perceived this news from the interpreter of dreams, he—glad, pleased, and joyful, &c.—spoke to them thus: (82)

'That is so, O beloved of the gods, &c. (see § 11, down to) as you have pronounced it.'

Thus saying he accepted the true meaning of the dreams, and honoured the interpreters of dreams with praise and plenty of food, flowers, perfumes, garlands, and ornaments. He made them a present in keeping with their station in life[1] and dismissed them. (83)

After this the Kshatriya Siddhârtha rose from his throne, went to the Kshatriyânî Trisalâ behind the curtain, and addressed her thus: (84)

'Now, O beloved of the gods, you have seen these fourteen great dreams, &c. (see §§ 79, 80, down to) emperor of the law.' (85, 86)

When the Kshatriyânî Trisalâ had heard and perceived this news, she—glad, pleased, and joyful, &c.—accepted the true meaning of the dreams. (87) With the permission of king Siddhârtha she rose from her chair of state which was decorated with arabesques of various jewels and precious stones,

[1] Or a life annuity.

and returned to her own apartments, neither hasty nor trembling, with a quick and even gait like that of the royal swan. (88)

From that moment in which the Venerable Ascetic Mahâvîra was brought into the family of the *Gñâtris*, many demons[1] in Vaisramana's service, belonging to the animal world, brought, on Sakra's command, to the palace of king Siddhârtha, old and ancient treasures, of which the owners, deponers, and families to whom they originally belonged were dead and extinct, and which were hidden in villages, or mines, or scot-free towns, or towns with earth walls, or towns with low walls, or isolated towns, or towns accessible by land and water, or towns accessible either by land or by water only, or in natural strongholds, or in halting-places for processions or for caravans, in triangular places, or in places where three or four roads meet, or in courtyards, or squares, or high roads, or on the site of villages or towns, or in drains of villages or towns, or in bazaars, or temples, or assembling halls, or wells, or parks, or gardens, or woods, or groves, or burying-places, or empty houses, or mountain caves, or hermits' cells, or secret places between walls, or in houses on an elevation, or houses for audience, or palaces. (89)

In the night in which the Venerable Ascetic Mahâvîra was brought into the family of the *Gñâtris* their silver increased, their gold increased; their riches, corn, majesty, and kingdom increased; their army, train, treasure, storehouse, town, seraglio, subjects, and glory increased; their real valuable property, as riches, gold, precious stones, jewels,

[1] *Gambhaya* = *Grimbhaka*; what they are is not said in the commentaries.

pearls, conches, stones, corals, rubies, &c., the intensity of their popularity and liberality highly increased. At that time the following personal, reflectional, desirable idea occurred to parents of the Venerable Ascetic Mahâvîra: (90)

'From the moment that this our boy has been begotten, our silver increased, our gold increased, &c. (see § 90, down to) the intensity of our liberality and popularity highly increased. Therefore when this our boy will be born, we shall give him the fit name, attributive and conformable to his quality—Vardhamâna[1].' (91)

Now the Venerable Ascetic Mahâvîra, out of compassion for his mother, did not move nor stir nor quiver, but remained quiet, stiff, and motionless. Then the following, &c. (see § 90, down to) idea occurred to the mind of the Kshatriyâ*n*î Tri*s*alâ: 'The fruit of my womb has been taken from me, it has died, it is fallen, it is lost. Formerly it moved, now it does not move.' Thus with anxious thoughts and ideas, plunged in a sea of sorrow and misery, reposing her head on her hand, overcome by painful reflections, and casting her eyes on the ground she meditated. And in the palace of king Siddhârtha the music of drums and stringed instruments, the clapping of hands, the dramatical performances, and the amusements of the people ceased, and mournful dejection reigned there. (92)

Then the Venerable Ascetic Mahâvîra, knowing that such an internal, &c. (see § 90, down to) idea had occurred to the mind of his mother, he quivered a little. (93)

[1] I.e. 'the increasing one' not as we should expect, and Stevenson translated, the Increaser.

Feeling her child quivering, trembling, moving, and stirring, the Kshatriyânî Trisalâ—glad, pleased, and joyful, &c.—spoke thus: 'No, forsooth, the fruit of my womb has not been taken from me, it has not died, it is not fallen, it is not lost. Formerly it did not move, but now it does move.' Thus she was glad, pleased, and joyful, &c.

Then the Venerable Ascetic Mahâvîra, while in her womb, formed the following resolution: 'It will not behove me, during the life of my parents, to tear out my hair, and leaving the house to enter the state of houselessness.' (94)

Bathing, making offerings to the house-gods, performing auspicious rites and expiatory acts, and adorning herself with all ornaments, the Kshatriyânî Trisalâ kept off sickness, sorrow, fainting, fear, and fatigue by food and clothing, perfumes and garlands, which were not too cold nor too hot, not too bitter nor too pungent, not too astringent nor too sour nor too sweet, not too smooth nor too rough, not too wet nor too dry, but all just suiting the season. In the proper place and time she ate only such food which was good, sufficient, and healthy for the nourishment of her child. She took her walks in places which were empty and agreeable as well as delightful to the mind; her desires were laudable, fulfilled, honoured, not disregarded, but complied with and executed; she most comfortably dozed, reposed, remained, sat, and laid on unobjectionable and soft beds and seats, and thus most comfortably carried her unborn child. (95)

In that period, in that age the Venerable Ascetic Mahâvîra[1]—after the lapse of nine months and

[1] The whole passage is in some disorder; for the subject is she (Trisalâ) and the object is 'boy,' yet 'the Venerable Ascetic Mahâ-

seven and a half days, in the first month of summer, in the second fortnight, the dark (fortnight) of *K*aitra, on its fourteenth day, [while all planets were in their exaltations, the moon in her principal conjunction, and the sky in all its directions clear, bright, and pure; while a favourable and agreeable low wind swept the earth; at the time when the fields were green and all people glad and amusing themselves][1] in the middle of the night while the moon was in conjunction with the asterism Uttaraphalgunî—(Tri*s*alâ), perfectly healthy herself, gave birth to a perfectly healthy boy. (96)[2]

End of the Fourth Lecture.

In that night in which the Venerable Ascetic Mahâvîra was born, there was a divine lustre originated by many descending and ascending gods and goddesses, and in the universe, resplendent with one light, the conflux of gods occasioned great confusion and noise. (97)[3]

In that night in which the Venerable Ascetic Mahâvîra was born, many demons in Vai*s*rama*n*a's

---

vîra' is also put in the nominative. It seems that the author or the copyists added the three words Samâ*n*e Bhagava*m* Mahâvîre because they usually followed the beginning: te*n*a*m* kâle*n*a*m* te*n*a*m* samae*n*a*m*. The same disorder occurs in all corresponding passages which we shall meet with later on.

[1] The passage in brackets seems to be a later addition; for it is wanting in my oldest MS., and the commentator says that it was not seen in many books. The occurrence of the astrological term exaltation (u*kk*a = ὕψωμα) in this passage proves it to be inserted after 300 A.D. For about that time Greek astrology had been introduced in India, as I have shown in my dissertation: De Astrologiae Indicae 'Hora' appellatae originibus, Bonn, 1872.

[2] Cf. Â*k*ârâṅga Sûtra II, 15, § 6.

[3] Cf. Â*k*ârâṅga Sûtra II, 15, § 7.

service belonging to the animal world, rained down on the palace of king Siddhârtha one great shower of silver, gold, diamonds, clothes, ornaments, leaves, flowers, fruits, seeds, garlands, perfumes, sandal, powder, and riches. (98)[1]

After the Bhavanapati, Vyantara, *G*yotishka, and Vaimânika gods had celebrated the feast of the inauguration of the Tîrthakara's birthday, the Kshatriya Siddhârtha called, at the break of the morning, together the town policemen and addressed them thus: (99)

'O beloved of the gods, quickly set free all prisoners in the town of Ku*nd*apura, increase measures and weights, give order that the whole town of Ku*nd*apura with its suburbs be sprinkled with water, swept, and smeared (with cowdung, &c.) that in triangular places, in places where three or four roads meet, in courtyards, in squares, and in thoroughfares, the middle of the road and the path along the shops be sprinkled, cleaned, and swept; that platforms be erected one above the other; that the town be decorated with variously coloured flags and banners, and adorned with painted pavilions[2]; that the walls bear impressions in Gosîrsha, fresh red sandal, and Dardara[3] of the hand with outstretched fingers; that luck-foreboding vases be put on the floor, and pots of the same kind be disposed round every door and arch; that big, round, and long garlands, wreaths, and festoons be hung low

[1] Cf. Â*k*ârâṅga Sûtra II, 15, § 8.

[2] According to the commentary this may also be translated: smeared (with cowdung) and whitewashed.

[3] Dardara is sandal brought from Dardara. All who have travelled in India will have noticed on walls the impressions of the hand mentioned in the text.

and high; that the town be furnished with offerings, &c. (see § 32, down to) smelling box; that players, dancers, rope-dancers, wrestlers, boxers, jesters, story-tellers, ballad-singers, actors[1], messengers[2], pole-dancers, fruit-mongers, bag-pipers, lute-players, and many Tâlâkaras[3] be present. Erect and order to erect thousands of pillars and poles, and report on the execution of my orders.' (100)

When the family servants were thus spoken to by king Siddhârtha, they—glad, pleased, and joyful, &c. (see § 58)—accepted the words of command, saying, 'Yes, master!'

Then they set free all prisoners, &c. (see § 100, down to) pillars and poles. Having done this, they returned to king Siddhârtha, and laying their hands on their heads, reported on the execution of his orders. (101)

The king Siddhârtha then went to the hall for gymnastic exercises, &c. (see §§ 60 and 61[4]). (After having bathed) the king accompanied by his whole seraglio[4], and adorned with flowers, scented robes, garlands, and ornaments, held during ten days the festival in celebration of the birth of a heir to his kingdom; (it was held) under the continuous din and sound of trumpets, with great state and splendour, with a great train of soldiers, vehicles, and guests, under the sound, din, and noise of conches,

---

[1] Lasakâ bhânda.

[2] Ârakshakâs talârâ, âkhyâyakâ vâ. The translation is conjectural.

[3] Tâlâkaras are those who by clapping the hands beat the time during a performance of music.

[4] The text has down to 'with his whole seraglio.' But as no such words occur in the passage in question, they seem to point to the description in § 115, which contains the latter part of this passage.

cymbals, drums, castanets, horns, small drums, kettle drums, Muragas, M*ri*dangas, and Dundubhis [1], which were accompanied at the same time by trumpets [2]. The customs, taxes, and confiscations were released, buying and selling prohibited, no policemen were allowed to enter houses, great and small fines were remitted, and debts cancelled. Numberless excellent actors performed [3] and many Tâlâ*k*aras were present, drums sounded harmoniously, fresh garlands and wreaths were seen everywhere, and the whole population in the town and in the country rejoiced and was in full glee. (102)

When the ten days of this festival were over, the king Siddhârtha gave and ordered to be given hundreds and thousands and hundred-thousands of offerings to the gods, gifts, and portions (of goods); he received and ordered to be received hundreds, thousands, and hundred-thousands of presents. (103) [4]

The parents of the Venerable Ascetic Mahâvîra celebrated the birth of their heir on the first day, on the third day they showed him the sun and the moon, on the sixth day they observed the religious vigil; after the eleventh day, when the impure operations and ceremonies connected with the birth of a child had been performed, and the twelfth day had come, they prepared plenty of food, drink, spices, and sweetmeats, invited their friends, relations, kinsmen, agnates, cognates, and followers, together with the *Gñ*ât*ri*ka Kshatriyas. Then they bathed, made

[1] Muragas, M*ri*dangas, Dundubhis are different kinds of drums.

[2] Samaga-*g*amaga-turiya.

[3] This is the translation of a varia lectio. The adopted text has: while courtezans and excellent actors performed.

[4] Cf. Â*k*ârâṅga Sûtra II, 15, § 11.

offerings (to the house-gods), and performed auspicious rites and expiatory acts, put on excellent, lucky, pure court-dress, and adorned their persons with small but costly ornaments. At dinner-time they sat down on excellent, comfortable chairs in the dining-hall, and together with their friends, relations, kinsmen, agnates, cognates and followers, and with the *G*ñât*ri*ka Kshatriyas they partook, ate, tasted, and interchanged (bits) of a large collation of food, drink, spices, and sweetmeats. (104)

After dinner they went (to the meeting hall[1]) after having cleansed their mouths and washed; when perfectly clean, they regaled and honoured their friends, &c. (see § 104, down to) *G*ñât*ri*ka Kshatriyas with many flowers, clothes, perfumes, garlands, and ornaments. Then they spoke thus to their friends, &c.: (105)

'Formerly, O beloved of the gods, when we had begotten this our boy, the following personal, reflectional, desirable idea occurred to our mind: "From the moment that this our boy has been begotten, our silver increased, our gold increased, &c. (see § 91, down to) Vardhamâna. Now our wishes have been fulfilled, therefore shall the name of our boy be Vardhamâna."' (106, 107)[2]

The Venerable Ascetic Mahâvîra belonged to the Kâ*s*yapa gotra. His three names have thus been recorded: by his parents he was called Vardhamâna; because he is devoid of love and hate, he is called *S*rama*n*a (i. e. Ascetic); because he stands fast in midst of dangers and fears, patiently bears hardships and calamities, adheres to the chosen rules of

[1] This is an addition of the commentator.

[2] Cf. Â*k*ârâṅga Sûtra II, 15, § 12.

penance, is wise, indifferent to pleasure and pain, rich in control, and gifted with fortitude, the name Venerable Ascetic Mahâvîra has been given him by the gods. (108)[1]

The Venerable Ascetic Mahâvîra's father belonged to the Kâsyapa gotra; he had three names: Siddhârtha, *S*reyâ*m*sa, and *G*asa*m*sa, &c. (see Â*k*ârâṅga Sûtra II, 15, § 15, down to) *S*eshavatî and Ya*s*o-vatî. (109)

The Venerable Ascetic Mahâvîra—clever, with the aspirations of a clever man, of great beauty, controlling (his senses), lucky, and modest; a *Gñ*â*tri* Kshatriya, the son of a *Gñ*â*tri* Kshatriya; the moon of the clan of the *Gñ*â*tri*s; a Videha, the son of Videhadattâ, a native of Videha, a prince of Videha—had lived thirty years in Videha when his parents went to the world of the gods (i. e. died), and he with the permission of his elder brother and the authorities of the kingdom[2] fulfilled his promise. At that moment the Laukântika gods, following the established custom, praised and hymned him with these kind, pleasing, &c. (see § 47, down to) sweet, and soft words: (110)

'Victory, victory to thee, gladdener of the world! Victory, victory to thee, lucky one! Luck to thee, bull of the best Kshatriyas! Awake, reverend lord of the world! Establish the religion of the law which benefits all living beings in the whole universe! It will bring supreme benefit to all living beings in all the world!'

Thus they raised the shout of victory. (111)

---

[1] See Â*k*ârâṅga Sûtra II, 15, § 15.

[2] Guru-mahattara is the original of the last words, which I have translated according to the explanation of the commentary.

Before the Venerable Ascetic Mahâvîra had adopted the life of a householder (i.e. before his marriage) he possessed supreme, unlimited[1], unimpeded knowledge and intuition. The Venerable Ascetic Mahâvîra perceived with this his supreme unlimited knowledge and intuition that the time for his Renunciation[2] had come. He left his silver, he left his gold, he left his riches, corn, majesty, and kingdom; his army, grain, treasure, storehouse, town, seraglio, and subjects; he quitted and rejected his real, valuable property, such as riches, gold, precious stones, jewels, pearls, conches, stones, corals, rubies, &c.; he distributed presents through proper persons, he distributed presents among indigent persons. (112)[3]

In that period, in that age, in the first month of winter, in the first fortnight, in the dark (fortnight) of Mârgasiras, on its tenth day, when the shadow had turned towards the east and the (first) Paurushî[4] was full and over, on the day called Suvrata, in the Muhûrta called Vigaya, in the palankin *K*andraprabhâ, (Mahâvîra) was followed on his way[5] by a train of gods, men, and Asuras, (and surrounded) by a swarm of shell-blowers, proclaimers, pattivallas,

[1] Âbhogika. It is inferior to the Avadhi knowledge. In a quotation it is said that (the knowledge) of the Nairayikas, Devas, and Tîrthakaras does not reach the Avadhi; it is total with them, but with others only partial.

[2] Nishkrama*n*a = pravragyâ.

[3] Cf. A*k*ârâṅga Sûtra II, 15, § 17.

[4] Yâma or time of three hours.

[5] Sama*n*ugammamâ*n*a-magge. The commentator divides sama*n*ugammamâ*n*am agge, and explains the passage thus: him who was followed by, &c., and surrounded by, &c. (agre parivr*i*tam) they praised and hymned, and the authorities spoke thus to him.

courtiers, men carrying others on the back, heralds, and bell bearers. They praised and hymned him with these kind, pleasing, &c. (see § 47, down to) sweet and soft words: (113)

'Victory, victory to thee, gladdener of the world! Victory to thee, lucky one! Luck to thee! with undisturbed knowledge, intuition, and good conduct conquer the unconquered Senses; defend the conquered Law of the *S*rama*n*as; Majesty, conquering all obstacles, live in Perfection; put down with thy devotion Love and Hate, the (dangerous) wrestlers; vigorously gird thy loins with constancy and overcome the eight Karmans, our foes, with supreme, pure meditation; heedful raise the banner of content, O Hero! in the arena of the three worlds gain the supreme, best knowledge, called Kevala, which is free from obscurity; obtain the pre-eminent highest rank (i. e. final liberation) on that straight road which the best *G*inas have taught; beat the army of obstacles! Victory, victory to thee, bull of the best Kshatriyas! Many days, many fortnights, many months, many seasons, many half-years, many years be not afraid of hardships and calamities, patiently bear dangers and fears; be free from obstacles in the practice of the law!'

Thus they raised the shout of victory. (114)

Then the Venerable Ascetic Mahâvîra—gazed on by a circle of thousands of eyes[1], praised by a circle of thousands of mouths, extolled by a circle of thousands of hearts, being the object of many thousands of wishes, desired because of his splendour, beauty, and virtues, pointed out by a circle of thousands of

[1] Literally, by thousands of circles of eyes, &c. &c.

forefingers, answering with (a salam) of his right hand a circle of thousands of joined hands of thousands of men and women, passing along a row of thousands of palaces, greeted by sweet and delightful music, as beating of time, performance on the Vînâ, Tûrya, and the great drum, in which joined shouts of victory, and the low and pleasing murmur of the people; accompanied by all his pomp, all his splendour, all his army, all his train, by all his retinue, by all his magnificence, by all his grandeur, by all his ornaments, by all the tumult, by all the throng, by all subjects, by all actors, by all time-beaters, by the whole seraglio; adorned with flowers, scented robes, garlands, and ornaments, &c. (see § 102, down to) which were accompanied at the same time by trumpets—went right through Kundapura to a park called the Shandavana of the *Gñâtris* and proceeded to the excellent tree Asoka. (115) There under the excellent tree Asoka he caused his palankin to stop, descended from his palankin, took off his ornaments, garlands, and finery with his own hands, and with his own hands plucked out his hair in five handfuls. When the moon was in conjunction with the asterism Uttaraphalgunî, he, after fasting two and a half days[1] without drinking water, put on a divine robe, and quite alone, nobody else being present, he tore out his hair and leaving the house entered the state of houselessness. (116)[2]

The Venerable Ascetic Mahâvîra for a year and

[1] I. e. taking only one meal in three days. He fasted therefore two continuous days and the first part of the third.

[2] Cf. Âkârâṅga Sûtra II, 15, § 22.

a month wore clothes; after that time he walked about naked, and accepted the alms in the hollow of his hand. For more than twelve years the Venerable Ascetic Mahâvîra neglected his body and abandoned the care of it; he with equanimity bore, underwent, and suffered all pleasant or unpleasant occurrences arising from divine powers, men, or animals. (117)[1]

Henceforth the Venerable Ascetic Mahâvîra was houseless, circumspect[2] in his walking, circumspect in his speaking, circumspect in his begging, circumspect in his accepting (anything), in the carrying of his outfit and drinking vessel; circumspect in evacuating excrements, urine, saliva, mucus, and uncleanliness of the body; circumspect in his thoughts, circumspect in his words, circumspect in his acts[3]; guarding his thoughts, guarding his words, guarding his acts, guarding his senses, guarding his chastity; without wrath, without pride, without deceit, without greed; calm, tranquil, composed, liberated, free from temptations[4], without egoism, without property; he had cut off all earthly ties, and was not stained by any worldliness: as water does not adhere to a copper vessel, or collyrium to mother of pearl (so sins found no place in him); his course was unobstructed like that of Life; like the firmament he wanted no support; like the wind he knew no obstacles; his heart was pure like the water (of rivers or tanks) in autumn; nothing could soil him like the leaf of

[1] Cf. Âkârâṅga Sûtra II, 15, § 23.

[2] Circumspect is samita, guarding gupta; the former relates to execution of good acts, the latter to the abstinence from bad ones.

[3] This is the triad manas mind, vâk speech, kâya body.

[4] Âsrava.

a lotus; his senses were well protected like those of a tortoise; he was single and alone like the horn of a rhinoceros; he was free like a bird; he was always waking like the fabulous bird Bhâru*nd*a[1], valorous like an elephant, strong like a bull, difficult to attack like a lion, steady and firm like Mount Mandara, deep like the ocean, mild like the moon, refulgent like the sun, pure like excellent gold[2]; like the earth he patiently bore everything; like a well-kindled fire he shone in his splendour.

These words have been summarised in two verses:

A vessel, mother of pearl, life, firmament, wind, water in autumn, leaf of lotus, a tortoise, a bird, a rhinoceros, and Bhâru*nd*a; I

An elephant, a bull, a lion, the king of the mountains, and the ocean unshaken—the moon, the sun, gold, the earth, well-kindled fire. II

There were no obstacles anywhere for the Venerable One. The obstacles have been declared to be of four kinds, viz. with regard to matter, space, time, affects. With regard to matter: in

---

[1] Each of these birds has one body, two necks, and three legs.

[2] The last three similes cannot be translated accurately, as they contain puns which must be lost in the translation. The moon is somalese, of soft light, but Mahâvîra has pure thoughts (le*s*yâ, manaso bahirvikâra); the sun is dittateo of splendent light, Mahâvîra of splendent vigour; gold is *g*âyarûva, a synonym of ka*n*aga gold, Mahâvîra always retains his own nature. It is worthy of remark that only two regular puns (for the second is but a common metaphor) occur in a passage in which a later writer would have strained his genius to the utmost to turn every simile into a pun. The difference of style is best seen on comparing this passage with e.g. the description of the nun Sarasvatî and of autumn in the Kâlakâ*k*ârya Kathânaka; see my edition, Zeitschrift der Deutschen Morgenl. Gesellschaft, XXXIV, pp. 260, 263.

things animate, inanimate, and of a mixed state; with regard to space: in a village or a town or in a wood or in a field or a threshing-floor or a house[1] or a court-yard; with regard to time: in a Samaya[2] or an Âvalikâ or in the time of a respiration or in a Stoka or in a Kshana or in a Lava or in a Muhûrta or in a day or in a fortnight or in a month or in a season or in a half year or in a year or in a long space of time; with regard to affects: in wrath or in pride or in deceit or in greed or in fear or in mirth or in love or in hate or in quarrelling or in calumny or in tale-bearing or in scandal or in pleasure or pain or in deceitful falsehood, &c. (all down to)[3] or in the evil of wrong belief. There was nothing of this kind in the Venerable One. (118)

The Venerable One lived, except in the rainy season, all the eight months of summer and winter, in villages only a single night, in towns only five nights; he was indifferent alike to the smell of ordure and of sandal, to straw and jewels, dirt and gold, pleasure and pain, attached neither to this world nor to that beyond, desiring neither life nor death, arrived at the other shore of the samsâra, and he exerted himself for the suppression of the defilement of Karman. (119)

---

[1] Ghare vâ, omitted in my edition.

[2] Different names of divisions of time; a Stoka contains seven respirations, a Kshana many (bahutara) respirations (according to another commentary a Kshana contains six Nâdikâs, it is the sixth part of a Ghatî), a Lava contains seven Stokas, and a Muhûrta seventy Lavas. This system of dividing time differs from all other known; compare Colebrooke, Misc. Essays, II², pp. 540, 541. Wilson, Vishnu Purâna, I², p. 47, note 2.—Expunge pakkhe vâ in my edition.

[3] The same passage occurs in the Aupapâtika Sûtra (ed. Leumann, § 87), but without an indication that it is not complete.

With supreme knowledge, with supreme intuition, with supreme conduct, in blameless lodgings, in blameless wandering, with supreme valour, with supreme uprightness, with supreme mildness, with supreme dexterity, with supreme patience, with supreme freedom from passions, with supreme control, with supreme contentment, with supreme understanding, on the supreme path to final liberation, which is the fruit of veracity, control, penance, and good conduct, the Venerable One meditated on himself for twelve years.

During the thirteenth year, in the second month of summer, in the fourth fortnight, the light (fortnight) of Vais*â*kha, on its tenth day, when the shadow had turned towards the east and the first wake was over, on the day called Suvrata, in the Muhûrta called Vi*g*aya, outside of the town *Gri*mbhikagrâma on the bank of the river Ri*g*upâlika, not far from an old temple, in the field of the householder Sâmâga[1], under a Sal tree, when the moon was in conjunction with the asterism Uttaraphalgunî, (the Venerable One) in a squatting position with joined heels, exposing himself to the heat of the sun, after fasting two and a half days without drinking water, being engaged in deep meditation, reached the highest knowledge and intuition, called Kevala, which is infinite, supreme, unobstructed, unimpeded, complete, and full. (120)[2]

When the Venerable Ascetic Mahâvîra had become a *Gi*n*a* and Arhat, he was a Kevalin, omniscient and comprehending all objects; he knew and saw all conditions of the world, of gods,

[1] Or Sâmâka.

[2] Cf. Â*k*ârânga Sûtra II, 15, § 25.

men, and demons: whence they come, whither they go, whether they are born as men or animals (*k*yavana) or become gods or hell-beings (upapâda), the ideas, the thoughts of their minds, the food, doings, desires, the open and secret deeds of all the living beings in the whole world; he the Arhat, for whom there is no secret, knew and saw all conditions of all living beings in the world, what they thought, spoke, or did at any moment. (121)[1]

In that period, in that age the Venerable Ascetic Mahâvîra stayed the first rainy season in Asthikagrâma[2], three rainy seasons in *K*ampâ and P*ri*sh*t*i*k*ampâ, twelve in Vai*s*âlî and Vâ*n*i*g*agrâma, fourteen in Râ*g*ag*ri*ha and the suburb[3] of Nâlandâ, six in Mithilâ, two in Bhadrikâ, one in Âlabhikâ, one in Pa*n*itabhûmi[4], one in *S*râvastî, one in the town of Pâpâ[5] in king Hastipâla's office of the writers: that was his very last rainy season. (122)

In the fourth month of that rainy season, in the seventh fortnight, in the dark (fortnight) of Kârttika, on its fifteenth day, in the last night, in the town of Pâpâ, in king Hastipâla's office of the writers, the Venerable Ascetic Mahâvîra died, went off, quitted the world, cut asunder the ties of birth, old age, and death; became a Siddha, a Buddha,

---

[1] Cf. Â*k*ârâṅga Sûtra II, 15, § 26.

[2] According to the commentary it was formerly called Vardhamâna, but it has since been called Asthikagrâma, because a Yaksha *S*ûlapâ*n*î had there collected an enormous heap of bones of the people whom he had killed. On that heap of bones the inhabitants had built a temple.

[3] Bâhirikâ?

[4] A place in Vagrabhûmi according to the commentaries.

[5] Ma*gg*h*i*mâ Pâpâ, the middle town Pâpâ.

a Mukta, a maker of the end (to all misery), finally liberated, freed from all pains. (123)

This occurred in the year called *K*andra, the second (of the lustrum)[1]; in the month called Prîtivardhana; in the fortnight Nandivardhana; on the day Suvratâgni[2], surnamed Upa*s*ama; in the night called Devânandâ, surnamed Nir*ri*ti; in the Lava called Ar*k*ya; in the respiration called Mukta[3]; in the Stoka called Siddha; in the Kara*n*a called Nâga; in the Muhûrta called *S*arvârtha-siddha; while the moon was in conjunction with the asterism Svâti he died, &c. (see above, all down to) freed from all pains. (124)

That night in which the Venerable Ascetic Mahâvîra died, &c. (all down to) freed from all pains, was lighted up by many descending and ascending gods. (125)

In that night in which the Venerable Ascetic Mahâvîra died, &c. (all down to) freed from all pains, a great confusion and noise was originated by many descending and ascending gods. (126)

In that night in which the Venerable Ascetic Mahâvîra died, &c. (all down to) freed from all pains, his oldest disciple, the monk Indrabhûti of the Gautama gotra, cut asunder the tie of friendship which he had for his master[4], and obtained the

---

[1] The yuga or lustrum contains five years; the third and fifth years are leap years, called abhivardhita, the rest are common years of 354 days and are called *k*andra. The day has 1262 bhâgas.

[2] Some MSS. and the commentary have aggivesa.

[3] Or Supta.

[4] Indrabhûti was on a mission to convert somebody when Mahâvîra died. Being aware that love had no place in one who is free from passion, he suppressed his friendship for his teacher and

highest knowledge and intuition, called Kevala, which is infinite, supreme, &c., complete, and full. (127)

In that night in which the Venerable Ascetic Mahâvîra died, &c. (all down to) freed from all pains, the eighteen confederate kings of Kâsî and Kosala, the nine Mallakis and nine Likkhavis[1], on the day of new moon, instituted an illumination[2] on the Poshadha, which was a fasting day; for they said: 'Since the light of intelligence is gone, let us make an illumination of material matter!' (128)

In that night in which the Venerable Ascetic Mahâvîra died, &c. (all down to) freed from all pains, the great Graha[3] called Kshudrâtma, resembling a heap of ashes, which remains for two thousand years in one asterism, entered the natal

became a Kevalin; he died twelve years after, having lived fifty years as a monk, and altogether ninety-two years.

[1] They were tributary to *Ketaka*, king of Vaisâlî and maternal uncle of Mahâvîra. Instead of Li*kkh*avi, which form is used by the Buddhists, the *G*ainas have Le*kkh*akî as the Sanskrit form of the Prâkrit Le*kkh*aî, which may be either.

[2] Pârâbhoya*m* or vârâbhoya*m*. The meaning of this word is not clear, and the commentator also did not know anything certain about it. He therefore tries three different etymological explanations, which are all equally fanciful. I have adopted one which makes vârâbhoya to stand for Sanskrit dvârâbhoga, which is explained prâdîpa, lamp; for this best suits the meaning of the whole passage. The *G*ainas celebrate the Nirvâ*n*a of Mahâvîra with an illumination on the night of new moon in the month Kârttika.

[3] It is not clear what is intended by this Graha, the thirtieth in the list of Grahas. Stevenson supposes it to have been a comet appearing at that time. There was a comet at the time of the battle of Salamis, as Pliny tells us, Hist. Nat. II, 25, which would answer pretty well as regards chronology. But it had the form of a horn and not that of a heap of ashes. We must therefore dismiss the idea of identifying it with the Graha in question, and confess that we are at a loss to clear up the mystery of this Graha.

asterism of the Venerable Ascetic Mahâvîra. (129) From the moment in which the great Graha, &c., entered the natal asterism of the Venerable Ascetic Mahâvîra, there will not be paid much respect and honour to the *S*rama*n*as, the Nirgrantha monks and nuns. (130) But when the great Graha, &c., leaves that natal asterism, there will be paid much respect and honour to the *S*rama*n*as, the Nirgrantha monks and nuns. (131)

In that night in which the Venerable Ascetic Mahâvîra died, &c. (all down to) freed from all pains, the animalcule called Anuddharî was originated: which when at rest and not moving, is not easily seen by Nirgrantha monks and nuns who have not yet reached the state of perfection, but which when moving and not at rest, is easily seen by Nirgrantha monks and nuns who have not yet reached the state of perfection. (132) On seeing this (animalcule) many Nirgrantha monks and nuns must refuse to accept the offered alms.

'Master, why has this been said?' 'After this time the observance of control will be difficult.' (133)

In that period, in that age the Venerable Ascetic Mahâvîra had an excellent community[1] of fourteen thousand *S*rama*n*as with Indrabhûti at their head; (134) thirty-six thousand nuns with *K*andanâ at their head; (135) one hundred and fifty-nine thousand lay votaries with *S*aṅkha*s*ataka at their head; (136) three hundred and eighteen

---

[1] The original has: ukkosiyâ sama*n*asa*m*payâ; ukkosiya is translated utk*ri*sh*t*a; in the sequel I abridge the similar passages which are all constructed on the same model as § 134. It is to be noticed that these numbers though exaggerated are nevertheless rather moderate. Compare the note to the List of the Sthaviras, § 1

thousand female lay votaries with Sulasâ and Revatî at their head; (137) three hundred sages who knew the fourteen Pûrvas, who though no *G*inas came very near them, who knew the combination of all letters, and like *G*ina preached according to the truth; (138) thirteen hundred sages who were possessed of the Avadhi-knowledge and superior qualities; (139) seven hundred Kevalins who possessed the combined[1] best knowledge and intuition; (140) seven hundred who could transform themselves, and, though no gods, had obtained the powers (*ri*ddhi) of gods; (141) five hundred sages of mighty intellect[2] who know the mental conditions of all developed beings possessed of intellect and five senses in the two and a half continents and two oceans; (142) four hundred professors who were never vanquished in the disputes occurring in the assemblies of gods, men, and Asuras; (143) seven hundred male and fourteen hundred female disciples who reached perfection, &c. (all down to) freed from all pains; (144) eight hundred sages in their last birth who were happy as regards their station, happy as regards their existence[3], lucky as regards their future. (145)

[1] Sambhinna. According to the commentary this word has been explained in two opposite ways. Siddhasena Divâkara makes it out to denote that knowledge and intuition functionate at the same time, while *G*inabhadraga*n*i in the Siddhântah*ri*daya says that in our case knowledge and intuition do functionate alternately.

[2] This is that knowledge which is called mana*h*paryâya or the knowledge which divines the thoughts of all people.

[3] Station (gati) is explained devagati, state of the gods, existence (thiti), devasthiti, devâyûrûpa, existence of the gods, having the length of life of the gods.

The Venerable Ascetic Mahâvîra instituted two epochs in his capacity of a Maker of an end: the epoch relating to generations, and the epoch relating to psychical condition; in the third generation ended the former epoch, and in the fourth year of his Kevaliship the latter. (146)[1]

In that period, in that age the Venerable Ascetic Mahâvîra lived thirty years as a householder, more than full twelve years in a state inferior to perfection, something less than thirty years as a Kevalin, forty-two years as a monk, and seventy-two years on the whole. When his Karman which produces Vedanîya (or what one has to experience in this world), Âyus (length of life), name, and family, had been exhausted, when in this Avasarpi*n*î era the greater part of the Du*h*shamasushamâ period had elapsed and only three years and eight and a half months were left, when the moon was in conjunction with the asterism Svâti, at the time of early morning, in the town of Pâpâ, and in king Hastipâla's office of the writers, (Mahâvîra) single and alone, sitting in the Samparyaṅka posture, reciting the fifty-five lectures which detail the results of Karman, and the thirty-six[2] unasked questions, when he just explained the chief lecture (that of Marudeva) he died, &c. (see § 124, all down to) freed from all pains. (147)

[1] The meaning of this rather dark passage is according to the commentary that after three generations of disciples (Vîra, Sudharman, *G*ambûsvâmin) nobody reached Nirvâ*n*a; and after the fourth year of Mahâvîra's Kevaliship nobody entered the path which ends in final liberation, so that all persons who before that moment had not advanced in the way to final liberation, will not reach that state though they may obtain the Kevalam by their austerities and exemplary conduct.

[2] This is the Uttarâdhyayana Sûtra.

Since the time that the Venerable Ascetic Mahâvîra died, &c. (all down to) freed from all pains, nine centuries have elapsed, and of the tenth century this is the eightieth year. Another redaction has ninety-third year (instead of eightieth)[1]. (148)

End of the Fifth Lecture.

End of the Life of Mahâvîra.

[1] To what facts the two dates in this paragraph relate, is not certain. The commentators confess that there was no fixed tradition, and bring forward the following four facts, which are applied at will to either date:

1. The council of Valabhi under the presidency of Devarddhi, who caused the Siddhânta to be written in books.

2. The council of Mathurâ under the presidency of Skandila, who seems to have revised the Siddhânta.

3. The public reading of the Kalpa Sûtra before king Dhruvasena of Ânandapura, to console him on the death of his son. Ânandapura is identified with Mahâsthâna by *G*inaprabhamuni, and with Ba*d*anagara by Samayasundara. Some scholars have assumed, but not proved, that this Dhruvasena is identical with one of the Valabhi kings of the same name.

4. The removal of the Pa*gg*usan by Kâlakâ*k*ârya from the fifth to the fourth Bhâdrapada.

LIFE OF PÂRSVA.

In that period, in that age lived the Arhat Pârsva, the people's favourite[1], the five most important moments of whose life happened when the moon was in conjunction with the asterism Visâkhâ: in Visâkhâ he descended (from heaven), and having descended thence, entered the womb (of his mother); in Visâkhâ he was born; in Visâkhâ, tearing out his hair, he left the house and entered the state of houselessness; in Visâkhâ he obtained the highest knowledge and intuition, called Kevala, which is infinite, supreme, unobstructed, unimpeded, complete, and full; in Visâkhâ he obtained final liberation. (149)

In that period, in that age, in the first month of summer, in the first fortnight, the dark (fortnight) of Kaitra, on its fourth day, the Arhat Pârsva, the people's favourite, descended from the Prânata Kalpa[2], where he had lived for twenty Sâgaropamas, here on the continent Gambûdvîpa, in Bharatavarsha, in the town of Benares; and in the middle of the night when the moon was in conjunction with the asterism Visâkhâ, after the termination of his allotted length of life, divine nature, and existence (among the gods), he took the form of an embryo in the womb of the queen Vâmâ, wife of Asvasena, king (of Benares). (150)

The knowledge of the Arhat Pârsva, the people's

[1] Purisâdânîya, explained: who is to be chosen among men because of his preferable karman.

[2] This is the tenth world of the gods.

favourite, (about this) was threefold, &c. (repeat §§ 3–95 after making the necessary substitutions, and omitting what exclusively applies to Mahâvîra, all down to) comfortably carried her unborn child. (151)

In that period, in that age the Arhat Pârsva, the people's favourite [1]—after the lapse of nine months and seven and a half days, in the second month of winter, in the third fortnight, the dark (fortnight) of Paushya, on its tenth day, in the middle of the night when the moon was in conjunction with the asterism Visâkhâ—(Vâmâ), perfectly healthy herself, gave birth to a perfectly healthy boy. (152)

In that night in which the Arhat Pârsva, the people's favourite, was born, &c. (repeat §§ 97–107 with the necessary alterations, all down to) therefore shall the name of our boy be Pârsva [2]. (153, 154)

The Arhat Pârsva, the people's favourite, clever, with the aspirations of a clever man, of great beauty, controlling his senses, lucky, and modest, lived thirty years as a householder. Then the Laukântika gods, following the established custom, addressed him with these kind, pleasing, &c., sweet, and soft words: (155)

'Victory, victory to thee, gladdener of the world!' (see § 111, down to) Thus they raised the shout of victory. (156) Before the Arhat Pârsva, the people's favourite, had adopted the life of a householder, &c. (see § 112, down to) indigent persons.

---

[1] As regards the construction of this passage compare § 96, note 1.

[2] This name was given him because before his birth his mother, lying on her couch, saw in the dark a black serpent crawling about. This is the account given by the commentator, who forgets to tell us how it comes to bear on the name Pârsva.

In the second month of winter, in the third fortnight, the dark (fortnight) of Paushya, on its eleventh day, in the middle of the night, riding in his palankin called Vi*s*âlâ, followed on his way by a train of gods, men, and Asuras, &c. (Pâr*s*va) went right through the town of Benares to the park called Â*s*ramapada, and proceeded to the excellent tree A*s*oka. There, &c. (see § 116, down to) five handfuls.

When the moon was in conjunction with the asterism Vi*s*âkhâ, he, after fasting three and a half days without drinking water, put on a divine robe, and together with three hundred men he tore out his hair, and leaving the house entered the state of houselessness. (157)

The Arhat Pâr*s*va, the people's favourite, for eighty-three days neglected his body, &c. (see § 117, down to) animals. (158)

Thereafter the Arhat Pâr*s*va, the people's favourite, was houseless, circumspect, &c. (see §§ 118–120, down to) meditated upon himself for eighty-three days.

During the eighty-fourth day—it was in the first month of summer, in the first fortnight, the dark (fortnight) of *K*aitra, on its fourth day, in the early part of the day, when the moon was in conjunction with the asterism Vi*s*âkhâ—Pâr*s*va, under a Dhâtaki tree, after fasting two and a half days without drinking water, being engaged in deep meditation, reached the infinite, &c. (see § 120, down to) highest knowledge and intuition called Kevala, &c. (see § 121, down to) moment. (159)

The Arhat Pâr*s*va, the people's favourite, had eight Ga*n*as and eight Ga*n*adharas (enumerated in a *S*loka):

*S*ubha and Âryaghosha, Vasish*th*a[1] and Brahma*k*ârin, Saumya and *S*rîdhara, Vîrabhadra and Ya*s*as. (160)

The Arhat Pâr*s*va, the people's favourite, had an excellent community of sixteen thousand *S*rama*n*as with Âryadatta[2] at their head; (161) thirty-eight thousand nuns with Pushpa*k*ûlâ at their head; (162) one hundred and sixty-four thousand lay votaries with Suvrata at their head; (163) three hundred and twenty-seven thousand female lay votaries with Sunandâ at their head; (164) three hundred and fifty sages who knew the fourteen Pûrvas, &c. (see § 138); (165) fourteen hundred sages who were possessed of the Avadhi knowledge; one thousand Kevalins; eleven hundred sages who could transform themselves, six hundred sages of correct knowledge, one thousand male and two thousand female disciples who had reached perfection, seven hundred and fifty sages of vast intellect, six hundred professors, and twelve hundred sages in their last birth. (166)

The Arhat Pâr*s*va, the people's favourite, instituted two epochs in his capacity of a Maker of an end: the epoch relating to generations and the epoch relating to psychical condition; the former ended in the fourth generation, the latter in the third year of his Kevaliship. (167)

In that period, in that age the Arhat Pâr*s*va, the people's favourite, lived thirty years as a householder, eighty-three days in a state inferior to perfection, something less than seventy years as a Kevalin, full seventy years as a *S*rama*n*a, and a hundred years on the whole.

[1] C. has Visi*tth*a, i. e. Vi*s*ish*t*a.

[2] Âriyadinna in the original.

When his fourfold Karman[1] was exhausted and in this Avasarpi*n*î era the greater part of the Du*h*shamasushamâ period had elapsed, in the first month of the rainy season, in the second fortnight, the light (fortnight) of *S*râva*n*a, on its eighth day, in the early part of the day when the moon was in conjunction with the asterism Vi*s*âkhâ, (Pâr*s*va), after fasting a month without drinking water, on the summit of mount Sammeta, in the company of eighty-three persons, stretching out his hands, died, &c. (all down to) freed from all pains. (168)

Since the time that the Arhat Pâr*s*va, the people's favourite, died, &c. (all down to) freed from all pains, twelve centuries have elapsed, and of the thirteenth century this is the thirtieth year. (169)

End of the Life of Pâr*s*va.

[1] See § 147.

LIFE OF ARISHTANEMI.

In that period, in that age lived the Arhat Arish*t*anemi, the five most important moments of whose life happened when the moon was in conjunction with the asterism *K*itrâ. In *K*itrâ he descended from heaven, &c. (see § 149, down to) obtained final liberation. (170)

In that period, in that age, in the fourth month of the rainy season, in the seventh fortnight, the dark (fortnight) of Kârttika, on its twelfth day, the Arhat Arish*t*anemi descended from the great Vimâna, called Aparâ*g*ita, where he had lived for thirty-six Sâgaropamas, here on the continent *G*ambûdvîpa, in Bharatavarsha, in the town of *S*auripura[1], and in the middle of the night when the moon was in conjunction with the asterism *K*itrâ, he took the form of an embryo in the womb of the queen *S*ivâ, wife of the king Samudravi*g*aya, &c. (the seeing of the dreams, the accumulation of riches, &c., should be repeated here). (171)

In that period, in that age the Arhat Arish*t*anemi—after the lapse of nine months and seven and a half days, in the first month of the rainy season, in the second fortnight, the light (fortnight) of *S*râva*n*a, on its fifth day, &c.—(*S*ivâ), perfectly healthy herself, gave birth to a perfectly healthy boy. (Repeat the account of the birth, substituting the name Samudra-

[1] The Prâkrit form is Soriyapura, which would correspond to Sanskrit *S*aurikapura. It is, of course, K*r*ish*n*a's town.

vigaya, all down to) therefore shall the name of our boy be Arishtanemi [1].

The Arhat Arishtanemi, clever, &c. (see §§ 155–157, all down to) indigent persons. (172) In the first month of the rainy season, in the second fortnight, the light (fortnight) of Srâvana, on its sixth day riding in his palankin called Uttarakurâ, and followed on his way by a train of gods, men, and Asuras, &c. (Arishtanemi) went right through the town of Dvârâvatî to the park called Revatika, and proceeded to the excellent Asoka tree. There, &c. (see § 116, down to) five handfuls. When the moon was in conjunction with the asterism Kitrâ, after fasting two and a half days without drinking water, he put on a divine robe, and together with a thousand persons he tore out his hair, and leaving the house entered the state of houselessness. (173)

The Arhat Arishtanemi for fifty-four days neglected his body, &c. (see §§ 117–120). During the fifty-fifth day—it was in the third month of the rainy season, in the fifth fortnight, the dark fortnight of Âsvina, on its fifteenth day, in the last part of the day, when the moon was in conjunction with the asterism Kitrâ—(Arishtanemi) under a Vetasa [2] tree on the summit of mount Girnâr [3], after fasting three and a half days without drinking water, &c., obtained infinite, &c., highest knowledge and intuition called Kevala, &c. (see § 121, down to) moment. (174)

---

[1] His mother saw in a dream a nemi, the outer rim of a wheel, which consisted of rishta stones flying up to the sky. Hence the name Arishtanemi.

[2] Vata in some MSS.; it is the Banyan tree.

[3] Ugginta in the original

The Arhat Arish*t*anemi had eighteen Ga*n*as and eighteen Ga*n*adharas. (175)

The Arhat Arish*t*anemi had an excellent community of eighteen thousand *S*rama*n*as with Varadatta at their head; (176) forty thousand nuns with Ârya Yakshi*n*î at their head; (177) one hundred and sixty-nine thousand lay votaries with Nanda at their head; (178) three hundred and thirty-six thousand[1] female lay votaries with Mahâsuvratâ at their head; (179) four hundred sages who knew the fourteen Pûrvas, &c.; (180) fifteen hundred sages who were possessed of the Avadhi knowledge; fifteen hundred Kevalins; fifteen hundred sages who could transform themselves; one thousand sages of vast intellect; eight hundred professors; sixteen hundred sages in their last birth; fifteen hundred male and three thousand female disciples who had reached perfection.

The Arhat Arish*t*anemi instituted, &c. (see § 146, down to) the former ended in the eighth generation, the latter in the twelfth year of his Kevaliship. (181)

In that period, in that age the Arhat Arish*t*anemi lived three centuries as a prince, fifty-four days in a state inferior to perfection, something less than seven centuries as a Kevalin, full seven centuries as a *S*rama*n*a, a thousand years on the whole. When his fourfold Karman was exhausted and in this Avasarpi*n*î era a great part of the Du*h*shamasushamâ period had elapsed, in the fourth month of summer, in the eighth fortnight, the light (fortnight) of Âshâ*dh*a, on its eighth day, in the middle of the night when the moon was in conjunction with the asterism *K*itrâ, (Arish*t*anemi), after fasting a month

[1] Read *kh*attîsa*m* in the printed text.

without drinking water, on the summit of mount Girnâr, in the company of five hundred and thirty-six monks, in a squatting position, died, &c. (all down to) freed from all pains. (182)

Since the time that the Arhat Arish*t*anemi died, &c. (all down to) freed from all pains, eighty-four thousand years have elapsed, of the eighty-fifth millennium nine centuries have elapsed, of the tenth century this is the eightieth year. (183)

End of the Life of Arish*t*anemi.

EPOCHS OF THE INTERMEDIATE TÎRTHAKARAS.

Since the time that the Arhat Nami died, &c. (all down to) freed from all pains, 584,979 years have elapsed, this is the eightieth year[1]. (184) Since the death of Munisuvrata this is the year 1,184,980. Since Malli[2] this is the year 6,584,980. Ara died 10,000,000 years before Malli; Kunthu a quarter of a Palyopama before Malli; *S*ânti three-quarters of a Palyopama; Dharma three Sâgaropamas before Malli; Ananta seven Sâgaropamas before Malli; Vimala sixteen Sâgaropamas before Malli; Vâsupû*g*ya forty Sâgaropamas before Malli; *S*reyâ*m*sa a hundred Sâgaropamas before Malli. *S*îtala died a krore of Sâgaropamas, less 42,003 years and eight and a half months, before the death of Vîra. Suvidhi, surnamed Pushpadanta, died ten krores of Sâgaropamas before *S*îtala; *K*andraprabha a hundred krores of Sâgaropamas before *S*îtala; Supârsva a thousand krores of Sâgaropamas before *S*îtala; Padmaprabha ten thousand krores of Sâgaropamas before *S*îtala; Sumati one hundred thousand krores of Sâgaropamas before *S*îtala; Abhinandana one million krores of Sâgaropamas before *S*îtala; Sambhava two million krores of Sâgaropamas before *S*îtala; A*g*ita five million krores of Sâgaropamas before *S*îtala. (185–203)

[1] The numbers are given in the same way as in § 183. I have abridged these tedious accounts. All Tîrthakaras except Mahâvîra have the title Arhat, which I have dropped in the sequel.

[2] Read Malli (for Mali) in the printed edition of the text.

LIFE OF *RI*SHABHA.

In that period, in that age lived the Arhat *Ri*shabha, the Kosalian[1], four important moments of whose life happened when the moon was in conjunction with the asterism Uttarâshâ*dh*â; the fifth, when in conjunction with Abhi*g*it: (204) in Uttarâshâ*dh*â he descended from heaven, &c. (all down to) in Abhi*g*it he obtained final liberation. (205)

In that period, in that age, in the fourth month of summer, in the seventh fortnight, the dark (fortnight) of Âshâ*dh*a, on its fourth day, the Arhat *Ri*shabha, the Kosalian, descended from the great Vimâna called Sarvârthasiddha, where he had lived for thirty-three Sâgaropamas, here on the continent *G*ambûdvîpa, in Bharatavarsha, in Ikshvâkubhûmi, and in the middle of the night, &c., he took the form of an embryo in the womb of Marudevî, wife of the patriarch[2] Nâbhi. (206)

The knowledge of the Arhat *Ri*shabha about this, &c. (all as in the case of Mahâvîra, but note the following differences: the first dream is a bull 'coming forward with his face,' the other (mothers of Tîrthakaras see first) an elephant. She (Marudevî) relates them to Nâbhi, the patriarch; there

[1] Kosaliya=Kausalika. He is thus called because he was born in Kosalâ or Ayodhyâ.

[2] Kulakara; these Kulakaras were the first kings and founders of families at the time when the rest of mankind were 'Yugalins.' The first Kulakara was Vimalavâhana; the seventh and last of the line Nâbhi.

are no interpreters of dreams; Nâbhi, the patriarch, himself interprets them). (207)

In that period, in that age the Arhat *Ri*shabha, the Ko*s*alian,—in the first month of summer, in the first fortnight, the dark (fortnight) of *K*aitra, on its eighth day, &c.,—(Marudevî), perfectly healthy herself, gave birth to a perfectly healthy boy. (208)

(The circumstances connected with the birth of *Ri*shabha are the same as in the case of that of Mahâvîra, only that the contents of §§ 100 and 101 do not apply to the present case.) (209)

The Arhat *Ri*shabha, the Ko*s*alian, belonged to the Kâ*s*yapa gotra, and he had five names: *Ri*shabha, First King, First Mendicant, First *G*ina, and First Tîrthakara. (210)

The Arhat *Ri*shabha, the Ko*s*alian, clever, with the aspirations of a clever man, of great beauty, controlling (his senses), lucky, and modest, lived two millions of former years[1] as a prince, and six millions three hundred thousand former years as a king. During his reign he taught, for the benefit of the people, the seventy-two sciences, of which writing is the first, arithmetic the most important, and the knowledge of omens the last, the sixty-four accomplishments of women, the hundred arts, and the three occupations of men[2]. At last he anointed his

---

[1] See Â*k*ârâṅga Sûtra I, 6, 3, § 2, note 1.

[2] The arts, as those of the potter, blacksmith, painter, weaver, and barber, each of which five principal arts is subdivided into twenty branches, are inventions and must be taught; while the occupations, agriculture, trade, &c. have everywhere developed, as it were, of themselves. The accomplishments of women are dancing, singing, &c. The commentator adds to these a detailed list of those questionable accomplishments which Vâtsyâyana has so curiously described, and refers the reader to the *G*ayamaṅgala for further details. The latter work, a still extant commentary on the

hundred sons as kings, and gave each a kingdom. Then the Laukântika god, following the established custom, &c. (see §§ 110–112, down to) indigent persons. In the first month of summer, in the first fortnight, the dark (fortnight) of *K*aitra, on its eighth day, in the latter part of the day, riding in his palankin called Sudarsanâ, followed on his way by a train of gods, men, and Asuras, &c. (*Ri*shabha) went right through the town Vinîtâ to the park called Siddhârtha Vana, and proceeded to the excellent tree A*s*oka. There, &c. (see § 116, down to) four handfuls. When the moon was in conjunction with the asterism Ashâ*dh*â, he, after fasting two and a half days without drinking water, put on a divine robe, and together with four thousand of high, noble, royal persons, and Kshatriyas, he tore out his hair, and leaving the house entered the state of houselessness. (211)

The Arhat *Ri*shabha, the Ko*s*alian, for one thousand years neglected his body, &c. (see §§ 117–120, down to) meditated upon himself for one thousand years. Thereupon—it was in the fourth month of winter, the seventh fortnight, the dark (fortnight) of Phâlguna, on its eleventh day, in the early part of the day, when the moon was in conjunction with the asterism Ashâ*dh*â, outside of the town Purimatâla, in the park called *S*aka*t*amukha, under the excellent tree Nyagrodha—(*Ri*shabha) after fasting three and a half days without drinking water, being engaged in deep meditation, reached the infinite, &c. (see § 120, down to) highest knowledge and intuition called Kevala, &c. (see § 121, down to) moment. (212)

Kâma Sûtra, must therefore be older than 1307, the date of *G*inaprabhamuni's commentary on the Kalpa Sûtra.

The Arhat *Ri*shabha, the Ko*s*alian, had eighty-four Ga*n*as and eighty-four Ga*n*adharas. (213)

The Arhat *Ri*shabha, the Ko*s*alian, had an excellent community of eighty-four thousand *S*rama*n*as with *Ri*shabhasena at their head; (214) three hundred thousand nuns with Brahmîsundarî at their head; (215) three hundred and five thousand lay votaries with *S*reyâ*m*sa at their head; (216) five hundred and fifty-four thousand female lay votaries with Subhadrâ at their head; (217) four thousand seven hundred and fifty sages who knew the fourteen Pûrvas, &c.; (218) nine thousand sages who were possessed of the Avadhi knowledge; (219) twenty thousand Kevalins; (220) twenty thousand six hundred sages who could transform themselves; (221) twelve thousand six hundred and fifty sages of vast intellect, &c.; (222) twelve thousand six hundred and fifty professors; (223) twenty thousand male and forty thousand female disciples who had reached perfection; (224) twenty-two thousand nine hundred sages in their last birth, &c. (225)

The Arhat *Ri*shabha, the Ko*s*alian, instituted, &c. (see § 146, down to) the former ended after numberless generations, the latter from the next Muhûrta after his Kevaliship. (226)

In that period, in that age the Arhat *Ri*shabha, the Ko*s*alian, lived two millions of former years as a prince, six millions three hundred thousand former years as a king, together eight millions three hundred thousand former years as a householder; a thousand (former) years in a state inferior to perfection, nine-and-ninety thousand former years as a Kevalin, together a hundred thousand former years as a *S*rama*n*a, and eight millions four hundred thousand years on the whole. When his fourfold Karman was exhausted, and in this Avasarpi*n*î era the Sushamadu*h*shamâ period had nearly elapsed, only three years and eight and a half months being left, in the third month of winter, in the fifth fortnight, the dark (fortnight) of Mâgha, on its thirteenth day, in the early part of the day when the moon was in conjunction with the asterism Abhi*g*it, (*Ri*shabha), after fasting six and a half days without drinking water, on the summit of mount Ash*t*âpada, in the company of ten thousand monks in the Samparyaṅka position, died, &c. (all down to) freed from all pains. (227)

Since the time that the Arhat *Ri*shabha, the Ko*s*alian, died, &c. (all down to) freed from all pains, three years and eight and a half months elapsed; thereupon one ko*t*i of ko*t*is of Sâgaropamas, less forty-two thousand and three years and eight and a half months, elapsed. At that time the Venerable Ascetic Mahâvîra died; after his Nirvâ*n*a nine centuries elapsed, of the tenth century this is the eightieth year.

End of the Life of *Ri*shabha.

End of the Lives of the *G*inas.

LIST OF THE STHAVIRAS.

At that period, at that age the Venerable Ascetic Mahâvîra had nine Ga*n*as and eleven Ga*n*adharas.

'Why, now, has it been said, that the Venerable Ascetic Mahâvîra had nine Ga*n*as, but eleven Ga*n*adharas?'

'The oldest monk of the Venerable Ascetic Mahâvîra was Indrabhûti of the Gautama gotra, who instructed five hundred *S*rama*n*as; the middle-aged monk was Agnibhûti of the Gautama gotra, who instructed five hundred *S*rama*n*as; the youngest was Vâyubhûti of the Gautama gotra, who instructed five hundred *S*rama*n*as. The Sthavira Ârya-Vyakta of the Bhâradvâ*g*a gotra instructed five hundred *S*rama*n*as; the Sthavira Ârya-Sudharman of the Agnive*s*yâyana gotra instructed five hundred *S*rama*n*as; the Sthavira Ma*nd*ikaputra[1] of the Vâsish*th*a gotra instructed two hundred and fifty *S*rama*n*as; the Sthavira Mauryaputra of the Kâ*s*yapa gotra instructed two hundred and fifty *S*rama*n*as; the Sthavira Akampita of the Gautama gotra and Sthavira A*k*alabhrât*ri* of the Hâritâyana gotra, both Sthaviras instructed together three hundred *S*rama*n*as each; the Sthaviras Metârya and Prabhâsa, both of the Kau*nd*i*n*ya gotra, instructed together

[1] Some spell this name Ma*ndit*aputra; he and Mauryaputra were sons of the same mother, Vi*g*ayadevî, but different fathers; the former of Dhanadeva, the other of Maurya. I do not know any legend which connects this Maurya with a king of the Maurya dynasty, which besides would be impossible from a chronological point of view.

three hundred *S*rama*n*as each[1]. Therefore, Sir, has it been said that the Venerable Ascetic Mahâvîra had nine Ga*n*as, but eleven Ga*n*adharas.' (1)

All these eleven Ga*n*adharas of the Venerable Ascetic Mahâvîra, who knew the twelve Aṅgas, the fourteen Pûrvas, and the whole Siddhânta of the Ga*n*ins, died, &c. (all down to) freed from all pains in Râ*g*agr*i*ha after fasting a month without drinking water. The Sthaviras Indrabhûti and Ârya Sudharman both died after the Nirvâ*n*a of Mahâvîra. The Nirgrantha *S*rama*n*as of the present time are all (spiritual) descendants of the monk Ârya Sudharman, the rest of the Ga*n*adharas left no descendants. (2)

The Venerable Ascetic Mahâvîra was of the Kâ*s*yapa gotra. His disciple was[2]:

1. Ârya Sudharman of the Agnive*s*yâyana gotra;
2. Ârya *G*ambûnâman of the Kâ*s*yapa gotra;
3. Ârya Prabhava of the Kâtyâyana gotra;
4. Ârya *S*ayyambha, father of Manaka, was of the Vatsa gotra;
5. Ârya Ya*s*obhadra of the Tuṅgikâyana gotra. (3)

In the short redaction the list of Sthaviras after Ârya Ya*s*obhadra is the following:

6. Ârya Sambhûtavi*g*aya of the Mâ*th*ara gotra and Ârya Bhadrabâhu of the Prâ*k*îna gotra;
7. Ârya Sthûlabhadra of the Gautama gotra;
8. i. Ârya Mahâgiri of the Ailâpatya gotra and

[1] The sum total of *S*rama*n*as is therefore 4711, while in § 134 it is stated to have been 14,000.

[2] I only give the facts. The names of those Sthaviras who continue the line are spaced. The names are given in their Sanskrit form which in many cases is well known, in others can easily be made out. In doubtful cases I have put the Prâkrit form in brackets.

ii. Ârya Suhastin of the Vâsish*th*a gotra;

9. Susthita and Supratibuddha, surnamed Ko*t*ika and Kâkandaka, of the Vyâghrâpatya gotra;

10. Ârya Indradatta (Indadinna) of the Kau*s*ika gotra;

11. Ârya Datta (Dinna) of the Gautama gotra;

12. Ârya Si*m*hagiri *G*âtismara of the Kau*s*ika gotra;

13. Ârya Va*g*ra of the Gautama gotra;

14. Ârya Va*g*rasena of the Utk*ri*sh*t*a gotra[1].

He had four disciples: Ârya Nâgila, Ârya Padmila, Ârya *G*ayanta, and Ârya Tâpasa, each of whom founded a *S*âkhâ called after his name, viz. the Âryanâgilâ *S*âkhâ, the Âryapadmilâ *S*âkhâ, the Ârya*g*ayantî *S*âkhâ, and the Âryatâpasî *S*âkhâ. (4)

In the detailed redaction the list of Sthaviras after Ârya Ya*s*obhadra is the following:

6. i. Ârya Bhadrabâhu of the Prâ*k*îna gotra, who had four disciples of the Kâ*s*yapa gotra:

a. Godâsa, founder of the Godâsa Ga*n*a[2], which was divided into four *S*âkhâs:

α. The Tâmraliptikâ *S*âkhâ,

β. The Ko*t*ivarshîyâ *S*âkhâ,

γ. The Pu*nd*ravardhanîyâ *S*âkhâ, and

---

[1] He is left out in some MSS.

[2] It is not quite clear what is meant by Ga*n*a, Kula, and *S*âkhâ. Ga*n*a designates the school which is derived from one teacher; Kula the succession of teachers in one line; *S*âkhâ the lines which branch off from each teacher. These terms seem to be disused in modern times, for the four principal divisions called after Nâgendra, *K*andra, Niv*ri*tti, and Vidyâdhara are generally called Kulas, but also occasionally *S*âkhâs. They go back to Va*g*ra according to some, to Va*g*rasena according to others. The modern Ga*kkh*a appears equivalent with the ancient Ga*n*a.

δ. The Dâsîkharba*t*ikâ *S*âkhâ.

b. Agnidatta,

c. *G*anadatta,

d. Somadatta.

ii. Ârya Sambhutavi*g*aya of the Mâ*th*ara gotra, who had twelve disciples:

7. a. Nandanabhadra,

b. Upananda,

c. Tishyabhadra [1],

d. Ya*s*obhadra,

e. Sumanobhadra [2],

f. Ma*n*ibhadra,

g. Pu*n*yabhadra [3],

h. Sthûlabhadra of the Gautama gotra,

i. *Rig*umati,

k. *G*ambû,

l. Dîrghabhadra, and

m. Pâ*nd*ubhadra;

and seven female disciples:

a. Yakshâ,

b. Yakshadattâ (Yakshadinnâ),

c. Bhûtâ,

d. Bhûtadattâ (Bhûtadinnâ),

e. Senâ (also E*n*â),

f. Ve*n*â,

g. Re*n*â.

8. i. Ârya Mahâgiri of the Ailâpatya gotra, who had eight disciples:

a. Uttara,

b. Balissaha, who both together founded the Uttarabalissaha Ga*n*a, which was divided into four *S*âkhâs:

---

[1] Tîsabhadda, translated Trida*s*abhadra.

[2] Or Sumanabhadra.

[3] Or Pûr*n*ibhadra.

α. Kau*s*ambikâ,
β. Sautaptikâ (Pr. Soittiyâ),
γ. Kau*t*umbinî (or Ku*nd*adharî),
δ. *K*andanâgarî.
c. Dhanarddhi (Pr. Dha*n*a*ddh*a),
d. *S*irarddhi (Pr. Siri*ddh*a),
e. Ko*d*i*n*ya,
f. Nâga,
g. Nâgaputra,
h. *Kh*aluka Rohagupta of the Kau*s*ika gotra, founder of the Trairâ*s*ika *S*âkhâ.

ii. Ârya Suhastin[1] of the Vâsish*th*a gotra, who had twelve disciples:

9. a. Ârya Roha*n*a of the Kâ*s*yapa gotra, founder of the Uddeha Ga*n*a, which was divided into four *S*âkhâs:
α. Udumbarikâ (Pr. Udumbari*gg*iyâ),
β. Mâsapûrikâ,
γ. Matipatrikâ,
δ. Pûr*n*apatrikâ (Pr. Punnapattiyâ, Panna°, Sunna°, or Suvanna°);

and into six Kulas:
α'. Nâgabhûta,
β'. Somabhûta,
γ'. Ullaga*kkh*a (or Ârdraka*kkh*a ?),
δ'. Hastilipta (Pr. Hatthili*gg*a),
ε'. Nândika (Pr. Nandi*gg*a),
ζ'. Parihâsaka.

[1] Suhastin is said to have converted Samprati, grandson and successor of A*s*oka. The correctness of this statement is open to doubt; but at any rate Suhastin must have been one of the most important patriarchs, for under and immediately after him the spread of *G*ainism must have been uncommonly vigorous, as is proved by the great number of Kulas and *S*âkhâs at that time.

b. Bhadrayasas of the Bhâradvâga gotra, who founded the Uduvâtika Gana, which was divided into four Sâkhâs:

α. Kampîyikâ (Pr. Kampiggiyâ),
β. Bhadrîyikâ (Pr. Bhaddiggiyâ),
γ. Kâkandikâ,
δ. Mekhalîyikâ (Pr. Mehaliggiyâ);

and into three Kulas:

α'. Bhadrayaska (Pr. Bhaddagasiya),
β'. Bhadraguptika,
γ'. Yasobhadra (Pr. Gasabhadda).

c. Megha.

d. Kâmarddhi (Pr. Kâmiddhi) of the Kundala gotra, who founded the Vesavâtika Gana, which was divided into four Sâkhâs:

α. Srâvastikâ,
β. Râgyapâlikâ (Pr. Raggapâliyâ),
γ. Antarañgikâ (Pr. Antariggiyâ),
δ. Kshemaliptikâ (Pr. Khemaliggiyâ);

and into four Kulas:

α'. Ganika,
β'. Maighika,
γ'. Kâmarddhika,
δ'. Indrapuraka.

e. Srîgupta of the Hârita gotra, founder of the Kârana Gana, which was divided into four Sâkhâs:

α. Hâritamâlâkârî,
β. Samkâsikâ,
γ. Gavedhukâ,
δ. Vagranâgarî;

and into seven Kulas:

α'. Vâtsalîya (Pr. Vakkhaligga),

β'. Prîtidharmika,
γ'. Hâridraka (Pr. Hâli*gg*a),
δ'. Pushyamitrika (Pr. Pûsamitti*gg*a),
ε'. Mâlyaka (Pr. Mâli*gg*a),
ζ'. Ârya*k*e*t*aka,
η'. K*ri*sh*n*asakha (Pr. Kanhasaha).

f. *Ri*shigupta Kâkandaka of the Vâsish*th*a gotra, founder of the Mânava Ga*n*a, which was divided into four *S*âkhâs:
α. Kâ*s*yapîyâ (Pr. Kâsavi*gg*iyâ),
β. Gautamîyâ (Pr. Goyame*gg*iyâ),
γ. Vâsish*th*îyâ (Pr. Vâsi*tth*iyâ),
δ. Saurâsh*t*rikâ;

and into three Kulas:
α'. *Ri*shiguptika,
β'. *Ri*shidattika,
γ'. Abhiya*s*asa.

g. and h. Susthita and Supratibuddha, surnamed Kau*t*ika and Kâkandaka, of the Vyâghrâpatya gotra, founders of the Kau*t*ika Ga*n*a, which was divided into four *S*âkhâs:
α. U*kk*anâgarî,
β. Vidyâdharî,
γ. Vagrî,
δ. Madhyamikâ (Pr. Ma*ggh*imilla);

and into four Kulas:
α'. Brahmaliptaka (Pr. Ba*m*bhali*gg*a),
β'. Vâtsalîya (Pr. Va*kkh*ali*gg*a, cf. e. α'.),
γ'. Vâ*n*îya (Pr. Vâ*n*i*gg*a),
δ'. Pra*s*navâhanaka.

Both Sthaviras had together five disciples:

10. a. Ârya Indradatta (Pr. Indadinna) of the Kâ*s*yapa gotra,

b. Priyagantha, founder of the Madhyamâ *S*âkhâ,

c. Vidyâdharagopâla of the Kâ*s*yapa gotra, founder of the Vidyâdharî *S*âkhâ,

d. *Ri*shidatta,

e. Arhaddatta (Pr. Arihadatta).

11. Ârya Datta (Pr. Dinna) of the Gautama gotra, who had two disciples:

12. i. Ârya *S*ântisenika of the Mâ*th*ara gotra, founder of the U*kk*anâgarî *S*âkhâ, who had four disciples:

a. Ârya Senika, founder of the Âryasenikâ *S*âkhâ,

b. Ârya Tâpasa, founder of the Âryatâpasî *S*âkhâ,

c. Ârya Kubera, founder of the Âryakuberâ *S*âkhâ, and

d. Ârya *Ri*shipâlita, founder of the Ârya*ri*shipâlitâ *S*âkhâ.

ii. Ârya Si*m*hagiri *G*âtismara of the Gautama gotra, who had four disciples:

13. a. Dhanagiri,

b. Ârya Samita of the Gautama gotra, founder of the Brahmadvîpikâ *S*âkhâ,

c. Ârya Va*g*ra of the Gautama gotra, founder of the Ârya va*g*râ *S*âkhâ,

d. Arhaddatta (Pr. Arihadinna).

14. i. Ârya Va*g*rasena, founder of the Âryanâgilâ *S*âkhâ,

ii. Ârya Padma, founder of the Âryapadmâ *S*âkhâ,

iii. Ârya Ratha of the Vatsa gotra, founder of the Ârya*g*ayantî *S*âkhâ.

15. Ârya Pushyagiri of the Kau*s*ika gotra

16. Ârya Phalgumitra of the Gautama gotra.
17. Ârya Dhanagiri of the Vâsish*th*a gotra.
18. Ârya *S*ivabhûti of the Kautsa gotra.
19. Ârya Bhadra of the Kâ*s*yapa gotra.
20. Ârya Nakshatra of the Kâ*s*yapa gotra.
21. Ârya Raksha of the Kâ*s*yapa gotra.
22. Ârya Nâga of the Gautama gotra.
23. Ârya *G*ehila[1] of the Vâsish*th*a gotra.
24. Ârya Vish*n*u of the Mâ*th*ara gotra.
25. Ârya Kâlaka of the Gautama gotra.
26. Ârya Sampalita and Bhadra, both of the Gautama gotra.
27. Ârya V*ri*ddha of the Gautama gotra.
28. Ârya Saṅghapâlita of the Gautama gotra.
29. Ârya Hastin of the Kâ*s*yapa gotra.
30. Ârya Dharma of the Suvrata gotra.
31. Ârya Si*m*ha of the Kâ*s*yapa gotra.
32. Ârya Dharma of the Kâ*s*yapa gotra.
33. Ârya *S*â*nd*ilya[2].

[1] A various reading has *Ge*t*th*ila = *G*yesh*th*a.

[2] This list in prose from 17 down to 33 is wanting in some MSS. I think that *S*â*nd*ilya is the same as Skandila, who was president of the council of Mathurâ, which seems to have been the rival of that in Valabhî; see notes to my edition of the Kalpa Sûtra, p. 117.

It deserves to be noticed that the gotra of *S*â*nd*ilya is not given, while that of the remaining Sthaviras is specialised. This seems to prove that his name is a later addition to the list.

After the prose list all MSS. have eight gâthâs, in which the names 16–32, given above, are repeated. Instead of translating these verses, which contain little more than a string of names, I only note down the differences from the above list. After 18 is added Dur*g*aya K*ri*sh*n*a, a Kau*s*ika; Nakshatra is shortened, metri causa, to Nakkha; the gotra of Saṅghapâlita is Kâ*s*yapa instead of Gautama; after 30 are inserted Hasta of the Kâ*s*yapa gotra and Dharma.

After these gâthâs follow five more, which are wanting in some MSS., and are not commented upon. The last (14th) gâthâ is

Bowing down my head, I pay my reverence to the Sthavira *G*ambû of the Gautama gotra, who possessed steady virtue, good conduct, and knowledge. ix.

I prostrate myself before the Sthavira Nandita of Kâ*s*yapa gotra, who is possessed of great clemency and of knowledge, intuition, and good conduct. x.

Then I adore the Kshamâ*s*rama*n*a De*s*iga*n*in of the Kâ*s*yapa gotra, who, steady in his conduct, possesses the highest righteousness and virtue. xi.

Then I prostrate myself before the Kshamâ*s*rama*n*a Sthiragupta of the Vâtsya gotra, the preserver of the sacred lore, the wise one, the ocean of wisdom, him of great virtue. xii.

Then I adore the Sthavira prince, Dharma, the virtuous Ga*n*in, who stands well in knowledge, intuition, good conduct, and penance, and is rich in virtues[1]. xiii.

I revere the Kshamâ*s*rama*n*a Devarddhi of the Kâ*s*yapa gotra, who wears, as it were, the jewel of the right understanding of the Sûtras, and possesses the virtues of patience, self-restraint, and clemency. xiv.

End of the List of the Sthaviras.

---

found in all MSS. It brings the list down to the president of the council of Valabhî. (The translation of the gâthâs ix–xiv is given in full in the text.)

[1] The Sthaviras named in verses ix–xiii are probably not to be regarded as following each other in a continuous line, but rather as famous Sthaviras praised here for some reason or other (pû*g*ârtham). At least the first, *G*ambû, seems to be the same with *G*ambû, the second of the list, who was also a Kâ*s*yapa.

RULES FOR YATIS[1].

1. In that period, in that age the Venerable Ascetic Mahâvîra commenced the Paggusan when a month and twenty nights of the rainy season had elapsed.

'Why has it been said that the Venerable Ascetic Mahâvîra commenced the Paggusan when a month and twenty nights of the rainy season had elapsed?' (1)

'Because at that time the lay people have usually matted their houses, whitewashed them, strewn them (with straw), smeared them (with cowdung), levelled, smoothed, or perfumed them (or the floor of them), have dug gutters and drains, have furnished their houses, have rendered them comfortable, and have cleaned them. Hence it has been said that the Venerable Ascetic Mahâvîra commenced the Paggusan when a month and twenty nights of the rainy season had elapsed.' (2)

As the Venerable Ascetic Mahâvîra commenced the Paggusan when a month and twenty nights of the rainy season had elapsed, so the Ganadharas commenced the Paggusan when a month and twenty nights of the rainy season had elapsed. (3) As the Ganadharas have done, so the disciples of the Ganadharas have done. (4) As they have done,

---

[1] Sâmâkârî.

so the Sthaviras have done. (5) As they have done, so do the Nirgrantha *S*rama*n*as of the present time. (6)

As they do, so our masters, teachers, &c. do. (7) As they do, so do we commence the Pa*gg*usan after a month and twenty nights of the rainy season have elapsed. It is allowed to commence the Pa*gg*usan earlier, but not after that time. (8)

2. Monks or nuns during the Pa*gg*usan are allowed to regard their residence as extending a Yo*g*ana and a Kro*s*a all around, and to live there for a moderate time. (9)

3. During the Pa*gg*usan monks or nuns are allowed to go and return, for the sake of collecting alms, not farther than a Yo*g*ana and a Kro*s*a (from their lodgings). (10) If there is (in their way) an always flowing river which always contains water, they are not allowed to travel for a Yo*g*ana and a Kro*s*a. (11) But if the river is like the Erâvatî near Ku*n*âlâ, such that it can be crossed by putting one foot in the water and keeping the other in the air, there it is allowed to travel for a Yo*g*ana and a Kro*s*a. (12) But where that is impossible, it is not allowed to travel for a Yo*g*ana and a Kro*s*a. (13)

4. During the Pa*gg*usan the Â*k*ârya will say, 'Give, Sir!' Then he is allowed to give (food to a sick brother), but not to accept himself. (14) If the Â*k*ârya says, 'Accept, Sir!' then he is allowed to accept (food), but not to give. (15) If the Â*k*ârya says, 'Give, Sir! accept, Sir!' then the patient is allowed to give and to accept (food). (16)

5. Monks or nuns who are hale and healthy, and of a strong body, are not allowed during the Pa*gg*usan frequently to take the following nine drinks: milk,

thick sour milk, fresh butter, clarified butter, oil, sugar, honey, liquor, and meat. (17)

6. During the Pa*gg*usan a collector of alms might ask (the Â*k*ârya), 'Sir, is (anything of the just-mentioned articles) required for the sick man?' he (the Â*k*ârya) says, 'Yes, it is.' Then (the sick man) should be asked, 'How much do you require?' The Â*k*ârya says, 'So much is required for the sick man: you must take so much as he told you.' And he (the collector of alms) should beg, and begging he should accept (the required food). Having obtained the quantity ordered, he should say, 'No more!' Perchance (the giver of food) might ask, 'Why do you say so, Sir?' (Then he should answer), 'Thus much is required for the sick man.' Perchance, after that answer the other may say, 'Take it, Sir! You may after (the sick man has got his share) eat it or drink it.' Thus he is allowed to accept it, but he is not allowed to accept it by pretending that it is for the sick man. (18)

7. In householders' families which are converted, devoted, staunch adherers (to the law), and honour, praise, and permit (the visits of monks), Sthaviras, during the Pa*gg*usan, are not allowed to ask, 'Sir, have you got such or such a thing?' if they do not see it.

'Why, Sir, has this been said?' 'Because a devout householder might buy it or steal it.' (19)

8. During the Pa*gg*usan a monk eats only one meal a day, and should at one fixed[1] time frequent the abodes of householders for the sake of collecting

[1] I.e. after the sûtra and artha paurushîs or the religious instruction in the morning.

alms, except when he does services for the Â*k*ârya, the teacher, an ascetic, or a sick man, likewise if he or she be a novice who has not yet the marks of ripe age[1]. (20) To a monk who during the Pa*gg*usan eats only one meal on every second day, the following special rule applies. Having gone out in the morning, he should eat and drink[2] his pure dinner, then he should clean and rub his alms-bowl. If his dinner was sufficient, he should rest content with it for that day; if not, he is allowed for a second time to frequent the abodes of householders for the sake of collecting alms. (21) A monk who during the Pa*gg*usan eats on every third day, is allowed twice to frequent the abodes of householders for the sake of collecting alms. (22) A monk who during the Pa*gg*usan eats one meal on every fourth day, is allowed three times to frequent the abodes of householders for the sake of collecting alms. (23) A monk who keeps still more protracted fasts, is allowed at all (four) times to frequent the abodes of householders for the sake of collecting alms. (24)

9. A monk who during the Pa*gg*usan eats one meal every day, is allowed to accept all (permitted) drinks. A monk who during the Pa*gg*usan eats one meal on every second day, is allowed to accept three kinds of drinks: water used for watering flour, sesamum, or rice[3]. A monk who eats one meal

---

[1] I. e. on whose belly, armpits, lips, &c. hair has not yet grown. The last part is also explained: except an Â*k*ârya, teacher, ascetic, sick monk, and novice.

[2] Pi*kk*â is the reading of the commentaries.

[3] Cf. Â*k*ârâṅga Sûtra II, 1, 7, § 7. The definitions given in our commentary are the following: the first is water mixed with flour, or water used for washing the hands after kneading flour; the

on every third day, is allowed to accept three kinds of drinks: water used for washing sesamum, chaff, or barley[1]. A monk who during the Paggusan eats one meal on every fourth day, is allowed to accept three kinds of water: rain-water, or sour gruel, or pure (i. e. hot) water. A monk who during the Paggusan keeps still more protracted fasts, is allowed to accept only one kind of drink; hot pure water. It must contain no boiled rice[2]. A monk who abstains from food altogether, is allowed to accept only one kind of drink: pure hot water. It must contain no boiled rice; it must be filtered, not unfiltered; it must be a limited quantity, not an unlimited one; it must be sufficient, not insufficient. (25)

10. A monk who during the Paggusan restricts himself to a certain number of donations[3], is allowed to accept (e.g.) five donations of food, and five of drink; or four of food, and five of drink; or five of food, and four of drink. He may accept one donation of salt for seasoning his meat[4]. He should

second, water with which squeezed leaves, &c. are sprinkled; the third, water used for washing threshed and winnowed rice (ta*nd*ula).

[1] Âkârâṅga Sûtra II, 1, 7, § 8. The first is water used for washing sesamum, or, in Mahârâsh*t*ra, husked sesamum; the second, water used for washing rice, &c. (vrîhyâdi); the third, water used for washing barley.

[2] The commentator says that the body of monks who fast longer than four days is usually inhabited by a deity; this seems to denote, in our language, mental derangement as a consequence of starving oneself.

[3] Datti. The commentator does not explain this word. It seems to denote the quantity of food or drink which is given by one man.

[4] The one donation of salt is meant to make up the five donations to which the monk confines himself. But he should not reckon

rest content for that day with the dinner he has brought together, and is not allowed a second time to frequent the abodes of householders for the sake of collecting alms. (26) During the Paggusan monks or nuns who restrict their visits to certain houses may go to a place where rice is cooked[1], if it is the seventh house from that where they are lodged. According to some, the lodging is included in the seven houses which such a mendicant must pass before he may participate in the festive entertainment; but according to others, it is not included in those seven houses. (27)

11. During the Paggusan a monk who collects alms in the hollow of his hand, is not allowed to frequent the abodes of householders, &c., if rain[2], even in the form of a fine spray, falls down. (28) During the Paggusan a monk who collects alms in the hollow of his hand, is not allowed to stay anywhere except in a house after having accepted alms, for it might begin to rain. But he should eat a part, and put back the rest (if it then begins to rain), covering his hand with the other hand, and laying it on his bosom or hiding it under his armpit[3]; then he should go to well-covered (places), to a cave or the foot of a tree, where no water or drops of water or spray of water falls in his hand. (29)

12. During the Paggusan a monk who collects

the donations of food above the fixed number as donations of drink if the latter have not yet reached the fixed number.

[1] Samkhadi, the word which, in the Âkârânga Sûtra II, 1, 2, &c., we have translated 'festive entertainment.'

[2] Rain is here and in the sequel called rain-body, i. e rain-drops considered as containing life, apkâya.

[3] To render kaksha.

alms in the hollow of his hand, is not allowed to collect alms if rain, even in the form of a fine spray, falls down. (30)

13. During the Paggusan a monk who uses an alms-bowl is not allowed to frequent the abodes of householders for the sake of collecting alms if it rains fast, but he is allowed to do so if it rains but little; but they must wear then an under and upper garment. (31) During the Paggusan, a monk who has entered the abode of a householder while there are single showers of rain, is allowed (when the rain ceases for a moment) to stand under a grove, or in his residence, or in the assembling-hall of the village[1], or at the foot of a tree. (32) If before his arrival a dish of rice was being cooked, and after it a dish of pulse was begun to be cooked, he is allowed to accept of the dish of rice, but not of the dish of pulse. (33) But if before his arrival a dish of pulse was being cooked, and after it a dish of rice was begun to be cooked, he is allowed to accept of the dish of pulse, but not of the dish of rice. (34) If both dishes were begun to be cooked before his arrival, he is allowed to accept of both. If both dishes were begun to be cooked after his arrival, he is not allowed to accept of either. He is allowed to accept of what was prepared before his arrival; he is not allowed to accept of what was prepared after his arrival. (35) During the Paggusan, &c. (see § 32, down to) tree; he is not allowed to pass there his time with the food he had collected before. But he should first eat and drink his pure (food and drink), then rub and clean his alms-bowl,

[1] Vikatagriha.

and, putting his things together, he should, while the sun has not yet set, go to the place where he is lodged; but he is not allowed to pass the night in the former place. (36) During the Pa*gg*usan, &c. (see § 32, down to) tree. (37) It is not allowed that there at the same place should stand together one monk and one nun, nor one monk and two nuns, nor two monks and one nun, nor two monks and two nuns. But if there is a fifth person, a male or female novice, or if that place can be seen (by those who pass) or doors open on it, then they are allowed to stand there together. (38) During the Pa*gg*usan, &c. (see § 32, down to) tree. It is not allowed that there at the same place should stand together a monk and a lay woman, &c. (through the four cases as in § 28). But if there is a fifth person, a Sthavira or a Sthavirâ, or if that place can be seen (by those who pass) or doors open on it, then they are allowed to stand there together. The same rule applies to a nun and a layman. (39)

14. During the Pa*gg*usan monks or nuns are not allowed to accept food, drink, dainties, and spices for one who has not asked them, and whom they have not promised to do so. (40)

'Why has this been said, Sir?' 'Because one who collects alms for another without being asked for it, might eat them or not, just as he lists.' (41)

15. During the Pa*gg*usan monks or nuns are not allowed to take their meals as long as their body is wet or moist. (42)

'How has this been said, Sir?' 'Seven places which retain the moisture have been declared: the hands, the lines in the hand, the nails, the top of the nails, the brows, the under lip, the upper lip.'

But when they perceive that the water on their body has dried up and the moisture is gone, then they are allowed to take their meals. (43)

16. There are these eight classes of small things which a mendicant ought diligently to perceive, observe, and inspect, viz. living beings, mildew, seeds, sprouts, flowers, eggs, layers, and moisture.

What is understood by the small living beings? The small living beings are declared to be of five kinds: black, blue, red, yellow, and white ones. There is an animalcule called Anuddharî, which when at rest and not moving is not easily seen by monks and nuns who have not yet reached perfection, which when not at rest but moving is easily seen by monks and nuns who have not yet reached perfection. Monks and nuns who have not yet reached perfection must diligently perceive, observe, and inspect this. Those are the small living beings. (44)

What is understood by small mildew? Small mildew has been declared to be of five kinds: black, blue, &c. There is a kind of small mildew which has the same colour as the substance on which it grows. Monks, nuns, &c. (see § 44, down to) inspect this. That is small mildew.

What is understood by small seeds? Small seeds are declared to be of five kinds: black, blue, &c. There is a kind of small seeds of the same colour as grain[1]. Monks and nuns, &c. (see § 44, down to) inspect this. Those are the small seeds.

What is understood by small sprouts? Small sprouts are declared to be of five kinds: black, blue, &c. There is a kind of small sprouts of

[1] Ka*n*ikâ.

the same colour as earth. Monks and nuns, &c. (see § 44, down to) inspect them. Those are the small sprouts.

What is understood by small flowers? Small flowers are declared to be of five kinds: black, blue, &c. There is a kind of small flowers of the same colour as the tree (on which they grow). Monks and nuns, &c. (see § 44, down to) inspect them. Those are the small flowers.

What is understood by small eggs? Small eggs are declared to be of five kinds: eggs of biting insects[1], of spiders, of ants, of lizards (or wasps)[2], and of chameleons[3]. Monks and nuns, &c. (see § 44, down to) inspect them. Those are the small eggs.

What is understood by small caves or lairs? Small caves or lairs are declared to be of five kinds: lairs of animals of the asinine kind, chasms, holes, cavities widening below like the stem of a palm tree, and wasps' nests. Monks and nuns, &c. (see § 44, down to) inspect them. Those are the small caves or lairs.

What is understood by small moisture? Small moisture is declared to be of five kinds: dew, hoarfrost[4], fog, hailstones, and damps. Monks and nuns,

---

[1] Udda*m*sa, mosquitoes, gadflies, bugs.

[2] Halikâ, explained by g*ri*hakokila, which I take to mean the same as g*ri*hagolikâ, a kind of lizard; and vrâhma*n*î, a kind of wasps, ditto, of lizards.

[3] Hallohaliyâ, which is declared by the commentator to be synonymous with ahilo*d*î, sara*d*î, and kakki*nd*î. Of these words only sara*d*î is known; for it seems to be the same with Sanskrit sara*t*a or sara*t*u, 'chameleon, lizard,' and Marâthî sara*t*a, 'hedge-lizard.'

[4] Hima*h* styânodaka*h*.

&c. (see § 44, down to) inspect this. That is small moisture. (45)

17. During the Paggusan[1] a monk might wish to frequent the abodes of householders for the sake of collecting alms. He is not allowed to go without asking leave of the teacher, or sub-teacher, or religious guide, or Sthavira, or head of the Gana, or Ganadhara, or founder of the Gana, or whom else he regards as his superior; he is allowed to go after having asked leave of one of these persons (in this way): 'I want with your permission to frequent the abodes of householders for the sake of collecting alms.' If he (the superior) grants permission, one is allowed to go; if not, one is not allowed to go.

'Why has this been said, Sir?' 'The teacher knows how to make good what has been done wrong.' (46) The same rule applies concerning the visits to temples and leaving the house for easing nature[2], or any other business, also the wandering from village to village. (47)

18. During the Paggusan a monk might wish to take some medicine; he is not allowed to take it without asking leave of the teacher, &c. (see § 47, down to) founder of the Gana; but he is allowed to take it after having asked leave of one of these persons (in this way): 'I want, Sir, with your permission to take some medicine,' viz. so much or so often. If he, &c. (see § 46, down to) wrong. (48)

---

[1] The whole of the seventeenth rule holds good not only for the rainy season, but also for the rest of the year (ritubaddhakâla).

[2] Vihârabhûmi and vikârabhûmi, which in the Âkârâṅga Sûtra I have, according to the explanation of the commentary, translated 'places for study and religious practices.'

The same rule applies if a monk wants to undergo some medical cure. (49) Also if he wants to do some exalted penance. (50) Also if he intends, after the last mortification of the flesh which is to end in death, to wait for his last hour without desiring it, in total abstinence from food and drink or in remaining motionless; also if he wants to go out or to enter, to eat food, &c., to ease nature, to learn his daily lesson, to keep religious vigils—he is not allowed to do it without asking leave. (51)

19. If during the Pa*gg*usan a monk wants to dry or warm (in the sun) his robe, alms-bowl, blanket, broom, or any other utensil, he is not allowed without asking one or many persons to frequent the abodes of householders for the sake of collecting alms, to eat food, &c., to visit temples or leave the house for easing nature, to learn his daily lesson, to lie down with outstretched limbs or stand in some posture. If there is somebody near, one or many persons, then he should say: 'Sir, please mind this (robe, &c.) while I frequent the abodes of householders, &c. (see above, down to) posture.' If that person promises to do it, then he (the monk) is allowed to go; if he does not promise it, then he is not allowed to go. (52)

20. During the Pa*gg*usan monks or nuns are not allowed to be without their proper bed or bench[1] This is the reason: A mendicant whose bed and bench are not reserved for his own use, are low and rickety, not sufficiently fastened, without a fixed place, and never exposed to the sun, and

[1] The commentator translates pi*th*a, 'stool,' and phalaka, 'bench;' they are of course not the property of the mendicant, but only temporally reserved for his use.

who is not circumspect in what he does, nor accustomed to inspect and clean the things of his use, will find it difficult to exercise control; (53) but on the contrary, control will be easy to him. (54)

21. During the Paggusan monks or nuns must always inspect three spots where to ease nature; not so in the summer and winter, as in the rainy season. 'Why has this been said, Sir?' 'For in the rainy season living beings, grass, seeds, mildew, and sprouts frequently come forth.' (55)

22. During the Paggusan monks or nuns must have three pots, one for ordure, one for urine, and a spitting-box. (56) Monks and nuns, who wear after the Paggusan their hair as short as that of a cow, are not allowed to do so during the Paggusan after that night (of the fifth Bhâdrapada); but a monk should shave his head or pluck out his hair[1]. Shaving with a razor every month, cutting with scissors every half-month, plucking out every six months. (57) This is the conduct chiefly of Sthaviras during the rainy season[2].

[1] After these words the text has pakkhiyâ ârovanâ, which is explained in two ways: 1. every half-month the tied strings on the bed should be untied and inspected; the same should be done with wicker-work (? davaraka; cf. Hindî daurâ, 'basket'); 2. every half-month prâyaskitta should be made. The commentator Samayasundara says that these words are not connected with the preceding and following ones; their import (paramârtha) should be learned from a well-instructed brother (gîtârtha). I think that pakkhiyâ is not connected with paksha, 'half-month,' but with kesapaksha, 'braid of hair, tresses;' the two words, or rather the compound, would in that case denote arrangement of (or in) tresses or braids, and relate to nuns who do not, as far as I know, shave their head. A precept for nuns is just what would be expected at this place, after one for monks (ârya) has been given.

[2] The last words are variously interpreted by the commentators.

23. During the Paggusan monks or nuns should not use harsh words after the commencement of the Paggusan; if they do, they should be warned: 'Reverend brother (or sister), you speak unmannerly.' One who (nevertheless) uses harsh words after the commencement of the Paggusan, should be excluded from the community. (58)

24. If, during the Paggusan, among monks or nuns occurs a quarrel or dispute or dissension, the young monk should ask forgiveness of the superior, and the superior of the young monk. They should forgive and ask forgiveness, appease and be appeased, and converse without restraint[1]. For him who is appeased, there will be success (in control); for him who is not appeased, there will be no success; therefore one should appease one's self. 'Why has this been said, Sir?' 'Peace is the essence of monachism.' (59)

25. During the Paggusan monks or nuns should have three lodging-places; (two) for occasional use,

---

Therakappa is said to mean 'old monks,' for young and strong ones must pluck out their hair every four months. It usually denotes the conduct of ordinary monks, in opposition to the *Gina*kappa; if taken in this sense, the whole passage is made out to mean that even one who, because of sickness of his scalp, is dispensed from tearing out his hair, must do it in the rainy season, for then the precept is binding both for *G*inakalpikas and Sthavirakalpikas. According to the interpretation I have followed the words sa*m*va*kkh*arie vâ therakappe are a sort of colophon to the rules 17–22, and indicate that these rules apply to Sthavirakalpikas, but not exclusively (vâ), as some apply to *G*inakalpikas also. The phrase sa*m*va*kkh*ariya therakappa occurs also at the beginning of § 62, and has there a similar meaning.

[1] According to the commentary, they should ask each other the meaning of the Sûtras.

which must be inspected; one for constant use, which must be swept[1]. (60)

26. During the Pa*gg*usan monks or nuns should give notice of the direction or intermediate direction in which they intend to go forth for the sake of begging alms. 'Why has this been said, Sir?' 'During the Pa*gg*usan the reverend monks frequently undertake austerities; an ascetic becoming weak and exhausted might swoon or fall down. (In case of such an accident the remaining) reverend monks will undertake their search in that direction or intermediate direction (which the ascetic had named them). (61)

27. During the Pa*gg*usan monks or nuns are not allowed to travel farther than four or five Yo*g*anas[2], and then to return. They are allowed to stay in some intermediate place, but not to pass there (at the end of their journey) the night. (62)

Of those Nirgrantha monks who follow, &c. (see Â*k*ârâṅga Sûtra II, 15, v end, down to) . . . . these (rules regulating) the conduct of Sthaviras in the rainy season, some will reach perfection, &c. (see § 124, down to) be freed from all pains in that same life, some in the next life, some in the third birth;

[1] I deviate from the interpretation of the commentators, who give veuvviyâ (or veu*tt*iyâ v. l.), which I have rendered 'for occasional use,' the sense of 'repeatedly.' But as they give sâi*gg*iya the meaning 'used,' and as the practice justifies my translation, I am rather confident about the correctness of my conjecture. The practice, as related by the commentator, is this: The Upâ*s*raya where the monks live must be swept in the morning, when the monks go out begging, at noon, and in the afternoon at the end of the third prahara; the other two Upâ*s*rayas must be daily inspected, lest somebody else occupy them, and be swept every third day.

[2] And this only in case of need, to fetch medicine, &c. In ordinary cases the third rule applies.

none will have to undergo more than seven or eight births. (63)

In that period, in that age the Venerable Ascetic Mahâvîra, in the town of Râ*g*agr*i*ha, in the *K*aitya Gu*n*a*s*ilaka, surrounded by many monks and nuns, by many men and women of the laity, by many gods and goddesses, said thus, spoke thus, declared thus, explained thus; he proclaimed again and again the Lecture called Paryusha*n*âkalpa with its application, with its argumentation, with its information, with its text, with its meaning, with both text and meaning with the examination of the meaning.

Thus I say. (64)

End of the Rules for Yatis.

End of the Kalpa Sûtra.

INDEX.

TRANSLITERATION OF ORIENTAL ALPHABETS ADOPTED FOR THE TRANSLATIONS OF THE SACRED BOOKS OF THE EAST.

CONSONANTS.	MISSIONARY ALPHABET.			Sanskrit.	Zend.	Pehlevi.	Persian.	Arabic.	Hebrew.	Chinese.
	I Class.	II Class.	III Class.							
Gutturales.										
1 Tenuis	k	. . .	. . .	क	𐬐	[illegible]	ک	ك	כּ	k
2 " aspirata	kh	. . .	. . .	ख	𐬑	[illegible]	. . .	. . .	כ	kh
3 Media	g	. . .	. . .	ग	𐬔	[illegible]	گ	. . .	גּ	. . .
4 " aspirata	gh	. . .	. . .	घ	𐬖	[illegible]	. . .	. . .	ג	. . .
5 Gutturo-labialis	q	. . .	. . .	. . .	. . .	. . .	ق	ق	ק	. . .
6 Nasalis	ṅ (ng)	. . .	. . .	ङ	{ 𐬢 (ng) / 𐬣 (N) }	. . .	. . .	. . .	. . .	. . .
7 Spiritus asper	h	. . .	. . .	ह	𐬵 (𐬓 hv)	[illegible]	ه	ه	ה	h, hs
8 " lenis	'	. . .	. . .	. . .	. . .	. . .	ا	ا	א	. . .
9 " asper faucalis	ʻh	. . .	. . .	. . .	. . .	. . .	ح	ح	ח	. . .
10 " lenis faucalis	ʼh	. . .	. . .	. . .	. . .	. . .	ع	ع	ע	. . .
11 " asper fricatus	. . .	*ʻh*	. . .	. . .	. . .	. . .	خ	خ	ח	. . .
12 " lenis fricatus	. . .	*ʼh*	. . .	. . .	. . .	. . .	. . .	. . .	. . .	. . .
Gutturales modificatae (palatales, &c.)										
13 Tenuis	. . .	*k*	. . .	च	𐬗	[illegible]	چ	. . .	. . .	*k*
14 " aspirata	. . .	*kh*	. . .	छ	. . .	. . .	. . .	. . .	. . .	*kh*
15 Media	. . .	*g*	. . .	ज	𐬘	[illegible]	ج	ج	. . .	. . .
16 " aspirata	. . .	*gh*	. . .	झ	. . .	. . .	غ	غ	. . .	. . .
17 " Nasalis	. . .	*ñ*	. . .	ञ	. . .	. . .	. . .	. . .	. . .	. . .

VOWELS.	MISSIONARY ALPHABET. I Class.	II Class.	III Class.	Sanskrit.	Zend.	Pehlevi.	Persian.	Arabic.	Hebrew.	Chinese.
1 Neutralis	0	...	...	...	...	...	...	...	ְ	ă
2 Laryngo-palatalis	ĕ	...	...	...	...	...	...	...	...	...
3 „ labialis	ŏ	...	...	...	...	𐭥 fin.	...	...	...	...
4 Gutturalis brevis	a	...	...	अ	𐬀	𐭠 init.	ـَ	ـَ	ַ	a
5 „ longa	â	(*a*)	...	आ	𐬁	𐭠	ـَا	ـَا	ָ	â
6 Palatalis brevis	i	...	...	इ	𐬌	...	ـِ	ـِ	ִ	i
7 „ longa	î	(*i*)	...	ई	𐬍	𐭩	ـِي	ـِي	ִי	î
8 Dentalis brevis	*li*	...	...	ऌ	...	...	...	...	...	...
9 „ longa	*lî*	...	...	ॡ	...	...	...	...	...	...
10 Lingualis brevis	*ri*	...	...	ऋ	...	...	...	...	...	...
11 „ longa	*rî*	...	...	ॠ	...	...	...	...	...	...
12 Labialis brevis	u	...	...	उ	𐬎	...	ـُ	ـُ	ֻ	u
13 „ longa	û	(*u*)	...	ऊ	𐬏	𐭥	ـُو	ـُو	וּ	û
14 Gutturo-palatalis brevis	e	...	...	...	𐬈(e) 𐬉(*e*)	...	...	...	ֶ	e
15 „ longa	ê (ai)	(*e*)	...	ए	𐬇, 𐬆	𐭩	...	...	ֵ	ê
16 Diphthongus gutturo-palatalis	âi	(*ai*)	...	ऐ	...	...	ـَيْ	ـَيْ	...	âi
17 „ „	ei (ĕi)	...	...	...	...	...	...	...	...	ei, êi
18 „ „	oi (ŏu)	...	...	...	...	...	...	...	...	...
19 Gutturo-labialis brevis	o	...	...	...	𐬊	...	...	...	ָ	o
20 „ longa	ô (au)	(*o*)	...	ओ	𐬋	𐭥	...	...	וֹ	...
21 Diphthongus gutturo-labialis	âu	(*au*)	...	औ	𐬆𐬎 (*au*)	...	ـَوْ	ـَوْ	...	âu
22 „ „	eu (ĕu)	...	...	...	...	...	...	...	...	...
23 „ „	ou (ŏu)	...	...	...	...	...	...	...	...	...
24 Gutturalis fracta	ä	...	...	...	...	...	...	...	...	...
25 Palatalis fracta	ï	...	...	...	...	...	...	...	...	...
26 Labialis fracta	ü	...	...	...	...	...	...	...	...	ü
27 Gutturo-labialis fracta	ö	...	...	...	...	...	...	...	...	

Dentales modificatae (linguales, &c.)										
38 Tenuis	...	*t*	....	ट	....	...	ط	ط	ט	...
39 " aspirata	...	*th*	....	ठ	....	...	ظ	ظ	...	...
40 Media	...	*d*	....	ड	𐬜	[illegible]	...	...	...	...
41 " aspirata	...	*dh*	....	ढ	....	...	...	ض	...	...
42 Nasalis	...	*n*	....	ण	𐬣	...	...	...	...	...
43 Semivocalis	r	...	....	र	𐬭	[illegible]	ر	ر	ר	...
44 " fricata	...	*r*	....	...	....	...	...	...	...	*r*
45 " diacritica	...	...	R	...	....	...	...	...	...	...
46 Spiritus asper	sh	...	....	ष	𐬴	[illegible]	...	...	...	sh
47 " lenis	zh	...	....	...	....	...	...	...	...	...
Labiales.										
48 Tenuis	p	...	....	प	𐬞	[illegible]	پ	...	פּ	p
49 " aspirata	ph	...	....	फ	....	...	...	...	פ	ph
50 Media	b	...	....	ब	𐬠	[illegible]	ب	ب	בּ	...
51 " aspirata	bh	...	....	भ	....	...	...	...	ב	...
52 Tenuissima	...	*p*	....	...	....	...	...	...	...	...
53 Nasalis	m	...	....	म	𐬨	[illegible]	م	م	מ	m
54 Semivocalis	w	...	....	...	𐬎	...	...	...	...	w
55 " aspirata	hw	...	....	...	....	...	...	...	...	...
56 Spiritus asper	f	...	....	...	𐬟	[illegible]	ف	ف	...	f
57 " lenis	v	...	....	व	»	[illegible]	و	و	ו	...
58 Anusvâra	...	*m*	....	अं	𐬅 ã	...	...	...	...	...
59 Visarga	...	*h*	....	अः	....	...	...	...	...	...

CONSONANTS (continued).	Missionary Alphabet. I Class.	Missionary Alphabet. II Class.	Missionary Alphabet. III Class.	Sanskrit.	Zend.	Pehlevi.	Persian.	Arabic.	Hebrew.	Chinese.
18 Semivocalis	y	...	...	य	𐬫, [illegible] init.	[illegible]	ي	ي	י	y
19 Spiritus asper	...	(ẏ)	...	...	...	...	...	...	...	...
20 „ lenis	...	(ẏ)	...	...	...	...	...	...	...	...
21 „ asper assibilatus	...	*s*	...	श	𐬱	[illegible]	ش	ش	...	...
22 „ lenis assibilatus	...	*z*	...	...	𐬲	[illegible]	ژ	...	...	*z*
Dentales.										
23 Tenuis	t	...	...	त	𐬙	[illegible]	ت	ت	תּ	t
24 „ aspirata	th	...	...	थ	𐬚	...	...	...	ת	th
25 „ assibilata	...	...	TH	...	...	...	ث	ث	...	...
26 Media	d	...	...	द	𐬛	[illegible]	د	د	דּ	...
27 „ aspirata	dh	...	...	ध	𐬜	...	...	...	ד	...
28 „ assibilata	...	...	DH	...	...	...	ذ	ذ	...	...
29 Nasalis	n	...	...	न	[illegible]	[illegible]	ن	ن	נ	n
30 Semivocalis	l	...	...	ल	...	[illegible]	ل	ل	ל	l
31 „ mollis 1	...	*l*	...	ळ	...	...	...	...	...	...
32 „ mollis 2	...	...	L	...	...	...	...	...	...	...
33 Spiritus asper 1	s	...	...	स	𐬯	[illegible]	س (ث)	س	שׁ	s
34 „ asper 2	...	...	s (ʃ)	...	...	...	...	...	ס	...
35 „ lenis	z	...	...	...	𐬰	[illegible]	ز (ذ)	ز	ז	z
36 „ asperrimus 1	...	...	z (ʒ)	...	...	...	ص	ص	צ	ȝ, ȝh
37 „ asperrimus 2	...	...	ẓ (ʒ)	...	...	...	ض	...	...	...